BREAKING AWAY

PATRICK O'SULLIVAN WITH GARE JOYCE

BREAKING AWAY

A HARROWING TRUE STORY OF RESILIENCE, COURAGE AND TRIUMPH

HarperCollins*Publishers*Ltd

Published by HarperCollins Publishers Ltd

First edition

HarperCollins books may be purchased for educational, business,
or sales promotional use through our Special Markets Department.

HarperCollins Publishers Ltd
2 Bloor Street East, 20th Floor
Toronto, Ontario, Canada
M4W 1A8

www.harpercollins.ca

Library and Archives Canada Cataloguing in Publication
information is available upon request

ISBN 978-1-44344-466-8

Printed and bound in the United States of America
RRD 9 8 7 6 5 4 3 2

CONTENTS

PART THREE

BREAKING AWAY

I

BREAKING AWAY

I was sixteen when I decided to fight back.

It was almost midnight. I was sitting in the back seat of the conversion van, staring out the window as we drove down the highway for five hours through the wind and snow. I was trying not to look at the driver. Every time he looked in the rearview mirror and saw that I wasn't paying attention to him, he grabbed anything that was handy—a can of Coke he hadn't opened, his thermos, his lighter, whatever was close—and threw it at my head. I was trying to tune him out, but I couldn't help hearing him insult and threaten me. Like he had for three hours before he even dragged me into the van.

"You fuckin' faggot," he yelled.

Minutes passed and I said nothing. There was silence in the van, interrupted only by the hum of the motor, windshield wipers squeaking and his hyperventilating. The van filled with smoke as he worked his way through a pack of Marlboros.

"You're fuckin' soft," he yelled.

More minutes passed and I said nothing. I had heard it all before. He yelled again.

"All my fuckin' time, all my fuckin' money."

He sped past cars. He floored it. He yelled again.

"You're never gonna amount to fuckin' anything. I'm pullin' you out of school and you're getting' a fuckin' job."

He gritted his teeth, his eyes open wide. I knew that look.

"It's fuckin' over," he said.

And he was right about that. It had to be over. I had to put an end to it. I had already made my mind up earlier that night, before he pulled out of the parking lot.

I knew what was coming.

I had a reasonable fear that one of us was going to die that night.

If I didn't fight back, it was going to be me.

It's not like his anger was ever going to pass. For years it had been the same way. The way he saw it, he was always right, the only one who knew what was right. He pushed people around and intimidated anyone who got in his way. I was the one always around, always in the way, so I had been afraid for my life every hour of every day. It had been the only life I'd ever known.

Some of the worst of it happened on the road, on the back roads going from one small town to another. On cold nights like this one, he would kick me out of the van and make me run beside or behind it for a mile, maybe two, maybe more. I had to run hard enough to satisfy him. He threatened to leave me behind if I didn't measure up. Sometimes he would drive off into the distance on the highway in the middle of the night until the van would be out of sight and I'd run down the soft shoulder not knowing if he was still out there. That started when I was eight or nine years old.

My life had been no easier at home. I never knew what I was going to have to do just to get by. I never knew when it would happen. It could be the middle of the night, three in the morning, even a school night, when he'd be coming home or just leaving for one of the shift-work jobs he picked up but couldn't keep. He'd make me run or do push-ups and sit-ups until I couldn't do one more and then he would slap me around. "Toughen you up, make you tough like me," he'd say.

I was never good enough, never tough enough, not as tough as he thought *he* was. He punched me and kicked me and humiliated me. I just had to suck it up. I couldn't even cry. If I did cry, he'd call me *faggot* or *pussy* and just beat me worse.

It never stopped. I'd go to school—grade 5, grade 6, right up to high school—and I'd be scratched or cut or bruised and would come up with an explanation if anyone asked. They almost never did. I'd go to school exhausted, barely able to sit up and keep my eyes open. I could have laid my head on a desk and fallen asleep anytime, but I didn't. I stayed awake, because there'd have been questions if I fell asleep, and my father didn't want anyone poking around our house.

The older I got, the clearer it was to me. It was only getting worse.

It was me or my father.

My mind was racing on the drive that night. He pulled off the highway at a gas station. Only a few cars were out at two a.m. There was no running from him, not in the middle of nowhere. I didn't even have a quarter to make a phone call and call the cops. Even if I did, what could I do until they got there, which might have been a half-hour, an hour, or maybe not at all?

He knew I didn't have options out on the road. He didn't need to handcuff me or tie me up or lock me in. I was stuck. He thought I couldn't run and had nowhere to hide, not at the gas station. He was right. He believed, really believed, that I was always going to have to give in to him. He was wrong.

I had made up my mind. It had to go down tonight.

An hour from the city, he was still going off, threatening to kick the shit out of me. If he had looked in the rearview mirror, he'd have seen my head turned away. I was hiding a smile. It wasn't that I was afraid of making him any madder. I don't think he could have got madder. Some fires are so big that throwing gasoline on them doesn't make them any bigger. That was the fire that night. No, I was hiding my smile because I didn't want to set him off just yet. I had to pick my spots. I didn't want him to see me smile or he would have pulled over and we would have had it out right then and there on the side of the road. Not the time yet, not the place. Soon.

When I was young, I would have run through walls for him or died trying. I believed every word he said. I thought he knew the way of the world and was one step ahead of everybody. That's what he wanted me to believe, and I guess that's what I wanted to believe too.

I was sixteen now, though. As much as he tried to control every second of my life, I'd been out in the world just enough to see who he was. *What* he was. Yeah, I was physically frightened of him. He was 230 pounds, maybe even 240. He had gone his whole life looking for fights, whether he was sober in the ring or drunk in the street. He had been in hundreds of fights, never backed down. He was tough that way but weak in so many others. I was old enough now to see just how pathetic he was. Had failed at everything he ever tried. Couldn't hold down a job, but it was always someone else's fault. Feared by everyone, respected by no one. In control of nothing in his life, nothing except me.

We reached the city. We were going to stop at the house for a couple of minutes and then get back out on the highway and drive five more hours to the border.

He pulled up in the driveway. No lights were on inside. The only ones on were up the street, Christmas lights that hadn't been taken down.

"Stay in the fuckin' car," he said as he put the van in park and left it running.

"No, this is it," I said. I opened the door, got out of the van and stood on the lawn in front of the house he had grown up in. "I'm not going. I'm staying here."

"Get in the fuckin' car."

"I'm not going anywhere. This is it. I'm done with it."

I could have run then. I could have outrun him, and I knew my way around the neighborhood. I could have run and hid or tried to get help. I had an out if I wanted it. I didn't run, though. Not as a matter of pride, just survival. I had to take a stand, not for a night but for my life, and whatever the price, I'd have to pay. We were going to have it out on the snow-covered lawn on a quiet suburban street under the streetlights.

He started throwing punches.

"You little fuckin' bastard. You piece of shit!"

He put everything he had behind every punch. He had meant it when he'd said "It's over."

I fought back, the first time in my life that I went all in. I punched back and flushed him a couple of times.

"You wanna take a punch at me, you faggot?"

It wasn't enough to stop him. He had more than sixty pounds on me. After a minute or so, I was on my back and he was standing over me, loading up on every punch. He pinned me on the ground. He beat the hell out of me until he was too tired and breathing too hard to keep punching. Five minutes, maybe longer. I was lucky to come away with my teeth in place and my jaw in one piece. He had toughened me up over the years, but I've never thought of myself as a street fighter or anything like that. Maybe that's the lesson I took from him—the uselessness and stupidity of being a fighter.

Lights went on at the house next door.

"Is that enough?" I said, practically asking for more, knowing he had nothing left.

I crawled away. I got up to my knees and then to my feet. My eyes were blurry and I could feel them swelling up. While he was bent over at the waist, trying to catch his breath, I made a break for it and ran into the house. The door wasn't locked. My sweatshirt was torn and wet and I left a trail of mud and blood behind me on the living-room floor.

I picked up the phone and dialed a number. It picked up on one ring. Ten seconds later, my father stood in the doorway.

"Fuck," he shouted.

And then he was gone.

2

A MEDAL AND A TROPHY

Four months later I was standing on the blue line beside my team-mates in an arena five thousand miles from home. We were singing along, or at least shouting along, to a recording of the anthem that came through a scratchy old PA system. We were watching the flag behind us be raised. We had gold medals draped around our necks. We had just beaten the Russians, who were lined up across the ice from us, shooting us dirty looks.

For two weeks we had played the top young players in the world. I was the leading scorer on our team, and the youngest on the roster. Players on our team and the others were only a few months away from signing NHL contracts and playing in the league. I was going to have to wait a couple of years before that could happen, but still, professional hockey had never felt closer. When I had gone to Europe with the team, I felt like I had a pro career ahead of me. With the gold medal around my neck I thought that it was more than that. I thought I had a real shot to be a star.

Those two weeks in Europe were the best time of my life to that point. The biggest thing I'd ever won. The best hockey I had ever played. The best teammates I had ever played beside. The best coach I had ever played for.

I tried to drink it all in. I tried to get lost in the moment, and I did—halfway, anyway. But then reality kicked in, *my* reality. I looked up in the stands to see if my father was out there. That had been my habit since I was eight years old. Back then I was trying to find him. But since that night in January of that year, I had looked up in the stands hoping *not* to see him.

I thought he might be up there.

So did the coaches—they knew all about him.

So did the U.S. marshal over by our bench.

All American teams traveling to international competitions were accompanied by federal security after 9/11. The marshal who traveled with us had an added surveillance assignment: he had to keep an eye out for a stalker who was considered dangerous.

People told me that there was no way my father would make it to Europe. I wouldn't put anything past him. He wasn't in his right mind. He thought we could patch things up. He'd told people that we were working things out, or that we had a good father–son relationship even though I hadn't said a word to him since that night I had fought for my life and a life of my own on the lawn.

* * *

Just a couple of weeks after coming home from Europe with my gold medal, I was standing in an arena again, this time by the bench and in a suit. I heard my name called and I walked across a carpet that was laid across the ice. I didn't look up in the crowd and didn't wave. I just shook the hand of the league official, who then handed me the trophy that goes to the top first-year player in Canadian major junior hockey. I posed for pictures and smiled, but then I looked up into the stands to see if my father was there, to see if he was going to try to crash my party. He had a peace bond against him and then a restraining order but still he had made it out to my games in Ontario and in Michigan, even though security at the entrances had photocopies of his mug shot.

That wasn't all. He had sent me letters that I didn't open. He had made phone calls that I never picked up and had left messages that I deleted without listening to them.

Reporters were waiting for the players who had been part of the trophy presentation. They asked me questions, the usual, about my background. I dodged any personal stuff. I hoped they would think I was shy rather than evasive. Then they asked me about my season. I told them I wanted to focus on what was ahead. "Next season should be our best year ever so it should be fun," I told them.

On the other side of the room, reporters lined up in front of a kid named Ray Emery. He had won the award as the best goaltender in the major junior ranks. Someone asked him about me—if he was surprised that I had won the best-rookie trophy. Emery said he expected it. He told the reporters how I had scored on the first shot I took on him.

"He snapped it past my shoulder," Emery told them. "I said, who's this guy?" *Who is this guy?* A question a lot of people asked.

3

NO MORE SECRETS

I don't talk a lot about that night. I don't talk a lot about the years leading up to it. I'm not a public person. I have a small circle of close friends. They know my story, so there's no point in retelling it. There's certainly no point in going into gritty detail about it with them. Take it from me: nothing kills a conversation like describing those times when you were abused, when you suffered, when you feared for your life.

My wife, Sophie, knows more about my story that anyone else, but I wasn't able to tell her about it in one sitting. It would have made her too uncomfortable. No, it took years to tell her the stories, as much of them as I could recall. Even before I started filling in the picture, she knew the effects of the years of abuse had on me before I ever gave her the blow-by-blow. She knew how difficult it was for me to understand people's feelings. She knew, unfortunately, how quickly I could get angry and frustrated and anxious—just the smallest thing could set me off. She tolerated an awful lot, more than almost anyone would, and she could almost always talk me past it. I owed it to her to open up. It wasn't that I was keeping secrets from her or hiding my past. It was just too hard to talk about, just too hard to go back there. And of course I was worried how she would take the unpacking of all my baggage: I wasn't trying to win her sympathy and I've never thought anything is owed me because something bad happened to me. I owed her truth even if it made her push me away. And it could have been enough to push her away because this wasn't just my past but my present and future, because it's always going to be there.

I had to tell her one story at a time, each one leaving her in a puddle of tears and me with my gut twisted into a knot. It had to be done—she had to know. There couldn't be any secrets between us. Still, I hated doing it. *Hated it.* Not just that it reopened my old wounds. No, it was like I was making my wounds hers. Like I was putting her though the same pain that I suffered.

That's the legacy of abuse, I guess—the gift that keeps on giving.

It would be easy to not tell my story, to just get on with the rest of my life. But I feel like I have to open up this one time. There were hundreds of nights when I felt like the loneliest kid in the world. I was alone, but I know now that I wasn't the only one going through what I did. By telling my story, I'm telling others' as well.

I'm thirty now. Sophie and I have two sons. I know it's time to get past the anger. For much of my childhood I lived with fear of my abuser and with anger at the unfairness of it all. Once I broke free of my abuser, only the anger remained. After everything that I had to go through, I believed that I deserved my just reward. I can see now how my life could have been better, how my professional career could have been better, how I might even still be playing, if the anger had been behind me, or if I could have stopped, taken a breath and put the anger behind me. I wouldn't have walked away from the game at twenty-eight, what should have been my prime. I had loved the game but in the end I couldn't love it enough to change.

It's too late now. I know I'm done for playing the game. I've made mistakes; they're on me; they're not on my past. It's just how I dealt with it. I hope people who are haunted by cruelty and abuse will take something away from my story and make better choices than some I've made.

I'm telling my story to encourage parents to take time to analyze how they are raising their children. A lot of reasonable people do unreasonable things. Sometimes they have lapses. Parents who want to motivate their kids will cross a line and end up punishing them instead. This book isn't a manual by any stretch—I'm not an expert qualified to tell parents how to raise their kids. I'm a survivor of exactly how *not* to raise a kid. I hope that parents who read my story will recognize when they're pushing their kids too hard, like I was pushed. I hope they'll know when to back off rather than risk doing damage to their children's psyches and destroying their families. If just one parent, just one reasonable person, knows to lighten up because of reading this book, then telling my story will have been worthwhile.

I'm also telling my story so that adults will be able to spot red flags, to identify kids who might be victims of abuse by parents or guardians. I expect that people who read this book will realize that being able to pick out the boy or girl at risk is only the first step. They'll know that they have to act; that the bar isn't set at proof conclusive but rather strong suspicion; that the onus should be on the witness to report to authorities; and that there should be zero tolerance, no waiting for the abuse to happen again. I understand why people aren't inclined to act: they base their decisions on the context they know, how their own parents raised them. They presume that all others have the same common sense and common decency. Reading my story, they'll realize that those qualities aren't quite as common as they think. If this book encourages just one adult to report an incident of abuse when he or she might have otherwise stood by silently, if just one boy or girl is spared any physical or psychological harm because a reader of this book better understands the stakes involved, then telling my story will have been worthwhile.

And finally, I'm telling my story for sons and daughters who endured continual torment like I did. Like I said, I know I'm not alone. They're out there. They could have been kids who were athletes like I was. They could have been music prodigies. They could have been gifted in any number of ways. And because of their exceptional gifts, parents pushed them to unacceptable lengths. Maybe the parents did it out of greed, hoping to cash in on their kids' gifts. Maybe they did it because their kids' successes were a vicarious way of making up for their own failures. Maybe they did it because of mental illness. All are true in my case. If this book spurs them to seek professional help to heal the damage like I did, then putting it all down on the page will have been worthwhile.

part two

4

THE O'SULLIVANS

To tell my story, I have to start with the story of my father and his parents.

John O'Sullivan was born in England in February 1960. He was the oldest son of Bernard and Florence, immigrants who came to Canada in the mid-sixties and settled in a blue-collar neighborhood in the sprawling Toronto suburb of Scarborough. Bernard was calm, reserved, even gentlemanly. He had short gray hair and glasses and seemed to want to blend into the background. Physically, though, he was a presence—thick chested, maybe a bit over six feet tall and around 240 pounds. He towered over his wife. Florence was a stay-at-home mom to my father, his younger brother, Barry, and their little sister, Donna. She had to go it alone raising the brood. She and my grandfather came to Canada on their own, with no extended family here. There was no clan, no big family for get-togethers.

From what I knew of them and what I was told by my father, Bernard and Florence weren't particularly social, either. They didn't mix with their neighbors in any way, didn't attend church, didn't belong to any clubs.

Bernard worked at the Coca-Cola plant in Toronto. He was a lifer who punched the clock, who worked this single job from his arrival in Canada until his retirement. He had no close friends from his workplace, but the nature of the labor would have had something to do with that—production-line drudgery that he'd just want to escape. Socializing with guys from the plant would only remind you of the grind that awaited you when it was time to punch in again. He would have a drink now and then. I suspect there was a time when he did a bit more than that, and he wouldn't have been the only guy who had a bottle to keep him company through the workday.

The one thing that stands out for me about my grandparents was something that I had just heard about over the years. At some point before I was born, Florence had at least a couple of nervous breakdowns. At least that's how they labeled it. I suspect that she wasn't clinically diagnosed with any particular condition and didn't receive much in the way of treatment, if anything at all. At the time she would have felt too much stigma to seek out professional help. Typical of her time, I suppose. And in the years after that, too much shame would have been risked to discuss it openly in front of her grandchildren. I guess that's understandable, avoiding the subject being their way of coping. So I have no idea if she had some sort of emotional crisis that set her down a very dark road. It could have been postpartum depression. It could have been stress about her kids. It could have been loneliness. It could have been any of these things or dozens more, any combination or nothing at all. She might have just been disposed to anxiety. I'm sure that Bernard would have been sympathetic and supportive even if he didn't fully understand exactly what she was going through. By the time I came along, it seemed to have passed and she seemed reasonable happy.

From what I could tell, Bernard and Florence weren't neglectful parents, but they weren't overly involved or overtly loving. They provided for their kids, putting a roof over their heads and clothes on their backs but offering nothing in the way of extravagances. They wished for the best for their kids but let them find their own way and fend for themselves, all in the cause of developing their independence.

It's not surprising, then, that even as a teenager, my father considered himself his own creation. Not an inheritor. Not a chip off the old block. No, he considered himself his own man. Where my grandfather's accent had faded and he had come to think of himself as a Canadian, my father embraced his Irish roots and the notion of his tribe being warriors by nature. He was a disagreeable, defiant kid, looking for a fight rather than for a way to avoid one. He joined a boxing gym, hit the heavy bag and sparred, not so much to blow off steam as to get in his licks. He was a decent student, quick to pick things up but with no academic ambitions, but did more than enough to graduate even with spending the bare minimum of time on his schoolwork. School was a low priority because it had no impact on what he envisioned his career was going to be: professional hockey. From the time that he came to Canada and put on skates in house league, he was bound and determined to play in the NHL, to make pro money, to win fame and live a far better life than his father's. That he was just one of a million Canadian kids thinking the same didn't matter to him. If just one kid was going to make it, it was going to be him. That he had a late start in the game didn't matter either. He could make up for lost time just by putting in more hours every day. He believed that he wanted it more than anyone else and that that would be enough to get him to the Show. The first half of that proposition might have been true; the second, not even close.

5

MY FATHER'S (NOT SO GLORIOUS) CAREER

My father played youth-league hockey in Toronto, but not with the top organizations and not in the tiers with the most talent. In his day, the Metro Toronto Hockey League was the world's largest hockey organization, with 30,000 players. It was far easier to get into the most exclusive private school than it was to make the Toronto Marlies or one of the other triple-A teams in any age group. If your marks weren't solid enough, you could buy your way into a school, but if you couldn't keep up on the ice, there was no way that you were going to make it with one of the elite teams. And in the Toronto area, the players who moved to major junior, the NHL track, came exclusively from those top AAA programs.

My father had no doubts about his ability. He believed he was as good as anyone he was on the ice with and that no one out there matched him for toughness or will. Still, he never made it onto one of the triple-A teams. He figured that he got too late of a start, which might have been a factor, and that he didn't have the family connections that other players did, which wouldn't have been a factor at all. On both counts it was a way he could scapegoat Bernard for his own failures.

Back in '77, my father turned sixteen and became eligible for the Ontario Hockey Association's entry draft (the league is now known as the OHL). Teams had their scouts out looking for talent all season long and had a network of insiders across the province. Talented players didn't fly under their radar. Three hundred players from across the province were selected. My father wasn't one of them.

Despite the overwhelming odds against it, my father assumed that every team in the league had made a terrible mistake and began calling them up for a tryout as a walk-on.

My father never told me all the details, but I know how it would have played out. He would have had to get a general manager on the phone and convince him that he wasn't wasting his time. The GM would have been skeptical, and for good reason—the odds of drafted players making the team were already long. Competing against players two and three years older than them, fewer than one hundred of those draftees would make the rosters of the OHA's twelve teams. Every team blew off my father's cold calls that season. The next year he called around again and one team invited him in for a tryout.

The Brantford Alexanders were the worst team in the OHA—the worst by far. They won only twenty-three of sixty-eight games. How much my father played with the Alexanders is anybody's guess, but it certainly wasn't a lot. He might have been on the roster but didn't skate in a game. He might have only made it into an exhibition game.

Brantford's records for that season are incomplete, but statistics show up for players who made it into as few as three games. If my father had scored a goal or recorded an assist or even taken a penalty, it would show up. He couldn't have stayed there long before he was released. I've talked to a couple of players from that team and they had no memory of him whatsoever.

When the last-place team has no use for you, not even as a little-used guy at the end of the bench, you'd think that you had exhausted your options, that it was time to turn the page. He could have kept on playing hockey in a lesser league, a recreational league, and taken a job or gone back to school. But he wasn't going to let go. My father was a glutton for rejection.

In the Canadian major junior leagues, you are pretty well stuck with your region of origin. Kids in Ontario, like my father, play in the Ontario league. Kids in Quebec and points east wind up in the Quebec Major Junior Hockey League. Kids west of Ontario end up in the Western Hockey League. There are few exceptions, mostly elite kids who moved away from home at a young age to play for top teams. Even fewer kids jump from one league to another. It's a mark of my father's desperation to play—and his frustrations—that he wounded up play-ing in all three major junior leagues. I don't know of anybody else in the modern history of the sport in Canada who could make that claim. It's like getting thrown out of two Ivy League schools and then getting accepted by a third. You know there's a story there.

It started in the east.

My father had to get a release from the Alexanders and receive an exemption from the QMJHL, permitting him to play in Quebec after time in the OHA. That might explain why his name is scrubbed from existing records with Brantford—any verifiable appearances in games could have made him ineligible to play in the Q. He landed with the Hull Olympiques, an even worse team than Brantford in an even weaker league: just ten wins in seventy-two games. Records show that he played eight games in Hull, picking up two goals and an assist. Not a bad line of numbers, but not enough for the Olympiques to hold on to him. They traded him to the Shawinigan Cataractes, the second-worst team in the Quebec league. Again, he found it tough to get into the lineup, picking up no goals and just three assists in six games. It's not clear if he made it through the season, but probably not. Shawinigan didn't bring him back for the next season.

That type of rejection would crush anyone else, but my father wouldn't take no or even *non* for an answer.

The following fall, my father had to petition the Western Hockey League for a chance to play. At this point he would have been honing his skills as a negotiator if not as a hockey player. Again he managed to persuade a team, the Saskatoon Blades, to give him a shot. There were two WHL teams worse than Saskatoon that season, but one of them, the Great Falls Americans, folded before Christmas.

I hope you'll never know and can only imagine my father's desperation at this point. Like he had in the Quebec league, he managed to get into a handful of games with Saskatoon. Unlike his previous stops along the way, he managed to get into a couple of fights in games. It's easy to picture how that came about. Dropping the gloves with an opponent has been almost a form of initiation in the WHL. He would have been making his bones by fighting. He also might have been trying to win a spot with his fists in the lineup, as a goon. Though he had spent years in the gym and had been in dozens of fights in the streets, trying to be an enforcer would have been a last resort for him—he thought of himself as a skilled player, despite evidence to the contrary. His thinking: if he won a spot with the team as a brawler, it would only be a matter of time before they recognized he could do so much more than that.

It didn't get far. He stuck with the Blades a few weeks and was released. His junior career was over.

Defeat like this would have sucked the ambition out of 99 percent of junior hockey players. Many who've had success also know when they've gone as far as they can. My father was, of course, in that 1 percent who can't accept the unanimous opinion of coaches and managers who have spent years in the game. He knew better. He believed he had a future in the game even if there was abundant evidence that he didn't even have a present.

* * *

My father lasted a couple of days in the Winnipeg Jets' training camp in the fall of '81. He didn't have a chance to win a job. No one in his position would have. He was just one of dozens of spare bodies that showed up when camp opened. The players who are going to be on the NHL roster know that going in. Everybody in camp does. It doesn't sound like much, but this would turn out to be the highlight of his hockey career—getting to skate through drills with a bunch of NHLers.

Maybe my father thought he could compete for a spot with the Jets' CHL affiliate in Tulsa. He'd have been just about the only one who thought that. Players on the Tulsa Oilers had been all-stars with the major junior teams that had cut my father loose or that wouldn't even give him a tryout. I'll never know how he talked his way into an invitation to the Jets' camp—it's not like he had an agent out there making his case for him. If a guy with my father's credentials can talk his way into all three major junior leagues and then into an NHL camp, he should be a salesman, not a hockey player. But that's where his powers of persuasion ran out: he couldn't talk his way into anything more than that.

To stick around in pro hockey, he had to lower his sights as low as they could go: the Atlantic Coast Hockey League, the bottom of professional hockey's food chain.

The ACHL has been out of business for twenty-five years now, and only a few diehard fans in the Carolinas and Virginia, where the teams were based, would have noticed. The ACHL was way below the American Hockey League, the waiting room for those almost ready for the NHL or the last stop for those who barely miss making the grade. The ACHL was way below the International Hockey League, where one or two players on a roster might have a slim chance of making their way to the NHL. The ACHL was below the Central Hockey League, where teams might have a player who spent some time in the NHL and was holding on, almost always in vain, for a chance to make it back. All that is to say that the only thing between my father and the NHL was seven hundred other players.

The ACHL took pro hockey to grungy little arenas in Maryland, Virginia and the Carolinas, markets where hockey was a novelty sport, where the audience couldn't tell the difference between the NHL and the most watered-down minor-league product. ACHL teams offered players season-long contracts at just a bit better than subsistence living, not even three hundred bucks a week. Your typical ACHL player would share an apartment with a teammate or two, would have a bit of drinking money and on road trips would try to stretch his daily ten bucks in meal money. It was a young man's league, where it was hard to find a twenty-five-year-old in a dressing room.

My father didn't even get a season-long contract in the ACHL.

As you'd expect, turnover was pretty high in the ACHL, guys deciding on a daily basis that all the work and physical risk just weren't worth it anymore. To try to fill those always-opening spots, my father jumped from team to team on tryouts for five-game contracts. He was never in one place long enough to rent an apartment, so he lived out of his suitcase in motels. If he could remember all the places he played, all the tryouts he had, no one else could. Like that blank space beside his name in the Brantford Alexanders' records, the gaps in my father's CV do show up in hockey databases.

He started out with the Baltimore Skipjacks in the fall of '81. Dave Herbst, then a veteran forward with the Skipjacks, says my father was "a hockey drifter" who rubbed his teammates the wrong way right from the start. "We were a loose bunch and liked to have a good time," Herbst says. "Guys hung out together. We knew who we were, just young guys who liked to play hockey and pretty well had gone as far as we could go. We still liked to have fun. Then this guy came in and was taking everything so seriously, didn't have the time of day for anybody. Maybe on some teams the veterans didn't get close to the guys on the five-game contracts because you were just going to have to say 'See you later' to them at some point, but we weren't like that. But this guy had attitude and took things way more seriously than we did, like he was going to steal our jobs. And that was never going to happen."

Herbst and the rest of the Skipjacks might have forgotten completely about my father if it hadn't been for an incident that came

toward the end of his second and last five-game contract with Baltimore. My father must have sensed that "Moose" Lallo, the coach, was
not going to extend his contract and planned to cut him loose unless
one of the players was injured. In the middle of what turned out to be
his last game with Baltimore, my father had the puck near center ice
and Lallo yelled at him to dump the puck into the other team's end and
come off the ice for a line change. That would have been standard stuff
in the situation. For reasons only my father knew, he turned toward
the bench and fired a slapshot toward the coach and the Skipjacks. "It
might have been Moose that he was trying to hit, but Moose ducked
out of the way and it caught me in the jaw," Herbst says.

Herbst managed to turn his head, but the shot still left him with
broken teeth and fifteen stitches. While the trainer was waving smell-
ing salts under Herbst's nose and getting ready to take him to hospital
for X-rays, Lallo told my father to go to the dressing room—he was
done. The Skipjacks on the bench told the coach that they were going
to walk out if he didn't axe my father. But by the end of the period,
when the team went back to the dressing room for the intermission,
my father had cleaned out his stall.

That would have made an unforgettable exit, but my father wasn't
quite done and neither were the Skipjacks. A few days later my father
signed a five-game contract with the Winston-Salem Thunderbirds.
No team at any level moved more players in and out of the lineup than
Winston-Salem—my father was one of fifty-one players who played
for Winston-Salem in that fifty-game season. He made it through one
five-game contract and signed another. He didn't exactly tear it up in
his ten games with the team. He picked up three goals and a couple of
assists. He did pick up sixty minutes in penalties, most of them in a

game against his former Skipjacks teammates. "We ran him all night," Dave Herbst says. "He would have had at least three fights that night. After what he did, guys were lining up to get a piece of him."

There was no third five-game contract with Winston-Salem that season and it didn't look like he had any future there, but it would turn out that North Carolina would become his home for a while. And it was in Winston-Salem that he met the girl who would become his wife.

* * *

Anyone who has known my father would find it hard to imagine him in a romantic setting. Hockey at all levels is full of ladies' men, but people who played with my father or coached him could never imagine him chasing skirts. He seemed the farthest thing from that, antisocial not just with the teammates but with society at large. If anything, my father spent his time away from the rink dreaming up ways to make money. Of course, he was undercapitalized, or not capitalized at all, but that didn't stop him dreaming about making a big score in business. He dreaded the idea of punching a clock and wasting years away in a factory like his father.

He met a woman who was perfect for him in a couple of ways. Cathie Martin was a couple of years older than he was, but she was a girl without much in the way of life experience. She was an only child, protected, sheltered and probably a bit spoiled by her parents. After graduating from high school, she didn't head off to college and didn't have any idea what she wanted to do with the rest of her life. I don't know how they met exactly, but I imagine that she was starving for attention and my father was starving for that and everything else.

Cathie Martin's parents were wealthy. Her father had been sheriff of a town near Winston-Salem. After he left office, he developed a business, a company that manufactured fittings for hoses, and had at least sixty employees on the payroll. The Martins were a pretty sharp contrast to the O'Sullivans in blue-collar Scarborough. Even if he had been easy to get along with and to like, my father wouldn't have been his in-laws' type of people.

Their courtship is hard, maybe impossible, for me to imagine. Cathie and her parents had no idea about professional hockey, so when my father told them that he wanted to keep playing in the ACHL and wanted a future in the game, they wouldn't have second-guessed him. They wouldn't have known that his ambitions to make a living in hockey were a pipe dream. They might have even respected his determination, as deluded as it was. Even if they had their doubts, my father would have told Cathie the one thing that she wanted to hear: that he wanted to have kids. And whatever made the Martins' daughter happy made them happy.

My father came back for a second season in the ACHL and landed a couple of five-game contracts with the Hampton Roads Gulls. Still, he couldn't get a full-time job in the league, never mind anything that would sustain a reasonable person's hope for moving up to higher tiers in the game. Over the course of a season or so, the Martins had to become more aware of the cold realities of their future son-in-law's career prospects and offered to help him start up a business of his own, underwriting the first of what would be many sandwich shops and greasy spoons that he'd own and operate.

At some point during the engagement or after the marriage, the relationship between my father and his in-laws started to turn hostile.

I can only suppose that it was some sort of slight that he felt, but he kept his distance from them and stopped going by their home. That would never change. It didn't stop the Martins from offering to help him out financially and never stopped him from taking advantage of their generosity, but my father would not be in the same room as them ever again. He never took up an invitation from them and he went out of his way to avoid them.

Where else my father played that year is, again, something that even hockey historians will likely never dig up, but for some reason he landed the next fall with a men's senior team in Thompson, Manitoba. This was at least another step lower than the ACHL and one step up from recreational hockey—not the professional game in any sense. It seemed the least likely place to get scouted by a professional coach, but Tom Watt, the coach of the Winnipeg Jets, spotted my father in a game. Watt remembered my father from that training camp a couple of years before. He had been the coach of the University of Toronto Blues in the seventies and kept close ties to the school. That fall, he got a call from of U of T, asking if he knew of any players who might be able to fill out the varsity roster. Look down university rosters in Canada and you'll find players who spent seasons in major junior and occasionally in the pro minors. Watt told the U of T coach, Mike Keenan, that he had seen my father but had no idea if his marks would meet the school's high standards. Watt put Keenan in touch with my father, and the team staff were surprised to find that he was in fact academically qualified. Most minor-leaguers wouldn't have the marks to get into U of T, especially those who bounced around in major junior, switching schools—or, in my father's case, switching provinces. No pro teams were prepared to give him another tryout, never mind a short-term contract, so at age twenty-three, my father went back to school, in what looked like a chance to get on with the rest of his life.

My father was older than most of his teammates and had played pro, but he wasn't a ringer or a star on the team. He was a center on the third line. If he thought that U of T was some sort of springboard to the NHL, he was right—it wasn't for him, but it was for the team's MVP, André Hidi, who would wind up signing with the Washington Capitals after the season.

Even though he wasn't competing with his teammates for a spot on the roster or a contract, my father didn't mix with his teammates any more than he had with teammates in the ACHL. Most of the other players were serious students—almost all of them finished their degrees or graduate studies and landed white-collar jobs when they graduated. That wasn't the direction my father was heading. Almost everyone on the team was single and liked to hang out at the campus pubs. My father had a wife at home and always seemed to be racing into practice at the last minute and racing out right after. His teammates had no idea about my father's life away from the rink until the day they went to the Mr. Submarine sandwich shop across the street from Varsity Arena on Bloor Street after practice. The players were surprised that my father went along. He stood at the end of the line while they were getting their orders filled. When his was the last to be filled, he didn't pay. One of the players asked him how he got his sandwich for free and he told them, "I own this place."

Only after that did it come out that my father had three businesses on the go while he was a full-time student in the University of Toronto general arts program. And it turned out that his wife was doing assignments for him when he couldn't squeeze in the time between showing up in class, practice and working behind the counter at his franchises. His teammates hadn't seen that coming, but early on they had learned not to be surprised by anything "Crazy John" said or did. "I guess every dressing room has a guy that's out of the box," one former teammate says. "John just had this crazy look in his eyes and this crazy laugh."

Mike Keenan has a reputation as one of hockey's hard-asses. The idea of Iron Mike in the same room as my father sounds like a potential disaster—if my father ever shot a puck at him like he did at Moose Lallo in Baltimore, people in hockey would expect Keenan to pull out a small-gauge sidearm. Yet they never crossed swords. In fact, Paul Titanic, Keenan's assistant coach, remembers that the two actually got along. "Mike was tolerant of guys who were different," Titanic says.

It would have been hard for Keenan to find much fault with anyone on his team: the Blues that year were one of the strongest teams ever in Canadian university hockey, losing only one game all season and winning the national championship game over Concordia 9–1.

Somehow my father kept his grades up and stayed academically qualified while running his submarine franchises.

When Mike Keenan landed a job in the NHL, the University of Toronto athletic department went looking for a coach to take over the team at the last minute. It happened that the Winnipeg Jets had just fired Tom Watt, the coach who had recommended my father to Keenan the year before.

"There were huge cutbacks in the athletic department and we had to cut a staff of four down to one," Watt says. "Because of that the dressing room ended up in pretty bad shape. The players weren't happy with it. I wasn't happy with it, but there was nothing I could about except apologize. John decided that he was going to stage a protest—he took a shit in the shower. Left it there in the middle of the floor as a protest. His teammates were disgusted by it. I found out who did it—as unhappy as the players were with the cutbacks, they were a hell of a lot unhappier with a guy shitting in their shower room. I called John in the next day and he had no explanation—he was pretty defiant and profane about it. He went crazy. But that was that. He was kicked off the team, and he was out of school right after that. I've had some players do some strange things over the years but that was the single strangest thing ever. John would be up there with the strangest guys I ever coached."

6

GETTING OUT OF THE GAME AND GETTING BACK IN

Winston-Salem, North Carolina, June 1990

My first memory of hockey is one of my first memories, period. I remember watching the Stanley Cup final between Edmonton and Boston. SportsChannel carried the playoffs that year. I was five years old. I remember that my favorite player was Andy Moog. I don't know why the Boston goaltender was my favorite, probably just because I liked the sound of his name. The TV set in our house would have been one of the few in Winston-Salem tuned in to the game. It might not have been what you're thinking, reading this—it might not have been my father watching the game and telling me about it. He might not have been watching it at all, or it might have just been on in the background. I don't remember my father talking that much about hockey before I played it.

It had been a while since he'd thought of himself as a hockey player. Not long after he was kicked off the University of Toronto hockey team and dropped out of school, back in 1984, my mother became pregnant. They might have wanted to go back to North Carolina—the submarine sandwich business wasn't doing great. They decided to stick around long enough that they would have their medical expenses covered by the province's health plan rather than be uninsured in the U.S. and on the hook for money they just didn't have.

When I was born the next February, my parents started the process to go back to Winston-Salem. As soon as my father could unload his businesses, they packed up and headed south. My mother had always wanted kids but she realized early on that she needed help, so having her parents nearby meant they could pitch in. It made it a little less uncomfortable to ask her father for money to make ends meet and, later on, to ask him to underwrite my father's latest venture, a greasy spoon. And no big coincidence: the move gave my father one last shot at playing minor-league hockey, a chance to go back to the Thunderbirds for a couple of five-game contracts.

My father had been a fish out of water playing Canadian university hockey—he still thought of himself as a pro. But he wasn't a good fit going back to the Atlantic Coast league either. It had been fine when he was fairly fresh out of junior, but the ACHL was a young man's league. Everyone else was in his early twenties, single, just out for a good time before getting on with the rest of his life. Only a couple of years had passed, but in that time my father had gone from the youngest guy in the room to the oldest. For the average ACHL player, a $300-a-week salary put a serious crimp on partying, but for the sole breadwinner in a family it wasn't just his hardship alone.

That sort of money put a couple with a baby below the poverty line.

The game ended for my father in Winston-Salem.

Rick Dudley, an ex-NHL tough guy, actually got along with my father even if he couldn't figure him out. As a player and even as a coach, Dudley might have been even more tightly wired than my father (and definitely more talented). "John was a strange guy," Dudley says. "He was talented enough to play [in the Atlantic Coast league], but what good was that going to do him? He talked about the things he was going to do away from the game. I don't know how much he believed it. I have to suppose he realized that he had taken it as far as it goes. With him, someone telling him it was over wasn't going to work, but when he figured it out himself, he'd walk away without looking back. That's what I figured, anyway."

With Dudley there was no blow-up like there had been with Moose Lallo or Tom Watt. Dudley stopped just short of apologizing when he told my father that he didn't have another contract to offer him. "I told him that I would have kept him on but I just didn't have any room for him on the roster," Dudley says. "I didn't know how he'd take it, but it ended up he was okay with it."

That might have been true, but it's hard to square with the story that he told about his last game, a story that he was seemingly proud of or at least not embarrassed by. Knowing that he wasn't going to get another contract offer from Dudley and that no other team had any interest in him, my father didn't go to the dressing room with the rest of the team after the game. He didn't change back into the clothes that he wore to the arena. Instead he walked out of the arena and into the parking lot in his full equipment, across the asphalt still in his skates. I have no idea what to read into that.

Years later he'd tell people that he gave up the game to raise a family, but I was in diapers when he was giving it his last shot, leaving my mother alone with me while he was heading out on road trips.

* * *

My father set up with another greasy spoon in Winston-Salem, another dead end that my grandfather threw money into. The business was a break-even deal on its best days. My father always seemed to have a money-making scheme going on. And whatever he was doing, he didn't share the details with my mother. He treated her like she wasn't smart enough to understand his business, though if it ever came down to getting money, he had no problem sending her off to her parents as if he were sending her to the nearest ATM.

After he played his last game with Winston-Salem, my father ignored hockey completely, my mother said. He ignored himself too. He had always thought that clean living habits were going to be his ticket to the NHL. In retirement there was no point to the sacrifice, and he let everything slide all at once. He had been a gym guy as a young man—not with a bodybuilder's weight-lifting routine, more like the boxing routine he'd put me through later on. But after hanging up his skates, my father was like a lot of players when they retire: he shut it down physically. He didn't work out and didn't watch what he ate, so he gained weight. Within a couple of years he was twenty or even thirty pounds over his playing weight. He had lived healthy and he had criticized anyone who didn't. With no reason to stay in shape, he started smoking in a big way. He had never been a big drinker. Now he drank, and hardly ever at home, mostly to get out of the house. He wasn't what you'd call a social drinker—he didn't have a lot of friends in Winston-Salem. He was more like an anti-social drinker. He just felt better about getting drunk if there were other people around getting drunk.

If people ever asked, my father would tell them that got out of the game for "family" or that he wanted "to raise them the right way." Throwing "family" out there was convenient. Like he was sacrificing his career, the thing he loved to do, for a noble cause. He claimed the higher ground but never admitted the truth, that the game defeated him, that the game kicked his ass all those years waiting for a big break that never came. By the time I was enrolled in kindergarten and my sister Kelley was a year away from going to school, my father had nothing to do with hockey. There were no photographs of him as a player hanging at home. He didn't need the reminder. I don't ever remember seeing him in a team picture—he rarely lasted with one team long enough to get in one. I'm sure the game and his career rarely came up in conversation. Maybe in a hockey town, people would have known and asked him for some old war stories, but in Winston-Salem they would be more likely to talk about baseball or hoops with guys who had been stars in high school.

It was only when I was watching an NHL game on television that my father told me that he'd played. I can't say that I was hooked at that moment—I was too young to remember. That became the story that my parents would tell people later on. They probably exaggerated a bit, figuring it would be like Wayne Gretzky when he was a little kid, staring at the television screen, following the puck with his finger. It made a good story and it might have been half true. The other kids I grew up with wanted to play baseball, basketball and football, the usual sports you'd expect kids in North Carolina to be interested in. And I was interested in baseball a bit. Still, from six or seven, I wanted to play the game that my father had.

Winston-Salem was a hockey backwater for pros, and it was probably even farther off the axis at the grass roots. There were only a couple of rinks around the city, and those wouldn't have been able to keep going without figure skating. There were a couple of house leagues for kids, but nothing serious—no top coaches, a practice a week, a game a week, really not much of a chance to get on the ice more than that. Wanting to get serious about hockey in North Carolina back in the nineties was sort of like wanting to become a championship golfer in the Yukon—it can be done, but it's not easy. Carolina would get a team, but not for another eight years.

My interest in hockey brought back some memories for my father, but it might never have gone anywhere, or maybe I would have moved on and found something else. Our family scraped by and we moved from one rental to the next in not the best neighborhoods. We didn't go without food, but it was hard to cover the bills and have much left over. The births of my sisters were big financial hits too—we had no insurance, so I'm sure that my mother's folks bailed us out again. My father took the attitude that doing without extravagances was a way to build character. Hockey would have counted as an extravagance. Any parent of a hockey player can tell you it's a pricey game, even just to play house league, putting a kid in new skates and new equipment every year. When my grandparents got wind of my interest, they stepped in and bought me equipment.

I was six years old when my father signed me up for house league—two years younger than everyone else on the ice. I didn't get the earliest start in the game by any stretch, not compared to kids in Canada or the northeast or Michigan or Minnesota, where kids are on the ice as soon as they can walk, at two or three or four. I wasn't one of those preschoolers playing with cut-off sticks and shooting on nets in their driveways or basements. I was probably about the age my father was when he came over with his parents from England, and he had always complained that his development had been handicapped by a late start. And even though it was house league—just recreational hockey, entry-level stuff with a game and a practice a week—I wasn't a star by any means. I was an average size for a kid my age, so I looked tiny out there with eight- and nine-year-olds. I kept up, maybe did a little better than keep up, but I wasn't a natural for the game. My first year in the game, you'd have to look pretty hard and see something that everyone else missed to think that I was gifted.

My father did. He was dead sure of it.

He started working with me every day after school. He hadn't pitched his equipment, but he hadn't picked up a stick or opened his hockey bag since his last game with the Thunderbirds. He didn't have the money to send me to summer hockey school to learn from top coaches, so he decided to do take on the work himself. He rented ice time, and I still don't know where he found the money to do that. He laced up skates that he had figured he'd never put on again. He had me do drills. Every little detail, he taught me. People who had seen him play and who saw me years later would always say that I carried my stick the same way he did, that it was obvious who taught me the game. When he was growing up, fathers in Scarborough had been on the ice with their sons, teaching them the game, and he told me how lucky I was that he was there for me. Really, he was saying how unlucky he had been to have to try to teach himself the game on his own, his father being new to the country and tied down by an afternoon shift that kept him away from his kids except at breakfast.

A lot of people didn't completely buy into my father's claim that circumstances had worked against him and had limited how far he could go in the game. There's no way that people could miss his bitterness. But I was too young to know the difference. When he explained to me how the odds had been stacked against him, I was six or seven, and of course I believed every word. However he described himself as a player, I bought it. I felt like he hadn't got what he deserved. More than that, I took it as a crime against our family. When you're that young, you can god up your father, and I did.

It's stating the obvious to say that my father started to live vicariously. Another thing might not be so obvious: I made it my mission to get justice for us. Before I knew what the word *vindication* meant, I was living it every time I stepped on the ice. I was going to be his proof. I was going to take him with me. I was going to *be* him, if everything had been laid out for him like he was laying it out for me.

Hockey school was beyond our means, but my father was determined that I wasn't going to want for anything else if it gave me a better chance at success. That started with equipment. Even though we were living on basics otherwise, he was going to spare no expense on my second pair of skates. He bought me the most expensive out there, Bauers, his favorite brand in his playing days. They would have been the only pair in house league in North Carolina, top-of-the-line skates that top older players would have worn. My father was going to be as particular for me as if he were outfitting himself, and he let me know that he was doing this. He told me it was up to me to play like I deserved those skates. He told me that I was wearing pro skates, so I should play like a pro and I should put in the time like one.

He filled my head. He told me what it was going to take to become a professional and how lucky I was to have an ex-pro as my father.

One thing hit home above all, though. I would have been seven or eight when he said it for the first of a thousand times—more, really.

"I'm doing all this for you."

I bought in the way only a kid can buy in. I wanted his attention. I wanted his approval. I was going to make it right.

I was going to be the epitome of all the virtues he claimed had gone unappreciated in him as a player. He claimed that no one had been tougher, no one more determined. He said that he hoped I'd be the same way, though he made that sound almost impossible. He'd say that he was worried that I might take after my mother too much—he made it sound like a joke, though he said it with a straight face, just enough to make me wonder if he really believed it.

I was going to do it all for him.

* * *

In my second year of hockey, age seven, still playing against kids a couple of years older than me, I led the Winston-Salem house league in scoring. A lot of parents would have been more than happy with their son enjoying a game and doing well, but not my father. He saw dark clouds blowing in.

As soon as I started doing well, he figured I was at risk of becoming his story turned inside out. He had grown up in the world's most competitive hockey environment without support from a parent who understood the game. I was growing up with all the support in a foreign place for the game. I could hit a ceiling just like he did.

There was some truth in that.

Even if I was the best player, it was house league in Winston-Salem, North Carolina. Kids in Toronto and other traditional hockey cities played more games against better players, practiced more with better coaches. Their top teams traveled to tournaments to play the best kids in Canada and the U.S. Everything was just more serious in those places. And those kids would pull away from me. Every week they'd have one or two more practices and one or two more games under their belt than I'd get in Winston-Salem. And those kids would be playing beside skilled kids who would make them better—in Winston-Salem, a lot of times, I had to slow down to play at my teammates' speed.

I'm sure that the level of the game in North Carolina is higher today than it was back in the early nineties. When the Carolina Hurricanes played the first NHL game in the state in 1997, hockey's profile took off. When the team won the Stanley Cup in 2006, a lot more kids were looking to play the game. And hockey's reach is growing now to places where the game has no traditions at all. Still, as of the early nineties, no player born in the Carolinas had ever played a game in the NHL. The culture of the game was going to change there, but not soon enough for me.

So my father made a big leap, the first of many. He decided that we were going to move to Toronto to advance my hockey career—if an eight-year-old with a couple of years in house league can be described as having a career.

It couldn't have been an easy move. He had railed against the place. Though he never said so, he had to associate the city with his failures. It wasn't home for him in any way. He did speak to his parents, but I wouldn't say that they were particularly close—in all the years we were in Winston-Salem, he'd gone back to see them no more than a couple of times. Though his sister had drifted away from the family, my father might have thought that moving back would give a chance to reconnect with his brother, Barry.

My father convinced my mother that the move wasn't just for hockey. He made a case that the schools were better and they wouldn't have to worry about medical bills. That would make life a little less tense. So would a little distance between my father and the Martins. At this point, my father had effectively cut himself off from them. In all my life I can't remember him ever going over to their home or them coming over to ours. It was always my mother taking us to their house. When my grandparents went on vacation to a resort in West Virginia, I'd go up there with Kelley and, later on, our little sister, Shannon, but my father would always stay behind. I never saw my father and the Martins in the same room, and I can't say that they ever spoke on the phone.

The move had its benefits in a lot of ways. Not that life would be better, just that it *could* be. But I'm sure that we wouldn't have gone to Toronto if it weren't for my chance to become a better player.

* * *

Over the years I've heard of families that shipped off their kids at a young age so that they could play at an elite level of hockey or another sport. It's done more now than you might suspect, but it's something that goes back a long time. Back when my father was playing peewee hockey, a twelve-year-old kid moved away from his family in Brantford, Ontario, to play for a team in Toronto. All the same reasons were in play: the kid's father, a former minor-league player, thought his son was being limited by the level of game that was played in his hometown and that he needed a bigger challenge. A lot of people thought his decision to send his son away crossed a line. They thought it was crazy for a kid to leave home for the sake of a game while he was still in grade school. It would have seemed crazy if he had crashed and burned. It seemed a lot less crazy when that twelve-year-old was named the NHL's most valuable player before his twentieth birthday. Yeah, they used to say that Wayne Gretzky was pushed too hard.

A lot of parents have followed Walter Gretzky's lead since then, and some of their kids have landed in the NHL. My father wasn't about to send me off at age eight, but he wasn't about to wait, either. His career, he thought, was the cautionary tale of the high cost of a late start. We were going to move, and again he made a decision and claimed the high ground: we were moving for my benefit and to keep the family intact. He made it sound like a sacrifice he was willing to make. Heartfelt stuff, the way he'd play it. Really, though, he didn't trust anyone else to coach me. It didn't matter if the coach had a record of winning teams and successful players—the way my father saw it, that coach might focus on other players and not give me enough ice time and attention. It didn't matter if the coach had played the game—the way my father saw it, he knew more about the game than anyone who was coaching in minor hockey. It didn't even matter if the coach had played in the NHL—the way my father saw it, a guy who had played in the NHL had only got the breaks that he hadn't.

My father thought he had to watch over me. He talked about getting only one chance to become a player, just one chance to get it right. One slip, a year wasted, and other kids would pass me and I'd never catch up. He hammered the message that every game was a matter of life or death. If I didn't play well, if I didn't make it, it wasn't going to be just *my* disappointment, *my* wasted chance. No, if I was anything less than the best, I was going to let him down, let the family down. That's what he sold me and that's what I bought, all in. "We're doing it all for you," my father said, meaning moving a thousand miles away and starting over. It might seem like my father was watching over me to protect my interests, but he was invested in my success. He had to watch over me to protect his own interests. And it was my father almost to the exclusion to my mother. Early on, he left packing my equipment to my mother but one time she forgot to pack my helmet and I couldn't play in a game. For years after that, my father took charge and my mother almost always stayed home when we went to the rink. It wasn't a family event for me, not like it was with other kids who went to the arena with either of their parents and most of the time both. It was my father's time, period.

Eight years after being bounced from the game, he was getting back in. It was at a lower level, the grass roots, but that was for just now, he thought. He was planning on getting all the way back in and more.

7

THE HOCKEY HANDBOOK

Toronto, Ontario, 1993

After we moved back to Toronto when I was eight, my father found a book that he would make his Bible: *The Hockey Handbook*, by Lloyd Percival. And because the book was my father's Bible, it was mine. I would know every page of it. I'd live every page of it growing up.

Percival hadn't been a hockey player—he had played tennis and cricket and had boxed. He was better known for founding the Fitness Institute, a training center in Toronto's west end that had attracted a lot of Olympic and professional athletes, including NHL players, back in the seventies when my father was growing up. It would have been out of my father's price range as a kid—another advantage other players had over him. They could get the top personal training and conditioning while my father had to make up his own program as he went along.

Percival had a lot of ideas that were way out of the box when he wrote the first edition of *The Hockey Handbook* back in the late fifties. Coaches in the NHL carved him and called the book bullshit and worse. The book would have been out of print when my father was growing up and taking up the game. Then in the eighties it came out that *The Hockey Handbook* was the training manual for the coaches of the Soviet Union's national program, which won Olympic gold medals and dominated the amateur game for a couple of decades. After that publishers printed a new edition of the book and my father picked up a copy.

My father didn't look for other textbooks and training guides. He thought that Percival book was the ticket. Every drill on every page wound up consuming hundreds of hours of my life. Whether it was a puck on the ice or a ball on the concrete floor in the basement, I'd spend hours every day doing what Percival called "shadow stickhandling" with a golf ball: like a fighter shadowboxes an opponent he imagines, I stickhandled through whole games without anyone else in the room except my father standing there, pushing me. In the basement he'd put a blindfold on me and have me stickhandle for hours more just on feel, also a drill out of Percival's book. My father would cover the net with a sheet of plywood with only small slots at the top and bottom corners; I had to hit the same slot four times in a row before moving to the next, or try to hit each of the four in four straight tries without a single miss. I counted shots by the hundreds and then counted them again into the thousands.

Hours laid together—whole weeks and months of my life—were given over to repeating the same drills. Wherever we lived for the next eight years of my life, it was the same routine: my father would push me through stickhandling and shooting drills out on the ice at an arena, away from team practice, or he would take me downstairs at home. After a few hours he'd have me doing push-ups or sit-ups or running intervals out on the street. Every time we were out on the ice, he'd push me through skating drills until it felt like my legs were filled with sand. Players at every level of the game dread "bag skates"—practices with long, drawn-out skating drills that are supposed to develop conditioning and punish teams for what a coach thinks is a lousy effort. Well, bag skates were my usual working day when I went to the rink for a private session with my father. I never felt physically pushed in practices with my teams growing up—that hour or hour and a half would fly by and be a lot of fun compared to those times I was on the ice alone with my father.

My father pushed me through *The Hockey Handbook*, and I didn't push back when I was eight or nine years old. I took it all as a challenge. He told me that if I did everything in the program every day and put the sweat in, I was going to make the NHL, and I bought it. He'd put me through a workout when my team had a day off. He'd put me through workouts before and after my team's practices. He'd put me through workouts after my team's games, all the while telling me what I had done out on the ice. And when my team went to weekend tournaments, playing four or even five games in a couple of days, he'd put me through workouts in the gaps on the schedule—while other kids were eating lunch or dinner, I'd be out in the parking lot stickhandling or at the arena running steps.

My father pushed me, but I could motivate myself for most of it. Those first years I took it all as a challenge. And, yeah, I loved the game—I just looked at this as the price I had to pay to play. I created challenges, little mind games, to get past the boredom. It would be different teams I was playing against every night when I was shadow stickhandling in the basement. I'd be racing imaginary players when I was out on the ice doing skating drills. I could try to make it new every day and night.

And the bottom line is that I didn't know any different. When I was a kid in North Carolina, I didn't know any real hockey players—my father told me there weren't any in the South. When I got to Toronto, I didn't get a chance to know the other kids on the team—my father told me that what I was doing was what they were doing, so I just figured that no one who played hockey seriously had the time to hang out with other kids.

It's easier to look back and put together what I was thinking when all this was going on. It's harder to get inside my father's mind. All those hours I spent working through *The Hockey Handbook*, and he had to watch it all. He didn't trust me to do the work in the basement on my own. He thought he had to be there in case I messed up or got lazy. He had to be there when he rented ice and put me through a private workout—a liability thing that required an adult to supervise a minor—but he felt like he had to be there anyway to make sure that I put the work in. Unlike me, he knew that there were other things in life, but this was the one thing he chose above all else—above my mother, above my sisters, above his family. He had no close friends, and those he did have he hardly ever saw except for a few beers and maybe to show me off, make me do the *Hockey Handbook* drills for them like some sort of a floor show. My playing and practicing took priority over everything else, and what little money we had he poured into the dues for my team and ice rental.

I've always wondered if Percival would have written the book if he knew the awful way that my father would use it. I'm sure a lot of players benefited from *The Hockey Handbook*, but I've always believed there had to be hundreds of other kids who were put through these drills the same way I was—until there was no sense of play or practice, just work, and in the worst cases, punishment. Percival must have expected that some coaches and parents might take his training program to an extreme, because at the end of the book he included a section on coaching philosophy, a section that speaks directly to people like my father. He laid out how coaches should exercise understanding and patience, how they should *encourage* rather than *threaten*, how they should be friends rather than the bosses of their players. He laid out rules that seem basic to being not just a good coach but also a decent human being. The section feels tacked on, and after a couple of hundred pages of technical stuff and X's and O's, a lot of readers might have not made it that far. Really, Percival should have used the first chapter to deliver the message or put an advisory on the cover. "It is better," Percival wrote, "to build a player's ego rather than knock it down, and in every case be prepared to substitute analysis for criticism. A player's failure is almost always the failure of his coach. Bawling out in public is not only bad for the player but also gives the coach an unpleasant reputation with the rest of the team."

I didn't get a chance to read *The Hockey Handbook* when I was a kid. It was my father's book, something he wouldn't trust me with. Looking at this paragraph twenty years after my father started putting me through the *Hockey Handbook* drills, it seems so strange that Percival believed that the coaches should take a paternal approach to players. Really he was saying that they should be supportive father figures for them. I suppose my father never had a chance to play for anyone like that in major junior or the minor pros—his coaches would have believed that they couldn't afford to be friends with players, not when they had to trade or cut them, stuff you don't do to friends.

In fact my father wound up doing the exact opposite—he treated me like a hard-ass minor-league coach would have treated him. Everyone in the game knows and hates the guy who is bitter about falling short of the Show and takes it out on the players who have to ride the bus with him. After games, games that I scored four or five goals in, my father would ream me out for minor stuff—he'd blow up and call me "a little fag" before I had any idea what it meant. When he'd rent ice and get on the ice with me, he would slap the back of my helmet and daze me if he thought I wasn't trying hard enough. It was as if he learned his fathering skills in the Atlantic Coast Hockey League. Maybe if he had ever played for a coach who had gone out of his way to help him out, maybe if he had stuck around with Rick Dudley in Winston-Salem, he might have turned out different—not just a better player, but a different sort of father.

8

THE TRAINING TABLE

Toronto, Ontario, 1994

The Hockey Handbook gave a coach and a player a lot of direction on skill development, but it made no mention of diet. Looking back, my life would have been a lot easier if Percival had laid out some sort of meal plan, something that balanced the food groups for better performance. My father didn't have a guidebook on that count, just his own lunatic theories: he was convinced that I would grow taller and get stronger if I ate super-sized portions at every meal. He gave me portions that would be appropriate for two adults or three kids, three meals a day. I wasn't allowed to snack, but he hardly had to enforce that—I felt so stuffed so often that I'd have to save up an appetite for the next sitting. That I was average-sized and stayed average-sized didn't faze him. Others would think that the experiment wasn't working, but my father just doubled down and heaped more food on my plate. It could have turned out to be a disaster if I didn't have a fast metabolism. I could have easily ended up obese or diabetic if I hadn't been burning thousands of calories every day.

Making all this tougher was the fact that my mother wasn't a great cook by any stretch. It was like the Three Bears taken to an extreme: one meal was undercooked, one was burnt and the third was the right temperature but tasteless. I used to look forward to the times when my father brought leftovers home from the greasy spoon. Still, I preferred to take my chances with her cooking than my father's. Thankfully, it was rare that he'd have to make dinner. But one time still makes me nauseous just thinking about it.

I'm not sure where my mother was—it might have been that she had to go to hospital with my sister and was kept there for hours. Whatever the case, dinner was left up to my father. He had never made a meal for himself in his life. Before my mother had done it for him, it had been *his* mother, then billet families that he stayed with in junior, then burger joints in the minors, then whatever his employees at the submarine sandwich shop or his fry cook at the greasy spoon whipped up. That night my father made what would have been a gruesome dinner even if a French chef had prepared it: Spam and baked beans.

My father heated up the Spam on the stovetop and put the baked beans in a pot. Then he piled it high on my plate. I don't know that I would have been able to keep it down if it were a normal-sized helping, probably not. But when I balked at eating it and told him that I wasn't hungry, he just put more on my plate and ordered me to finish it.

Soon I was on my knees in the kitchen, throwing up on the floor.

That would have been bad enough but it got worse. At that point my father scooped my vomit onto a plate and told me to eat it. I started to cry and he slapped me in the back of the head and said there was more of that waiting if I didn't clean my plate. And so I did. I ate my vomit.

And I vomited again.

And again, my father scooped up my vomit and made me try again to finish up.

I ate again, vomited again, was slapped again, cried again and again.

Eventually, I managed to keep my food and the vomit down, though I almost choked a few times with the food coming back up. As overstuffed as I was so many other nights, I actually hurt when I went to sleep that night. It probably wasn't even going to sleep so much as passing out from the effort. Just the eating and re-eating had left me exhausted and sweating like I had a fever.

And to this day, just the smell of baked beans makes me dizzy and sick to my stomach.

9

HIS DO-OVER

I'm sure that when I first skated in a tryout with the Toronto Marlies AAA atom team, players and parents and coaches were wondering who I was and whether I really did come from North Carolina. The Marlies were probably the highest-profile atom-age team in the city—all kinds of history, kids who went on to play in the NHL, a program for ten-year-olds that was as professional as a lot of college teams. I was eight years old and I'm sure that the Marlies' staff were ready to brush my father off when he approached them about getting me a tryout. It was going to be the first of many times that my father managed to find his way and mine past a coach who thought I wouldn't be able to keep up with older players and wouldn't be able to stay out of harm's way on the ice.

My father was wound up so tight at home and with me when he was on the ice putting me through a workout, but he was a different guy at the arena when the Marlies practiced or played. He talked to other fathers and mixed with other families after games. He made jokes in a way that he would never do when we were home or alone together. He played the role of a cool dad, the guy who is rough around the edges, will swear in front of the kids on the team, making their dads seem uptight by comparison. And they *were* uptight—and successful. Most of the fathers were white-collar professional, executive types. They had done well with their lives, and my father couldn't possibly fit in with them, so he tried being something else: the guy who had been there and done that. I'm sure a lot of the parents could see right through it, but the kids ate it up.

My father talked a lot about his playing days—this was back before there were hockey databases where you can look up anyone who has played a professional game, so I know that my father padded his credentials and improved on the truth, as much as he could. Still, even if he stuck close to the truth, he would have made it farther than most of the other fathers—he had played for a national champion at U of T.

In other words, my father mounted a charm offensive. He had a sense that he had to tone down his act and get along with the coaches and the other players' families or else he'd wear out his welcome and mine. That charm offensive lasted right up until the drop of the puck and it picked up again at the final buzzer, but during the game, while I was out on the ice, he turned into a different guy completely.

It's not that my father wasn't self-aware—he knew enough to move away from the families when the game started and to stand alone in a corner of the rink. Whenever I was on the ice, I could hear him shouting at me. In fact, everyone in the arena could hear him shouting at me. It had to turn heads in the stands, but I had heard it before—he was no different during our games from during my workouts.

Not that he yelled at opponents or my teammates or the ref. No, he yelled only at me. There's a voice in your head when you play that tells you where to go and what to do next—well, the voice in my head had to compete with the shouting from the corner of the arena where my father was standing.

My father's ambition—that is, his ambition for, with and through me—really crystallized my year with the Marlies. Before we'd left North Carolina he was convinced—or at least had convinced himself—that I was going to make it as a professional player. It's a hell of a leap to see a seven-year-old in house league and be able to project him to professional hockey. It's an even bigger leap when that house league is in Winston-Salem. I was coming from a vacuum as far as hockey went and, with the Marlies, I made an elite team two years ahead of my class. It was something like going from grade 10 at a vocational school to making the honor roll in physics at MIT. It can be done, but it really shouldn't happen. Making the Marlies and playing well proved him right—to his mind, anyway.

That said, it wasn't all about what I had done. It was also about his life at that point. He had thought all those years that hockey was going to be his profession, but seven years had gone by since he'd cashed his last puny check from the Thunderbirds. Coming back to Toronto, he didn't even have a job that was as reliable as his father's. Short of the tap that he could get my mother to turn on with her parents, he had nothing going on to be optimistic about. It wasn't just that he saw something in me—he was desperate to see something good in his own life somewhere, anywhere. Coming back to Toronto and seeing me succeed where even he'd admit he struggled by comparison, he had reason to believe, when not long before he had just about given up.

He talked about how I was only going to get one chance to make good in the game. The fact was, he *had* a second chance. I was his do-over.

* * *

We were a good team but not a championship team that year, something that would become a theme in my career. I'm sure that my game improved over the course of the season—the move to Toronto was a boon to my skills development, pushing me harder than any competition in North Carolina or even in states with a much better quality of minor hockey might have. Still, my father wasn't satisfied with the progress I was making. Kids in minor hockey often stick with one organization all the way from atom to midget, from age ten to sixteen. Once a kid made a Marlies team, he'd have the inside track to making the squad the next season. But after I played as a double underager with the Marlies, my father started to look for other teams for me to play for the next season. I don't know exactly what went on behind the scenes, but the coaches and organizers had had their fill of my father's act. No matter how much my father tried to fit in, he didn't.

Minor hockey is pretty tolerant of "involved" parents—that's the word that you'll always hear coaches use, their shorthand for "over-involved" or "meddling." Involved parents are hockey's equivalent of stage mothers in the entertainment business. And that was my father. He was the most involved of the Marlies parents that year. He rubbed the coaches the wrong way. They thought he was way over the top with how he behaved at games. Even though AAA hockey is the most serious level of the game in minor hockey, all but the involved parents don't lose sight of the fact that it's kids who are out on the ice—in the case of Marlies that year, kids in grades 4 or 5. All but the involved parents understand that the game might be important but that not every game is life or death. My father took notes during our games so that on the trip home he could go over, point by point, what I did wrong—and it was always what I did wrong.

My father had been a professional hockey player of no big distinction. With the move to Toronto, he became a professional parent. He was a problem. Coaches and teams can deal with some of their players' problems and try to avoid others. When a parent is a problem, they try to steer clear of it. Someone might have said something directly to my father about toning down his act at the arena, but even if no one did, the message from the coaches and other parents would have been pretty clear to my father. *It just isn't done.* And my father would have brushed that off. His attitude would have been: *They don't know anything. They never played the game. You don't like me—who needs you?* They were at cross-purposes. They wanted him to back off; he wanted a bigger role. He wanted to be able to take an active hand with me. He wanted to be on the ice with me.

So my father looked for another place for me to play—something else that would become a theme in my career, just like it had been in his. He had never played for the same team or even the same league from one season to the next. A lot of the time he hadn't even lasted a season with a team. That was going to be how it would be for me. With him managing me—and he looked at it as just that, *managing*—it was inevitable that this was going to be "like father, like son." It wasn't a matter of influence, like how with all his coaching I ended up carrying my stick just like him or picked up some of his mannerisms on the ice. No, this was a matter of control. I was going to pick up pretty much where he'd left off as a player.

I ended up with the Toronto Red Wings that next season, and my father worked as an assistant coach with the team. The Red Wings would be the best team that I played with through minor hockey—we lost only a couple of games all season. We had a bunch of kids who went on to play in major junior. A couple, like Chris Campoli, made it to the NHL. It should have been all good memories that I took away from that season, but one thing stuck with me that has always bothered me and that would be best evidence of his screwed-up values, at least within the dressing room of a team that I played for.

One day during a practice my father took me aside to tell me to drop my gloves during practice and fight another kid, one of my linemates. I'll just call him Steve.

"Punch him the first chance you get," he said.

He didn't say why, and I knew not to ask him. I also knew that if I didn't, I was going to be in all kinds of shit afterward. Either I was going to fight Steve or my father was going to thump me later on. I was resigned to the fact that my father was going to slap me around at some point, but I was prepared to do whatever it took to avoid it for as long as I could. And that's how I looked at it with Steve. If it meant slugging a kid I liked, a kid who'd invited me for a sleepover, a kid I considered a friend, then I didn't have much of a choice. Suckering Steve was a matter of self-defense.

I'll admit that I wasn't a Boy Scout. My father had taught me how to fight on the ice and how to fight in the street. I had a lot of fights on the playground at school, stuff that I never told my father about. Maybe I did it because I was wound up like a golf ball, with all the shit I was dealing with at home. I have to accept the blame for those. And I had been a willing participant in a lot of my fights in games. My father might have told me to go out on the ice and go after a kid, but often he was just authorizing me to do what I already wanted to do.

That wasn't the case with Steve, though. And that wasn't the case when my father told me to do the same thing with other teammates in minor hockey later on. I've seen Steve a bunch of times in all those years since. I wouldn't say that we're close friends, but I worked out with him a few times in the off-season when we were both playing pro. We never discussed that fight.

I've never understood why my father had me pop Steve. Was it something that Steve said to my father, or a look he gave him? Was it something between my father and Steve's father? Was it that my father thought he needed to wake me up? Or just to prove to himself and to me that he was in complete control? I'll never know. But with everything that came out after, I suspect Steve never brought up the fight because he had a pretty good idea that anything I did was whatever my father wanted. If I did impulsive things, a lot of the time it was my father's impulses that I felt I had to act on.

You wouldn't say that a father telling his son to punch out a teammate was trying to clean up his act. After being uninvited by the Marlies, my father didn't feel like he had to tone down his act with the Red Wings. Because he was one of only a few fathers who could make it out to every practice and game, my father wound up as an assistant coach with the Red Wings. Parents who coach their kids usually go out of their way to avoid the perception of favoritism, but my father either couldn't help himself or couldn't be bothered. Nominally he was an assistant coach, but really he held the position so that he could coach me directly, like a personal coach. He gave some attention to my linemates but spent most of his time telling me what to do.

Word about my father had made it around the Greater Toronto Hockey League when I played for the Marlies, but some people might have been willing to give him the benefit of the doubt, thinking that someone with an axe to grind might have been spreading bad rumors about him. My father's act with the Red Wings left no doubt about it. More people had seen it up close. If it had been based just on my play, the Red Wings would have had me back, moving me up with my teammates to peewee. But the top teams not only had the pick of the players—they had the pick of the parents. The Red Wings wouldn't have wanted my father back behind the bench again. No team in Toronto would have been interested in having me if that was the condition my father attached.

My father had moved our family to Toronto to give me a chance to play with and against the best level of competition. Within two years he had earned a reputation as the Hockey Father from Hell. No team would put up with his level of "involvement." So we were going to have to move again. The first time, we had moved for a better opportunity for me on the ice. This time we were moving so that my father could stay involved. We had to go where they knew nothing about my father's reputation—even outside Toronto, the word would have made it around.

So we packed up and headed off to Sterling Heights, Michigan. Not that we had any roots or connections there. And not like there were a lot of jobs in a state where the automakers were laying off workers ten thousand at a time. We moved there for my hockey career. My father was doing it all for *me* again, even though I was the one who was switching schools and trying to make a new set of friends. My mother wasn't doing it all for me—she was just doing it because my father said that's what we were going to do. Even if it didn't make sense to her, she wasn't going to question him. Both my sisters were dragged along, again with no say and no consideration from my parents.

Another season, another team, another league and this time crossing the border—another theme from my father's career that was becoming one of my own. I was a hockey drifter at age nine.

10

KICKED OUT OF PRACTICE

Michigan, 1996

My family was able to move pretty freely across the border—my father had a Canadian passport and my mother was a U.S. citizen. I think Customs officers didn't give them too much attention going back and forth. Being in Sterling Heights made for an easy commute across the border to Windsor. If any of us got sick and needed to see a doctor, we just had to drive through the tunnel to see one, my father claiming that we still lived in Ontario and using his parents' address. That's how we lived in so many way—things were pretty sketchy, and my father made things up as he went along. He had a bunch of fake IDs and fake paperwork, whatever he needed to get work and keep a car on the road. He also had my mother's parents, who were ready to step in if ever the electricity was going to be turned off.

That first year in Michigan, my father didn't try to get me a tryout with the top teams. Compuware, Little Caesars and HoneyBaked were established sponsored outfits that played against the top teams in Toronto and traveled across the U.S. for elite tournaments. If I had landed with any of those three teams, it wouldn't have been a step down from the GTHL at all. Those teams might have been leery about letting a ten-year-old try out for a team of twelve-year-olds. They would also have a network of contacts in the GTHL who would have given them the lowdown on my father. Instead my father lined up a tryout with the Michigan Nationals, a new program and team overmatched against Compuware, Little Caesars and HoneyBaked. Again he'd convince a coach that I was up to playing against players two years older than me—very few kids are. My father couldn't find any real problem with the Nationals' coach, Dwight Foster. Dwight had been a first-round NHL draft pick and played ten years in the NHL. He would have lasted longer if an injury hadn't cut his career short.

Dwight was skeptical at first about a double underager trying out for his team, and he was skeptical when my father told him that he had bounced around the minor leagues. But after I skated with the team in a couple of practices, I convinced him that I was going to be able to keep with the bigger kids—I wasn't the best player on the team, but I could help. My father also convinced Dwight to take him on as an assistant coach, telling him how successful the Red Wings had been with him behind the bench the previous season. The Nationals didn't have any other assistant coaches, so Dwight could use any help that he could get. My father helped for a while but then he didn't. He became a problem again.

It was the same story as in Toronto with the Red Wings—my father was supposed to work with the team but focused almost exclusively on me. By age ten, I had stopped following my father blindly. Stuff that I had accepted as my lot in life I had started to question. I had put it together that not all hockey players went through what I had to with my father, no matter what he said. I had seen enough and got to know enough talented kids to realize that being miserable wasn't a prerequisite to being a good player. I knew that suffering wasn't the same as working hard. It might be hard to imagine that it took me that long to put things together, but that's how much I was sheltered. In fact before I realized that, I knew that there was something wrong with all the attention that my father paid to me at practice. Dwight's son was on the team, and Dwight treated him like he would any other player. My father didn't follow his lead—and I told him that I didn't like it. I lipped off to him at practice even though I knew he'd slap me around when we got in the van or got home. It might sound strange, taking physical abuse so casually or accepting it. At age ten I had resigned myself to it. If I was asking for trouble by mouthing off, I figured that it was just getting the inevitable over with now rather than later.

Dwight tolerated a lot from my father because he needed the help—managing sixteen 10-year-old kids alone is tough even if you did play in the NHL. But one practice my father blasted me and I started chirping back. Dwight stopped practice and told both of us to get off the ice. I've been with teams when a coach has thrown a player who was dogging it out of practice. I've never heard of an assistant coach getting ordered out of practice. I'm sure there are only a few times in the history of the game at any level that a player and a coach have got tossed out for behaving badly. A father-and-son combination—I have to believe it had never happened before and hasn't since.

After practice, Dwight came into the room before the other players were off the ice and within earshot. He laid down the law: he told us that things had to change or I couldn't be on the team; that it wasn't fair to the other players on the team when my father and I were a distraction. And he told my father that he was done as the assistant coach, that he'd find someone to help out, but if it meant trying to manage sixteen 10-year-olds on the bench or at practice himself, he was willing to try. He made it clear that he wasn't going to take any more shit from my father and probably had taken too much already. That wasn't up for discussion. If I wasn't at the next practice, then he was prepared to move on.

To put it mildly, my father didn't take this well. A couple of F-bombs later we were gone. I knew I was in for trouble that night, and I really thought I was done with the Nationals.

It wasn't really a power struggle, what my father had with Dwight Foster. Dwight was in charge. My father physically intimidated a lot of people at the arena. He gave them good reason to think that he was going to boil over. Dwight wasn't intimidated. He wasn't going to take any shit from my father. Some other places, an assistant coach has cut out a head coach—that happens, but it wasn't going to happen with the Nationals. It was the first time, and just about the only time, I had seen anyone stand up to my father. Dwight knew he had the cards: my father wanted me to play, and he didn't have any other options halfway through a season—it was the Nationals or nothing. Dwight knew that my father had a hate-on for him but had no way to bail out. So my father drove me to the next practice and didn't acknowledge Dwight. There was going to be no apology, no tail-between-his-legs act, no plea to get back his spot as an assistant coach. He wasn't about to go down peacefully, though.

For that practice and for every game and practice left in that season, my father acted out even more than ever before. He would literally climb onto the boards, in games, in practice. That was his way of making a statement that he wasn't going to back down, that he wasn't going to let Dwight show him up. He ran down Dwight at every opportunity. He'd say that Dwight really didn't know that much about coaching. He said it to me again and again, and he told any parent he crossed paths with the same thing—not that they would buy that from a wild man who seemed completely irrational whenever the team was on the ice.

It would have been easy for Dwight to drop me from the team. Sometimes he had to have wished, when my father was shouting at the top of his voice, trying to show him up, that he'd done that. I respect the fact that Dwight gave me a chance to play rather than cut me loose. I'm sure that would have only made things worse for me. If I hadn't been able to play again that season after Dwight told us to get off the ice, my father would have blamed me and taken it out physically on me. If I hadn't be able to finish the season with the Nationals, my father would have had to cook up some sort of way for me to train that would have made the usual grind seem like a walk in the park by comparison. As it was, my father stepped up his "program" for me away from the arena.

II

NIGHT WORK

When my father worked in Michigan, it was usually a night shift. He had different jobs—maintenance in a retirement home was one—none of them paying that well, most of them not lasting very long, all of them with flexible hours that allowed him to take me to games or put me through his private workouts. In Toronto it had seemed like he had a workout planned for my every waking hour. It had often left me on the verge of exhaustion. In Michigan, though, it intensified. My waking hours weren't enough to accommodate his program.

My father would come home at three or four in the morning from his job, a lot of the time half-drunk or worse, and he'd wake me up for a workout while I was still in my pajamas. I was barely able to keep my eyes open, but he'd have me down on the floor doing push-ups until my arms gave out and I did a face-plant on the floor. He'd have me doing sit-ups until my stomach cramped. He would sit there with a beer and a smoke and bark at me. If he didn't think I was trying hard enough, he'd punch and kick me. A few times in the dead of winter, he would kick me out of the house and lock the door, leaving me standing in the snow in my PJs and bare feet. "This will toughen you up, you little fag," he'd say, or something to that effect. I knew not to beat my fists on the door or shout for help—if I did anything like that, he'd have come out the door and given me an even worse beat-down. There was no help coming, just more of the same.

Dozens of times I went to school almost asleep on my feet and with bruises and cuts on my face. Dozens of times I laid my head on my desk and slept, my teachers never asking why I was so tired. Dozens of times he'd come to my school and sign me out of class so that he could push me through workouts that lasted a couple of hours. Dozens of times I'd be sore and trembling from fatigue when I'd go to practices and games for the Nationals or for Belle Tire, the team that I would play for the next season in Michigan. And dozens of times my father would have me run after we left the rink—if he didn't like how I played, he would kick me out of the van, often while I was still in my full equipment and running shoes, and then make me chase it as he drove down back streets. If I was out of my equipment because I'd changed at the arena, it wasn't any easier. My father would kick me out of the van, throw my equipment bag at me on the street and then make me lug it over my shoulder while I ran.

That's what my life was like: I had to struggle to keep up, but even when I did there'd be no rest.

In some ways the worst part was the not-knowing.

When I went to school, I never knew when I might be paged over the PA because my father was waiting to take me for a workout—he'd say that I had a doctor's appointment or something else that never was questioned by anyone in the principal's office.

When I went to bed, I never knew if I'd get a night's sleep, and I'd roll around in my bed, worried that my father was going to come home and lock me outside. I worried even more when the winter weather was at its worst.

When I came off the ice after practice or a game, I never knew exactly what was next, but I knew it was going to be bad. While other kids went with their parents to grab a hamburger or ice cream, I'd be looking at an hour or two or more of my father's conditioning program, running the steps in the arena stands like a hamster on a treadmill or chasing after the van for two or three miles. If he didn't think that was toughening me up, he'd slap me around. Every year he was ramping it up: a slap in the face when I was eight; a slap with more force and a kick in the ass when I was nine; a punch when I was ten; a big right hook on my jaw and a kick in the gut or ribs until I was gasping when I was eleven, twelve and thirteen. And if that weren't enough, he'd grind a cigarette out in my face or come up with other ways to punish and humiliate me.

12

WITE-OUT

Ann Arbor, Michigan, August 1998

USA Hockey's Under-15 Festival is one of its biggest annual events, bringing in the top fourteen-year-old kids on regional all-star teams from across the country. We were still living in Sterling Heights, but at the U15 Festival I played for the Atlantic-Southeast team, kids from North Carolina, Washington, Georgia and other points south. We had, as you'd expect, the weakest team in the tournament. I didn't play for the Southeast because of my time in Winston-Salem. Given that I had played the previous season for Belle Tire, I was a Michigan player in the eyes of USA Hockey. But my father had tried to sign me up to try out for the Michigan team that summer and was turned down. I wound up with the Southeast because my father played there.

It starts with the rules that were on USA Hockey's books at the time: only players who were fourteen years old on January 1, 1998, were eligible to play in the festival. No older, obviously, but no younger either—the rule was hard and fast. Underage players had to sit the festival out and wait for their turn. I turned thirteen in February of that year, so the wait would have been for two more years, even though I had played with and against the players on the Michigan team.

My father thought the rule was unfair. He wanted the Michigan coaches to go to USA Hockey and argue for making an exception for me. He had always been able to talk the teams in Toronto and Michigan into allowing me to try out even though I was a year or two younger than everyone else on the ice. For a lot of coaches, the idea of a double-underage player went against their better judgment. They worried about a little kid getting physically banged up against players a head taller and fifty pounds heavier. They also worried about a little kid getting discouraged if things didn't work out. And they couldn't see the necessity of it—what was the rush, after all? But my father thought that if you weren't rushing, you weren't trying. He had always been able to get his way by being pushy. Or at least it seemed that way until he tried to get me into the U15 Festival with Michigan.

My father couldn't accept the idea that players I had skated with and against, players no better than me, were getting a chance to play and I was shut out. It wasn't like I had to sit out a season, like I would fall behind a year. It was a short tournament, a few games. It should have been no big deal in the grand scheme of things, nothing to go to war over. Still, my father thought that even that was giving an advantage to the other kids, that with just those few games I was falling behind. This was something he wasn't prepared to accept.

My father prided himself on being a do-whatever-it-takes kind of guy, someone who would bend the rules if he could and break them if that was what it took. The only thing that was keeping me out of the tournament was my birth certificate, so my father decided to change it.

Looking back now, it's laughable that he thought he could get away with it. My ID was white type on a dark background. My father got some Wite-Out, the stuff used to hide mistakes in type, and a Magic Marker. With a couple of tiny brushstrokes, 1985 became 1983. He had made me two years older. That was the first step.

My father knew there was no hope of going to the Michigan officials with the doctored birth certificate, and most of the teams in neighboring states would have been on to the scam pretty fast as well. The officials in the Southeast, though, didn't know me. He called them up and made the case that he and I were moving back into the area, using my grandparents' address in Winston-Salem. He gave them some line about his ex-wife living there and a court ordering the move as part of a custody ruling. He also told them that I had played for Belle Tire's bantam team the previous season but didn't mention that I was an underager. And when it came time to fill out the forms and send in the documents, my father faxed a photocopy of my birth certificate. No one who held the original in his hand and looked at it hard would have been fooled, but a blurry photocopy blurred again when faxed might have been able to pass. Whether the blurry copy did the trick or he had already fooled the Southwest officials over the phone, either way my father had got what he wanted. I was registered even though I was ineligible.

When we went to the team's tryouts in West Chester, Pennsylvania, the coaches were surprised. I was easily the smallest kid on the ice. I was also the only one whose voice hadn't broken yet. Those were red flags. So was my father's act. It really wasn't different, just that they hadn't seen it before. He never let me out of his sight for a second, and he was in their faces the whole time as well. As the *U.S. Hockey Report*, an amateur hockey newsletter, said a few weeks later when the con job was exposed, "Good scammers are nothing if not vigilant."

The coaches were worried about how I'd hold up at the festival— they thought I was one of most skilled players they had, but I was 140 pounds. Still, I made the cut. They needed players. The Southeast coach, John Riley, told the newsletter, "His hands, shot, and his hockey sense were superior to a lot who made the team—never mind the kids we cut."

When the tournament started in Ann Arbor, I wound up scoring the winning goal. We beat Massachusetts 4–1, and nothing tripped an alarm. None of the local minor-hockey officials or parents of local players were at the game, so I wasn't recognized—and neither was my father, who was yelling at the top of lungs in an arena where I had played dozens of times over the last three winters. The next game, though, all hell was going to break loose, and he knew it would when the schedule was announced: Southeast-Atlantic versus Michigan.

As soon as the teams skated onto the ice, the parents of the Michigan players started talking among themselves about filing a protest with tournament officials, telling them that Southeast-Atlantic had an ineligible player in the lineup. One of the Michigan Selects was Bobby Kukulka, a kid on my team at Belle Tire. They would have completely busted me. The parents didn't wind up filing a protest, though, because Michigan won and advanced to the medal round, so the Southeast coaches and festival officials were still in the dark. The truth came out only after we played our last game, a loss to New England. It was a complete embarrassment for USA Hockey.

The officials realized pretty quickly that the Southeast coaches weren't in on the scam and that my father had duped them. And my father didn't deny it. In fact, when the officials cornered him at the arena, he gloated about getting one over on USA Hockey, like he was trash-talking an opponent after a fight he had just won. They could slap his wrist, he said, but so what? He told them to do whatever they wanted, because he was taking me and moving on. He told them that I was going to be playing for a Junior B team in Petrolia, down the road from Sarnia on the other side of the border. "They think he's an '83 but you guys know, don't you?" he said and laughed in their faces.

USA Hockey pushed back hard. They banned my father indefinitely from coaching any U.S. youth-hockey team (he was still listed by Belle Tire as an assistant coach). When the newsletter wrote up the story of the tournament and the fraud my father had perpetrated, the story referred to him as "the Duke of Deception." Others would be embarrassed, but my father just laughed it off. None of that mattered to him. He had other plans for me. By his demented way of thinking, USA Hockey couldn't kick him out if he quit first, and if they understood how good I was going to be, they'd be breaking the rules too.

13

A BOY AMONG MEN

Alvinston, Ontario, October 1998

Petrolia didn't work out. It was one thing to use fake ID to get a thirteen-year-old into a tournament of fifteen-year-olds. It was completely another thing to throw me in against players seven and even eight years older, one level below major junior. Rather than looking to put me into a league with players closer to my own age, though, my father targeted the Great Lakes Junior C league in southwestern Ontario—again, players as old as twenty-one but a step down in skill from Petrolia's Junior B league.

Almost all pros played against kids reasonably close to their own age growing up. A few would have been like me in Toronto and Michigan—always in with players a year or two older. Going to Junior C was a lunatic idea. Over the years a few fourteen-year-olds have been able to stick in junior hockey, but mostly they were in mold of Denis Potvin: boys with men's bodies. I was an average-sized thirteen-year-old at best. I'd stood out as undersized with the Southeast team at the U15 Festival but looked like the stickboy when I walked into an arena where Junior C teams held their tryouts.

The coaches of Junior C teams in Blenheim and Walpole Island told my father to take a hike after just one practice. They didn't need to see anything more. The third team I skated with was in Alvinston, a little farm town about 150 miles from Ann Arbor. The Flyers were so bad that they actually needed help any way they could get it, and I was more skilled than anyone they had. The Toronto Red Wings were the only championship team I had been part of, but I had never played with a team as outmatched as Alvinston—we won six out of forty games that season.

For my father, a losing team wasn't an issue, so long as I was playing up—in this case, way up. And it didn't matter to him that every game and practice sucked up five hours on the road, more in bad weather and with lineups at Customs. It didn't matter that games and practices sometimes conflicted with my school days—he'd drive by the school and yank me out of class early. It didn't matter that after late games or trips to other teams' rinks we wouldn't get home until after midnight. My father was going to do whatever it took to get me on the ice. My hockey career—if you can say a thirteen-year-old has a career—took priority over everything.

Time away from my mother and sisters: it was no issue for my father, and frankly, the time he was out of the house was a relief to them.

Work: my father went through a bunch of jobs through this stretch—night shifts cleaning carpets, days shifts as a super and janitor—but any job that he took had to have flexible hours, something that would let him come in late or leave early.

The physical grind on me: my father thought that there was no limit to what I could physically handle, so he kept up with and even intensified the routine that had started with the move to Michigan, which left me so exhausted that I would fall asleep at my desk in school or feel like my legs were full of sand out on the ice. It seemed like I didn't have a home-cooked meal that season. My mother sent me out to the van with sandwiches to eat on the drive to the games while she stayed home with my sisters.

By the time I started playing with Alvinston, hockey had become a 24/7 experience for me. You might have heard other pros describe their childhood that way—it would be their way of saying that they would dedicate hours and days to practicing the game on their own time. For me, it was different. Yes, I loved the game the same way that they did and, given a spare hour or two, I would be in our basement or in the driveway, stickhandling and shooting pucks at targets, just like thousands of other kids.

My father, though, made it something more than the usual 24/7 dedication—he would *ambush* me with the game. Those times when he'd roll home from work before dawn and wake me up to do push-ups and sit-ups became more frequent and more intense. Same thing went for the workouts in the middle of school days. He kept upping the stakes. Everything became more urgent. He raised his standards. A bad game had meant getting slapped around afterward, but by the time I was playing with Alvinston, just one or two bad shifts would have him slapping me around. After games in Toronto and in Michigan, he used to make get out of the van and run behind it if he didn't like how I played, but that was always on city streets. That season with Alvinston, he started kicking me out of the van and making me chase it on back roads—I'd be shivering while I ran after him in my sweaty tracksuit on winter nights. No other cars would be on those roads after dark, so my father didn't have to worry about being seen by other drivers or by police. And he became even bolder about it—he took it from the back roads onto the 402, the four-lane highway to the U.S. border. Rather than crawl along on the soft shoulder, he kicked me out of the car and drove ahead a mile or more down the road, pulled over and parked the van while having a smoke.

The difference between other pros describing their boyhoods as "hockey 24/7" and my experience is the difference between guys on the street saying they love their country and a Navy Seal putting it on the line. They're using the same words to describe the way they see their lives, but the contexts couldn't be farther apart. It's one thing to play the game as a kid, another to play it just to survive another day without a beating. That's what the game became to me—all about survival.

It might sound like hyperbole, but that's the way it felt on the ice and off. In games I landed in situations that you'd never put a thirteen-year-old in. I went into one game afraid for my life: a road game on the Walpole Island Native reserve. The age limit in the league was twenty-one (a year older than major junior), but the Alvinston players and coaches were sure that some guys on the reservation team were twenty-four. They were a bunch of huge guys, and most of them were looking for fights as much as for goals or wins. In the arena parking lot before the game, fans were drinking, starting bonfires and shouting threats at my father and me when I was pulling my equipment bag out of the back of the van. They pounded and yelled that I was going to get killed. It was the one time that I couldn't hear my father in the arena. The kids I went to school with were going to the Quebec peewee tournament and for pizza with their families after games, while I was skating into the middle of a street fight or barroom brawl between grown men a foot taller and a hundred pounds heavier than me.

Looking back on it now, I was lucky to get out of that season without getting seriously hurt. I knew enough about the game to stay away from the places where someone might take a run at me, and I could skate fast enough to get away from a goon who was trying to splash me against the boards. I'm sure that a lot of the tough guys in the league were happy just to let me be or to throw a scare into me—they wouldn't have taken any satisfaction from flattening a little kid. Still, the game was faster and the bodies were so much bigger than what other thirteen-year-olds were skating against—nobody would have had to go out of his way to put me on a stretcher. Even an accidental collision, even one with a teammate, could have knocked me out.

That season I went out on the ice knowing that I was in real physical danger—the stakes were that much higher. Job one was just being in one piece at the end of the game. Still, I was Alvinston's leading scorer. Really, I was just happy that season ended—no more long drives, no more games against grown men, no more long runs on the back roads or along the highways' soft shoulders. At least until the next season.

14

JUNIOR B

Strathroy, Ontario, December 1999

Even a season after the birth certificate debacle at the Under-15 Festival, most of the best minor midget and midget programs in Michigan or anywhere in the U.S. would have had no interest in me playing for them if my father was included in the package. And at that point, no matter how well I played, no team would have had me on his terms: he had always managed to get out of paying registration fees and ice charges and all the rest. No one would have wanted to take on a well-known headache like him and pick up the tab at the same time.

My father didn't tell me how he got me a tryout with the Strathroy Rockets. He didn't look for my input on decisions like that. He would have been looking for a step up to Junior B, but probably not to Petrolia if he'd been turned down there the year before. Even if there had been no hard feelings, Strathroy would have been more attractive to my father because Pat Stapleton had run the Rockets. Stapleton had been a defenseman with the Chicago Blackhawks back in the sixties and seventies and played for Team Canada against the Soviets back in '72. Stapleton had managed and coached the team for almost twenty years and probably could have found a job in the pros but didn't want to leave his farm behind and work for someone else. He wasn't behind the bench when I was with the Rockets, but they were still his team. The Rockets weren't the biggest thing, but they were all his. My father, an ex-minor-leaguer who never played a full season of major junior, thought he knew more about the game than an ex-NHLer like Dwight Foster. Still, he had to concede that Pat Stapleton probably knew as much about hockey as he did. He criticized the way the team used me, but never within Stapleton's earshot.

I was happy not to be in Alvinston another season and happy that I was moving up to a higher level of the game, but in every other way it was more of the same. I'd hoped that I'd never have to spend five hours in a car for every game and practice again, but the drive to and from Strathroy was as far if not farther, and the Rockets practiced more and played more games. The grind was brutal: it was routine for us to have a game Friday night and another early Saturday afternoon. With all the hours on the road, I'd be home after midnight Friday and have time for only four or five hours of sleep before heading out again. When we went out on the ice for those Saturday games, my teammates would be warming up while I was trying to wake up.

Again, physically, I was a mouse in the house with my teammates and the opposition. This time, though, I was in against a better class of players. My father had tried to get me to Junior B after the U15 Festival, a giant step up. If I was a year behind his unrealistic expectations at fourteen, I was years ahead of every fifteen- and sixteen-year-old I had grown up skating with and against in Toronto and Michigan. Again, like in Alvinston, I was on the ice with grown men—there might have been a sixteen- or seventeen-year-old on the ice, but the rest were four or five years older than me. One guy on my line was twenty-one and had a wife and two kids. I was a high school freshman; a few on my team were out of school and holding down jobs. It wasn't only a matter of age and physical maturity, though. The best in the league were just a cut below major junior and were looking to play college hockey in the U.S. or for university teams in Canada. In against Alvinston, Strathroy would have won by double digits.

I never really got to know anyone on the Rockets. I had no time to say anything more than hi. I'd arrive with just enough time to lace up my skates and I'd leave right after we came off the ice, just putting on my running shoes and tracksuit and walking out to the van—I was still so young that I didn't even shower after games. The Rockets traveled to games in a couple of vans, but I never went with them. Separated from the team, I never had any idea what they thought of playing with a kid. I understood that I had to be seen and not heard. I would speak when spoken to and would do as I told. Even if I was playing on the first or second line, I still felt like a guest. I had earned my spot on the team, but they were making a big exception for me. Pat Stapleton didn't ever speak to me directly: it didn't seem to matter to him that I was four-teen. He didn't even really acknowledge the fact. I was just a player, and if he went about his business like there weren't any risks involved, from day one he just sent me out there to sink or swim.

I adapted. I scored a goal—a slapshot from the wing—on my first shift in my first game, and the season went that way. I was no novelty or mascot. I'd never recommend throwing a fourteen-year-old in with men, but on the ice Strathroy was a good hockey experience, a lot better than Alvinston for my development. And it was clear from the start of the season that we had a better team: we'd compete for a league title.

That season the Rockets were a pretty big deal in Strathroy. They'd get a good crowd of ticket-buying customers to the arena, what passed as an alternative to *Hockey Night in Canada* in towns like that. It was a business—a small business, but still professional in a way that youth hockey isn't. In Strathroy I landed on the radar of the pro hockey's big business, and the chance of that happening had to have figured into my father's motive to get me to Junior B as soon as possible. A fourteen- or fifteen-year-old in Junior B is going to attract the attention of hockey agents, and a stringer for one of the biggest agencies in the sport spotted me in Strathroy. By mid-season, two agents from Newport Sports, one of the biggest agencies in pro hockey, were standing beside my father at Rockets games and ended up striking a handshake deal with him to represent me. Newport's agents told my father everything he wanted to hear, and my father soaked up all of it. For him, an agency's interest just proved that his plan for me was working. The agents must have put it together that my father was high maintenance even though he would have kept them in the dark about the physical abuse.

Any benefits from playing in Strathroy were offset by the quality of my life when I left the arena. Early on that season, it was clear that my father was raising the stakes yet again. He had the same act at the arena: "Crazy John" yelling at one end of the rink, as usual, only toned down a bit when the Newport agents were around. He didn't socialize with other parents—in any case, it's more buddies and girlfriends who come out to junior games than parents. My father would hang around the dressing room before and after the game, making jokes, not being "an issue" so that Stapleton wouldn't chase him away. Once we left the arena, though, it was *on*. The trend that had played out every step of the way over the years increased: the beat-downs were more frequent and more intense, the punches and kicks were harder and aimed to leave bruises and welts. We'd barely be out of the arena and he'd start—out on Highway 402 he'd kick me out of the van and then drive a mile or two ahead, turning off the lights so that I didn't know where he was or if he hadn't just driven off and left me behind.

Our season came down to game 7 of the league final and we ended up a goal short. The Rockets had a bunch of events away from the arena over the course of the season, but my father avoided them, though he did drive me up for the year-end banquet, where I was given the team's rookie of the year award. That night the younger players talked to me about coming back in the fall and winning it all. They told me that another fifteen-year-old hotshot, Jeff Carter, would be joining the Rockets, and they'd be the favorites to win a league title.

I didn't know that I had played my last game for Strathroy. My father had other plans, but he didn't let me in on them.

15

EXCEPTIONAL

Sterling Heights, Michigan, May 2000

During my season in Strathroy, my father started talking to Newport Sports about exceptional-player status, a designation that would have allowed me early entry into the Ontario Hockey League. By the rules on the books, players eligible for the 2000 OHL draft would have been 1984 birthdays. Only a handful of times in recent years had the major junior leagues allowed fifteen-year-olds to play. It's a lot to ask of an underage player. Even though I'd been playing against twenty-year-olds in Alvinston when I was thirteen, the competition had been Junior C players, a completely different class of talent, at least three cuts below the future NHLers who skate in major junior. Still, my father wanted the agency to pursue it for him. The standard for the exceptional player is ridiculously high: he must be certifiably the best player in his birth year but also better than any player a year older than him in Ontario and the U.S. Midwest. He has to be what they always call a "generational player," a talent that comes along once in a generation. That's what my father presumed I was. He took it for granted that I was a prodigy, like the nine-year-old kid who plays Carnegie Hall or the middle-school kid who goes directly to MIT.

Exceptional-player status was a natural extension of my father's first principle of manufacturing a NHL star: always play against the best of the oldest players as soon as possible. My father wasn't unique on that count. It might not be the conventional wisdom, but a lot have bought into that strategy and a lot more will. "Too much too soon" is what you think about *other* parents' kids. Still, it's one thing in a league of top local kids in Toronto or Michigan—the difference between ten- and twelve-year-olds might be pretty small, in skill close to a wash. At the major junior level, it's another thing entirely to ask a fifteen-year-old to skate against nineteen-year-olds already under contract to NHL clubs, some who've already played a few NHL games.

Being cleared to play in the OHL at fifteen wasn't going to send me to play away from home. A precedent had been set the year before: a player designated for exceptional status had to play with the team nearest to his home. The league had granted Jason Spezza exceptional-player status for the 1999–2000 season, and because the Spezza family had just bought a house in Brampton, he played for the Brampton Battalion. Optics were a factor. The league didn't want to be seen as shipping kids away from home at fifteen—some still think it's pretty cold-hearted to do it with sixteen-year-olds, but then again, every year dozens of kids move away from home to play in better leagues at younger ages, even twelve- and thirteen-year-olds. Wayne Gretzky moved from Brantford to Toronto when he was thirteen. Still, the OHL had its stay-at-home rule for exceptional-status players in order to head off moralizing media criticism about the game being a brutal business.

My father didn't ask me if I thought I was ready for it or if I wanted to do it. If he wanted me to do it, I was going to have to do it. It was going to be no different from any other season. What did I know? He knew better, even if he hadn't been able to get into a game for the Brantford Alexanders back in his day. Newport Sports went along with my father. If they hadn't, he would have shopped around for another agency. Newport Sports gave the application credibility with the OHL. Newport had a good relationship with the league. Over the years, hundreds of its players had played in the OHL and had gone on to play pro.

Even today I don't know what the procedure was. I never sat in on a meeting. I was never interviewed. In retrospect, it seems pretty strange that the people who were making such big decisions about my health and welfare relied on what they heard in meetings and from second-hand reports. There was no video back then, no highlights of me playing for the Strathroy Rockets. Today a kid up for exceptional status would have highlight plays all over YouTube. There was no media coverage, no buzz, about my father's application. Today a fifteen-year-old's name would be out there on websites, and hockey fans would have been talking about him for months before.

I have to imagine that when my case came up in front of the OHL executives in the Toronto offices, Newport Sports took the lead. Even though it felt like my entire career was driven by my father's ego, he would have been smart enough to know that he wouldn't be the best spokesman. And if he were spokesman, he'd have had to worry about the league doing a background check on him—he wouldn't have wanted any questions about his act at arenas in Toronto or about the incident with the forged birth certificate. The league executives could have made a couple of phone calls and poked around into my father's history and realized that my father was a crank.

My father's application for my exceptional-player status was one of two that the league had for review. The other came from the family of Nathan Horton, another fifteen-year-old, who had been playing in the Golden Horseshoe Junior B league down toward Niagara Falls, a league that was probably a step down from the one Strathroy played in.

I'm not sure how seriously the league took either of the exceptional-player applications, but one thing was clear: the 1984 birthdays didn't make for a strong OHL draft class.

It wasn't the strongest year in the OHL draft. The top-ranked kid was Pat Jarrett, who wound up playing only one minor pro season and a few seasons in Europe after his OHL career. The second-ranked, Tim Brent, would make it into two hundred NHL games down the line; but the kid right behind him in the rankings, a defenseman named Richard Power, didn't get drafted by an NHL team at eighteen and ended up playing some university hockey.

Still, the OHL decided against granting either Horton or me exceptional-player status. League officials didn't give an explanation and didn't have to, but a couple of things were working against the application Newport Sports made for me.

One: because I was living in the Detroit area, my rights would have gone to the Plymouth Whalers, a strong program but one unpopular at the time with league executives. The Whalers were owned by Peter Karmanos, a guy who had made hundreds of millions in computer tech and used it pretty liberally for any advantage he could get for his team—including recruiting American prospects who wouldn't report to teams in Ontario but would bypass the NCAA to play in a nice suburb of Detroit for an owner who would underwrite their college education at a school of their choice down the line. Karmanos landing an exceptional-status player wouldn't have sat well with small-town teams that were community-owned, kitchen-table operations.

Two: playing in Strathroy meant that few executives in the league's Toronto offices had seen me. OHL executives didn't know much about the league. They would have seen me play if I had been coming out of a Toronto-area program like Jason Spezza had. There would have been media hype. OHL officials had to think that they shouldn't be granting exceptional status based on word of mouth.

Looking back now, it doesn't look like either Horton or I were head and shoulders above the other players in our own draft year, the 1985 class. One of the players who would go into the top five of the OHL draft the next year, Corey Perry, would be named the most valuable player in the NHL one season and win two Olympic gold medals and a Stanley Cup. Another, Mike Richards, would win two Cups.

Missing out on exceptional status was a disappointment but probably not a complete surprise. My father always knew better than everyone else. It was always Him against the World. For OHL executives, this would be their introduction to my father, and not the last time his name would come up in conversation in their offices. The exceptional-status application was just his way of dropping off his business card—high-maintenance parents have a way of announcing themselves often, and early.

In the end, though, the OHL's passing turned out to be a break for me. It wound up opening a door that I thought was going to be shut on me.

16

ALL-AMERICAN BOY

Ann Arbor, Michigan, October 2000

My father had gone all in on exceptional status. He didn't have a fall-back option for me. It looked like I was going to be back for another year in Strathroy playing for Pat Stapleton—either that or my father would find another Junior B team in another league. It would be a holding-pattern year. There might have been options back in Toronto, but my father's reputation was too well known. No one there would have wanted to take me on when it meant having to deal with him. I dreaded the idea of another year in Strathroy. I would have nothing to look forward to other than more beatings and more chasing after the van on the 402. I would still be the youngest kid in the room by at least two years. I would be on the team but my father wouldn't let me be part of it—he wouldn't let me move in with a billet family in Strath-roy, wouldn't let me ride the bus with the team, wouldn't let me get to know the players away from the arena. Another season in Strathroy would mean another year commuting, another year completely under his thumb. It looked like I was in for the worst season ever.

It turned out to be the best so far, maybe the best hockey experience I'd ever have. And it was a fluke, nothing that had ever been in my father's plans for me.

In September, USA Hockey had tryouts for its under-17 program and cut its roster down to twenty-four players, all of them born in 1984. This had been the end of a process that had been months, even years, in the works. The under-17 team's manager and coaches had been keeping tabs on eligible players and talking to parents the previous winter. They had scouted tournaments. The organization had its team set and players had reported in time to enroll for the academic year at the local high school.

But an opening came up a couple of weeks into the school year, before the under-17s had played a game on their schedule: Zach Parise, one of the key players among the '84 birthdays, told USA Hockey that he wanted to go back to Shattuck–St. Mary's, the Minnesota private school where his father, former NHLer J.P. Parisé, managed the hockey program. The timing couldn't have been any worse for the organization. All the top American players who had been the last cuts in tryouts were already committed to other teams, whether in prep schools like Shattuck or in age-group programs.

I'm sure that the manager of the program swallowed hard before he called my father. After all, he was still under the seven-year ban, a death sentence for minor hockey that had been handed down when he had forged my birth certificate for USA Hockey's Under-15 Festival. My father never had a better chance to gloat than when he took that call. As a player, he had been chewed up and spat out by the game, always "Don't call us, we'll call you." Now, as a father, he had a national program reaching out to him, saying that all was forgiven, commuting the death sentence and pardoning me.

My father didn't need much convincing. It was the next best thing to exceptional-player status in the OHL. In fact, it was the equivalent of it: one of the goaltenders on the team was a 1985 birthday like me, but everyone else was an '84. The program had never recruited under-age players before. Like with the Under-15 Festival, USA Hockey had a policy that not only discouraged playing up but avoided it without exception. On my count, they were making their first exception with a skater. It wasn't just a bragging point for my father but something that conformed to the basic tenet of his plan for my development: putting me in with the best available older players, forcing me to catch up. Though the players in Ann Arbor were younger than those I skated with in Strathroy and even Alvinston, they were clearly a cut above in talent. They were ticketed for top NCAA schools. A bunch would be high draft choices and NHL players down the line. The challenge wasn't quite as forbidding as the OHL, but it was stiff enough. The program had facilities as good as those at a lot of Division I schools and had coaches who could have stepped right into NCAA programs and pro organizations. The program also offered an extensive travel schedule with no cost to players' families, the tab picked up by USA Hockey, which used funds gathered from players in leagues across country. On all these counts, Ann Arbor would be a huge step up from Strathroy.

* * *

Though everyone in the under-17 program was a lot closer in age to me than the players in Alvinston and Strathroy had been, I was still as much of an outsider in Ann Arbor. It wasn't just that I was the kid who'd been parachuted in. Even if you didn't know the ugliest of the family secrets, I stood apart from the rest.

All of them had played with high school, prep school or age-group teams. None of them had experiences in the game like mine, playing like I had in Strathroy with a linemate who was married with kids. None of their families had skipped from one city to the next looking for a team.

The vast majority of them had stable families, a lot of them really well-to-do, flying in to Michigan for home games and traveling elsewhere first-class. My father and I stood out—we were the closest thing to hardscrabble you'd find in the program. Some of my teammates drove Beamers that would cost six times the book value of my father's van. Their parents made sure that they had the best of everything and spared no expense, while my father, since my days in Toronto, was cutting deals, getting teams to comp my registration fees and give me equipment. Other players knew only security, while our family got by, barely, and not all on my father's limited income working nights as unskilled labor. We ate but not well. We lived luxury free in a three-bedroom rental. I never spent one summer in a house with air-conditioning. When money was short for the bills, my mother made a call to her parents to get over the hump.

Yeah, some of the other parents were "involved"—it would be very hard to get this far in the game and into the Ann Arbor program without a lot of support. Many of the fathers had played the game and had been on the ice with their sons. Many of them had coached their sons at some point, some all the way through. Still, the level of my father's involvement registered with them. Some of the players' parents made it to Ann Arbor only once a month. My father was the only one who came out not just to every game but to every practice, and when he was there he didn't try to blend in with the scenery. He shouted at me just like had at every other stop on the way. My teammates never took shots at me about it, but their expressions, headshakes and eye rolls told me that they sympathized with me—or at least were thankful *their* fathers weren't making spectacles of themselves.

They didn't know the half of it, of course. At home my father stuck to his usual methods of toughening me up. I was too old to lock out of the house in my pajamas in the dead of winter. I would have been a threat to walk away and get a cab to a teammate's house. Still, my father would push me every waking hour to be working out. But I didn't just give in like I had when I was younger. I was starting to fight back—and that meant he had to raise his game. What used to be slaps became punches, with all his weight behind them.

I was able to break away to socialize more with my teammates than I had when I was younger—the team rule that everyone had to travel with the team cut me a break on that. The more time I spent with my teammates, the more I understood how much I had missed growing up. I wasn't used to making friends. I could be cut-throat when I spoke to teammates because I had no idea about their feelings. My life's experiences had been limited by my father's obsession. I wasn't a worldly kid. I had never gone to a school dance. I had never gone to a school football or basketball game or any other social event. My father thought that those things were a waste of precious time, time that had to be spent training. They were distractions from the goal. My father aspired to an unbalanced life.

People who didn't know me would read that I was remote, even aloof, and that was an easy takeaway given my father's attitude and behavior. Patrick Eaves and the other players I became closest to on the team knew different and did what they could to put all that to rest.

The players were good to me, and they thought they understood my situation. But I never opened up about the worst of it, or even, really, the basics. Everyone was trying to follow the script that our coach, an ex-NHLer named Moe Mantha, laid out. Moe gave us chapter and verse from the USA Hockey playbook, all the stuff about team play, sacrificing for the greater good, not worrying about personal stats. And Moe had it right—when our team was at its best, we won that way, beating teams in our age group and older that had more talent on the ice but didn't play so well together. But Moe's message was exactly the opposite from what I heard from my father.

"Don't give a damn about your teammates until you get to the NHL," my father would tell me. That was one of his favorites. Another: "Just get your goals. That's what you have to do if you're going to make it."

17

ROAD GAME

Truro, Nova Scotia, and Chicago, Illinois, January 2001

When I was offered a spot on the under-17 team, the coaches thought I wouldn't play a lot. I was in as a spare part, an extra forward who would spend most of the time on the bench, not much more than a practice player. Our schedule was made up almost entirely of junior and college teams—our entire team was "playing up," and we struggled. Every game, we were fighting above our weight class, so the role of an underage player should have been minimal. The coaches saw me as an investment in the program's future—a year in waiting would prepare me for a central role with the 1985 birthdays the next season. It didn't work out that way, though.

Going into the World Under-17 Challenge, the biggest event of our season, I played on the first line and led the team in scoring. Not that this dialed back the pressure I faced from my father. Even if we won, even if the coaches told me I played well, I knew my father would find some sort of issue with my game. If I scored a goal, I should have scored two; if I scored two, it should have been more. Thankfully, he didn't tell me to run a teammate or sucker someone.

Up until that season, USA Hockey programs had had no success in international tournaments, not even podium finishes. A lot of people in the game thought that Ann Arbor was a failed experiment and that the under-18 and under-17 programs should be dismantled and rebuilt. The organization needed a good result out of the Under-17 Challenge in Nova Scotia. And my father thought I needed a good tournament too—the day after Christmas, when all my teammates were still coming back from their holiday break, he called up our assistant coach, John Hamre, and asked him to open up the arena so that I could get in a skate. Hamre thought it was strange but went along with it.

I was leaving with the team for Nova Scotia on the morning of the 27th, but my father pulled out of our driveway a few hours after the workout at our rink. The under-17 tournament was a twenty-hour drive from Sterling Heights, not counting time lined up at a border crossing and any winter weather you might hit en route. My mother had to stay home with my sisters, so he'd have to do all the driving himself. Still, I had no doubt about my father driving out to Nova Scotia. Not flying—driving. I know that he had issues with both his license and his credit card, so even if he could fly into Halifax like the team did, he'd basically be stranded there, unable to rent a car. It would be the longest road trip that he would have made to see me play, but it was also the biggest event I had played in to that point—dozens of NHL scouts were going to be attendance. The best of the '84 birthdays, players like Rick Nash and Eric Staal, first and second overall picks in the NHL draft, were going to be playing.

We ended up going 6–0 in the tournament and we won most of those games in a walk. In the final, a game broadcast on TSN, we played the team from Alberta and British Columbia. Off the opening face-off, just fourteen seconds in, I let loose a slapshot from the left wing and put it over the goalie's shoulder—1–0, a lead we wouldn't give up. I ended up leading the tournament in scoring. And still it gave me no relief from my father's criticism.

I was carrying my gold medal out of the dressing room when he pulled me aside.

"Be fuckin' ready to play in Chicago," he yelled.

His tirade didn't last long. Our next game was against a really weak team in Chicago— nothing remotely meaningful, but it was scheduled less than forty-eight hours after the gold-medal game. My father knew that with a full twenty-four hours on the road, he had to get on the road ASAP to make it in time.

When our bus pulled to the arena in Chicago, I saw my father's van in the parking lot. He hadn't even stopped at our house on the way.

18

THE PITCHES

Ann Arbor, Michigan, February 2001

Even before the season in the USA Hockey program was done, my father started to look ahead to the next, when I would be sixteen turning seventeen. Though the exceptional-status application had been snuffed out on him, he stilled aimed high. This time he was looking at the International Hockey League. As the top professional minor league without direct ties to the NHL, the IHL was free to sign underage players. The league had recently opened the door to a bunch of East European sixteen- and seventeen-year-olds who collected six-figure paychecks rather than playing for pocket money in major junior. My father figured I could be the first North American teenager to play in the IHL. The hard, cold cash looked good to my father, and the level of competition, pros mostly in their mid- to late twenties, would have been a step up from major junior. A lot of the players in the league would have NHL experience. Again, it would seem a bit strange, but really no stranger than my experiences in Alvinston and Strathroy—it would be playing up again, just on a bigger stage. He thought that I could play for the IHL team in Detroit, the Vipers. He used to take me to Vipers games when I was eight or nine years old, part of my immersion studies. The Vipers back then had a teenage Czech player, Petr Sýkora, who went on to be a first-round NHL pick. My father thought I could play in the IHL at sixteen, and that all the hype would translate into endorsement money.

If he reached out to the Vipers, they didn't return his calls, at least as far as I knew.

* * *

My father's act wore out coaches and officials in the Ann Arbor program, but he kept up appearances at the rink. The scenes he made weren't as over the top as in Strathroy or in minor hockey before that. He exercised control that I didn't think he possessed. He had put it together that his act could have a negative effect on me—or at least on my stock with the NCAA recruiters who came out to scout the under-17 and under-18 teams.

USA Hockey had good relations with college coaches. The Ann Arbor program made for one-stop shopping for the top NCAA Division I programs. Coaches were already making overtures to my father even though I was too young to recruit officially—the schools couldn't offer me expenses-paid visits but what they could do within the rules, they did. Still, Michigan and Boston College, two NCAA heavyweights, had expressed interest to my father and, quietly, to the USA Hockey coaching staff. Both had strong cases. Michigan would let me stay close to home, which was important to my father. I liked BC because Patrick Eaves, my linemate and best friend in the program, was heading there.

Either way, my father liked the idea of me heading off to play in the NCAA at seventeen. He could see me making a splash in the media, being the youngest ever recruit at a big college in a traditional hockey market like Detroit or Boston. He also liked that he could attach dollar figures to the scholarships the schools would offer: tuition and expenses at $40,000 a year. He liked the idea even if I wasn't going to stick around for four years to get a degree. He liked it enough to push me hard to graduate a year ahead of my class—to carry a 50 percent larger course load than other sophomores, in class from the first bell to the last without a lunch break or any study hall. All that plus practice and games with the under-17 team and my father's workouts, which could still come unannounced at three in the morning when he got home from work. I was on a treadmill turned up high without a stop button to push.

The rush to graduate ahead of my class ended up being pointless in the end—I would graduate a year early, but I would never go through the recruiting process at the NCAA schools. My father had his head turned by a big name and a chance for me to make a splash where he as a player had not even made a ripple.

* * *

After the under-17s, coaches and scouts from a few OHL teams started to come out to my games in Ann Arbor and talked to my father. I was going to be eligible for the OHL's entry draft that spring, and everyone knew that I had the option of staying on in Ann Arbor to book a ticket to the NCAAs. Teams pitched my father on opting instead for major junior—what had been his first choice at the start. The NCAAs gave my father leverage, and OHL execs tried to get him on board with promises of cash—up to $100,000 in one case—along with use of a car, a computer, a cellphone and some of the expenses for my family's travel.

The league that didn't want my father when he was eighteen seemed to be bending down to kiss his ass. I was going to the OHL only on the terms of a guy who couldn't cut it there himself. I was my father's payback.

Don Cherry and his lawyer, Trevor Whiffen, started to come out to games in Ann Arbor. Cherry, the television personality, owned the Mississauga IceDogs. He was old school, talking a lot on *Hockey Night in Canada* about his years in hockey's minor leagues, making it sound like the game's glory days. He wanted to have a team that was in line with hockey's traditions. He mocked European players, saying he wouldn't have them on his team, accusing them of stealing jobs from Canadian and American kids. His formula wasn't working in Mississauga, though. The team he sent out on the ice was the worst argument for his vision of the game, and critics were able to throw it back in his face. That season the IceDogs were setting major junior records for losing, winning just three games in the sixty-eight-game season. Cherry's famous name and reputation didn't matter to a lot of the top prospects—since the franchise came into the league, a lot of prospects let the IceDogs know not to bother drafting them because they wouldn't report. Even worse for the team, though, was the fact that Mississauga had trouble keeping its best players. No one liked losing that much, and pro prospects thought they weren't developing. Some, like Jason

Spezza, would give it a shot until they realized they weren't getting out of it what they put in, then demand to be traded.

The IceDogs were going to own the first overall pick in the OHL draft that spring, and they didn't want to be in the same position as they had been with Spezza. A former No. 1 pick demanding to be traded would have been a public relations disaster. Cherry and Whiffen didn't say that when they approached my father. They softened the message, telling him that it was a critical year for the franchise and that they wanted to know early whether I was going to come if the IceDogs made me the first overall pick in the draft.

I'm sure my father wasn't the only parent Cherry and Whiffen talked to, and I'm sure those two heard "Thanks, but no thanks" a few times.

My father was there to be swayed. If it had been anyone else in charge of a two-win team, my father would have told them to take a hike and would have positioned himself to negotiate an offer from another team with money attached and a better chance to win—he had already heard from some teams promising six-figure payouts and lots of perks if I'd commit to them. Or he would have leveraged my chance to go to college as a way of extracting a better offer. Because it was Cherry, he heard them out. He was like a star-struck schoolgirl. My father played the hard-ass, plain-talking tough guy, and unless John Wayne were coming along to recruit me, no one was more my father's style than Cherry. I don't know how my father's motivations could have been divided into fractions—money and fame were big pieces of the puzzle, but so was the chance to rub elbows with hockey heroes, and Cherry fit the profile. He knew that Cherry had coached Bobby Orr. He had watched Cherry on *Hockey Night in Canada*. Now Cherry was slapping him on the back. Turn my father's head? Cherry put it on a swivel. My father knew how Cherry had talked Spezza up on television when he drafted him, and he would have imagined Cherry doing the same with me. My father knew Cherry brought media attention to the team, knew he'd have a chance to bend reporters' ears. He would have imagined that Cherry would even work in a mention of his top prospect's father, one career minor-leaguer paying tribute to another.

Even though going to major junior had been a key part of my father's plan for me, even though going No. 1 was a big attraction, my father didn't sign on right away. It wasn't going to be that easy. It was a big leap for him. If I signed with the IceDogs, he was going to lose control of me. He'd had complete control of me all the way through Strathroy. He had his special deal with USA Hockey that kept me living at home and under his watch. Mississauga was another story.

My father said he didn't want to leave Michigan. Kelley was playing tennis there, and he had hopes of her landing a scholarship and probably playing pro down the line too. It might have been more than that, though. I suspect that he had gone to Sterling Heights one step ahead of creditors. So he made a proposal: rather than living with a billet, I would live in a townhouse with my uncle, something that the team could arrange for him. The team would have to give me the best education package that they could offer—my complete college education paid for even if I signed a pro contract (which usually voids any guarantee of underwriting college expenses). I don't know if my father had any illusions about working for Cherry, his newfound friend. I suspect that my father didn't push it. Since his experience with Dwight Foster, he felt he didn't need to be on the ice with my team to put me through my paces.

I don't doubt that my father was at least as qualified as the IceDogs' staff. That much was clear from the first practice, when I reported in August. Cherry's nephew Steve had been coaching girls' high school hockey. He had zero major junior experience. I laughed the first time he stepped on the ice: he could barely skate. Joe Washkurak was the other assistant, a Toronto policeman who coached minor hockey in Toronto but hadn't coached in major junior either. Joe basically ran the practices and Don parachuted in occasionally, coming in for most games that didn't conflict with broadcasts. Other OHL teams had former NHL players behind the bench, even a few former NHL coaches. Going to major junior should have been like advanced studies, but it turned out to be like going back to grade school, a big step back from Ann Arbor. In fact, a big step back from Strathroy and Pat Stapleton. Even in atom I'd played for a coach, Dwight Foster, more qualified than the staff on the ice with this team at most practices.

19

SUITCASE

Mississauga, Ontario, September 2001

When the IceDogs started playing pre-season games back in September 2001, my father got top billing in the headline over a story in the *Toronto Star*'s sports section.

Suitcase Sully's son goes to the 'Dogs

The nickname "Suitcase Sully" is one that I never heard anyone call my father. I never heard him mention it before. I know Suitcase Smith used to be the nickname of Gary Smith, who played for the Toronto Maple Leafs and then six other NHL teams as well as a bunch of minor-league stops back in the sixties and seventies. I suppose a lot of minor-leaguers get tagged with something like that.

The story's lead was more accurate than the reporter could have known: "Every aspect of Patrick O'Sullivan's life is engulfed by hockey. For the rest of the O'Sullivan family, their lives are completely consumed by his game."

There was no doubt about the facts, though it put a pretty cheery spin on my life story, a script that my father could have dictated. The paper also described how we had moved eight times in sixteen years, all to advance my career. Of course, moving four times in a *season* was what my father's first year of junior hockey had looked like. Again, the emphasis was on dedication and on my father's and family's sacrifice for my sake. It drove home the idea that my father had been there once, and now was going through it as a parent. He had been a hockey nomad and now was there to guide me through it—a minor-leaguer whose love of the game was unrequited had become the selfless hockey father. He wasn't quoted saying it, but I have no doubt that at some point he'd dropped his favorite line about *doing it all for his son.*

If you read between the lines, the story wasn't really all that flattering to me, mind you. I came off looking pretty self-involved, a kid who puts his own interests ahead of his family's. *I* was the one who had us living out of suitcases. Because of me, my family had the zipper blues. Not that my father would clear that up or worry that I was getting thrown under the bus. He really wasn't worried about people getting a good impression about me. So long as he looked good, he was good.

The *Star* story made a passing mention of the "controversy" with USA Hockey and the Under-15 Festival. Again, it was entirely my father's version of events: "According to [John O'Sullivan], he only became aware of the age limitation after the final cuts were made." The way he told it and the newspaper presented it he had made an innocent mistake. USA Hockey's side of the story didn't make it into the article.

One small, dark cloud did show up on the radar: the *Star* story mentioned that my father had a reputation for "meddling" wherever I played. Don Cherry downplayed any rumors about my father. In fact, he gave my father his personal endorsement. "Some of the things I heard (about John O'Sullivan) were not complimentary, to say the least," Cherry said. "I went and talked to him, and I guess John's got the same reputation as me. I think he's great, but maybe it's two guys who are a little nuts together."

The IceDogs were coming off the worst season in the history of Canadian major junior hockey. They needed some good news. They needed positive publicity. Thankfully, they didn't portray me as the franchise savior or a wonder boy or anything like that. I wasn't a player who could single-handedly turn around a franchise, and I'm not sure if anyone could have for that team. But the IceDogs managed to get out a feel-good story that didn't even brush up against the truth. They endorsed me when they used their draft pick to select me and when they signed me. Effectively, though, at the media day they gave my father their character reference.

20

DEBUT

Mississauga, Ontario, September 21, 2001

"I wonder how they're going to put a negative spin on this," Don Cherry said. He was standing outside our dressing room and reporters were taking down notes after we won our home opener 9–1 over Peterborough. Cherry was telling the press how we had given him the game puck for his first win behind the bench with a major junior team and how he had promised to buy us new sweatsuits for playing so hard. He stopped short of saying *I told you so.*

While Cherry was holding court and crowing, my father had cornered me down the hall. He was giving me his post-game analysis of everything I had done wrong. I had scored two goals, assisted on two others. "What the fuck were you thinking on that play?" he said. "Where was your fuckin' head?" I looked around to see if anyone heard him going off on me. Everyone in the area was focused on Cherry.

A former NHL coach of the year, the owner of the franchise, was celebrating and accepting congratulations for what looked like a brand-new day for the IceDogs. For me, in the post-game, it was more of the same.

I had expected major junior to be a tipping point, that my father would have less control and less influence over me. And it had looked that way in the first few weeks after training camp opened in August. My family was still in Ann Arbor. My father had driven up for our first game of the season the week before—we opened in Sudbury, a good eight hours of driving each way for him. He made a point of whistling and catching my eye while fans were only starting to file into the arena during the warm-up. He made a point of pointing to his seat in the corner—the same place he'd parked himself for any of my games over the years. And all during the game, I could hear him shouting—again, his usual routine. And he was there after the game.

This was just more of the same. There was one big difference, though: after twenty minutes of standing there in my face and shouting until I had to wipe the spit off my tracksuit, I was able to turn and walk away and get onto the bus. I'd have four hours of peace and quiet and then sleep, knowing that he was going to drive all night to get back to Michigan. In Ann Arbor, all the players had had to ride the bus as a team rule for road games, but I was still living at home. It was just postponing the inevitable. I felt more independent with the IceDogs. Not completely, but a least a little more.

Through training camp and the first week of the season, I wouldn't see him Monday to Friday. I did have to listen to him once or twice a day on school nights, when he'd phone me up and go off for half an hour or more about being *tough enough*, about junior being a different game than I ever had to play before. That shit I could deal with. His opportunity to take things out on me physically seemed pretty limited.

Turned out that I was overoptimistic on that count.

My father had a key to the townhouse where I was living with Barry. He had ended up getting there before me after the loss in Sudbury, and we'd got into a fight there. And he was going to be there after the win against Peterborough. He was going to have me doing pushups and sit-ups, or he was going to drive me into the wall if I refused or if I didn't work hard enough. And he'd stick around to watch our team practice the next day. Hovering. Just reminding me, *I'm out there.* And that's how it was going to play out that fall—maybe there'd be some relief during the week, but it would be the same old shit on the weekends. If we had a single road game, he'd be there. After the bus had dropped us off at the arena parking lot and I drove back home, he'd be waiting for me. And it would start over again. And it was worse than any time before. Now my father didn't hold anything back, maybe because I was big enough that I was able to trade punches with him, maybe because he couldn't make me run after the van, maybe because he couldn't lock me out in my pajamas.

Major junior wasn't quite the escape that I had hoped for, but it was still an improvement. From Monday to Friday I got a taste of how I could hope things would turn out down the line—one day I was going to be off on my own, where he couldn't make it to every game, where he'd be cut off from the dressing room by a rope and arena security guards, where I'd be able to go home and lock the door behind me.

Major junior was the last stop on the way to the pros, I thought. And it was looking like that was exactly where I was heading at eighteen. Almost every first overall pick in the OHL draft ends up playing in the NHL, a lot of them in the first year they're eligible. Not all of my games were four-point nights like the opener against Peterborough, but I was having a lot of success. Sixteen-year-olds, even top picks coming into major junior, are expected to struggle playing against bigger, faster nineteen- and twenty-year-olds. I had first played against guys that age when I was thirteen in Alvinston. I didn't rattle. I would lead all rookies in scoring that fall—I'd be the only sixteen-year-old in the top ten in the league in scoring and be named the OHL and CHL rookie of the year.

A couple of years and all this shit was going to be behind me, I thought. My chance to break away was going to be out there. Life was going to be better after that. It was going to be pretty sweet.

My father was going to make it to every game that fall. He'd gone a lifetime without missing one, and I was resigned to the fact that that streak was going to hold up during my junior career.

More of the same: I was going to be able to deal with that. I figured it had gone as far as it could.

It was going to go places I had never imagined.

21

JOB APPLICATION

Sterling Heights, Michigan, October 2001

My father was consistent. He had done strange things all his life, but he had done them for a single purpose: getting me to the NHL. The same way, he had a view of me that never changed: he thought I lacked the character necessary to make it to the top of the game. *You don't want it enough.* And more to the point, he thought *he* had possessed that drive as a player but had been undercut by bad breaks and a late start—nothing that was any fault of his own, of course. His message: *If you want it as much as I did, you can be the greatest player in the game.* He thought character was teachable—or at least something that could be conditioned. He was going to instill it in me by ordeal. Waking me up in the middle of the night to do push-ups and sit-ups wasn't about strength at all. It was about determination. *What doesn't kill you makes you stronger.* He was going to impose his attitude on me until it became mine too. *It will always be Us against the World. Never quit.*

114

It was always like that—with one exception.

I didn't think about it at the time. My life with my father wasn't conducive to analysis. I was just too busy trying to survive the latest ordeal and get through the day to ask: *Why?* But my father broke from character late that fall. In retrospect, it seems so unlike him.

The IceDogs had a break in the schedule around Canadian Thanksgiving, and we were given three days off practice. We had no school Monday and I had nothing to do in Mississauga, so I went home to Sterling Heights to pick up my winter clothes. This was my first trip back to Michigan since late August—I had never been away from home that long before. I wasn't homesick, not even a little bit. In fact, the routine that I had settled into with the IceDogs was the closest thing that I had ever felt to autonomy. Not that I had been on my own. My father would still show up at every game, driving four hours each way to our home games, driving more if necessary. If he had to stay over at Barry's—and he did once or twice a week—he'd sleep on an air mattress or maybe pass out on the living-room couch. Those times it didn't feel like much had changed. When he wasn't up in Mississauga, he'd be in my ear on the phone every day, morning and night. Still, I felt for a few days that if it was only a phone call I had to listen to, if it was only hearing him yelling from the stands at a game, if it was only having him wait for me next to the team bus for a ten-minute critique of my play after games, I could deal with it. I felt like I was getting out from under his thumb. Staying over a night or maybe two in Sterling Heights over that Thanksgiving break seemed like something I could handle.

I expected the same harangues from my father. I expected that he was going to be either pushing me to go to the gym to work out or renting ice and pushing me through a practice. I was too old and had been pushing back too hard to have him throw me out of car and make me chase after it. At that point, I would just tell him to fuck off. I was turning the Us-against-the-World defiance he had taught me against him. Still, I counted on more of the same from him, and I figured I'd go through it, suck it up for a day or two knowing that I was going back to Mississauga the first chance I got and wouldn't look back in the rearview mirror.

Instead he was completely different.

Yeah, as expected, he said I was playing like shit even though I was in the top ten in scoring in the league, no other rookie even close. And I heard all about how I was soft, not tough like him.

This time, though, he said nothing was ever going to change. He said it made no sense for him to keep trying to change me. He was conceding, admitting *his* failure. In the battle of Us against the World, he was caving, waving the white flag, surrendering. He couldn't turn me into the best hockey player in the world. If there's one thing he would have hated being called, it was quitter. He would have scrapped with anyone who accused him of it. Look back on his career in junior hockey and the minors, you couldn't accuse him of quitting. He was always the guy who didn't know when to quit. But now, with every-thing pointing in the right direction, he was going soft.

It had always been anger. Now there wasn't a trace of anger, just disappointment. He basically came out and said that he pitied me—but he pitied himself at least as much.

"You're never going to play," he said. "You just aren't good enough. There's nothing that I can do for you. You're just going to have to plan on doing something else with your life."

Somehow my father had erased any memory of the season before, when he had gone to the Ontario league, pushing me as an "exceptional player," when I was the leading scorer on the best team of sixteen-year-olds in the world, when junior teams were prepared to give me money if I jumped to junior rather than return to Ann Arbor and go to college. Now, according to him, I had no future in the game.

"There's no sense pushing anymore," he said. "It's just not going to happen."

He had played hundreds of mind games on me over the years, but never this one. The message was mournful. *Woe is me. I've wasted all this time and money, my whole life.* He seemed depressed, like his hockey career had been a fool's errand and mine was becoming the same for him.

"You might as well pack up your shit in Mississauga and come home," he said.

Like that was ever going to happen.

"No sense getting you in school here," he said. "That's not for you."

Even though I was going to graduate high school a year ahead of my class. Right.

I waited for the next shoe to drop—I knew there had to be one. It wasn't one that I expected.

My father told me to clean up, put on a clean shirt and comb my hair. When I was presentable to his standards, he told me to get in the van. I knew this was going to be good. I went along with it even though I had no idea what it was going to be.

My father drove to the Taco Bell nearest to the house and pulled up in the parking lot.

"Go inside and ask for a job application," he said. "Come back out here with it."

I suspect that he wanted some reaction from me. I gave him none. Maybe he wanted me to get angry, but I wasn't about to do that. It was all I could do to keep a straight face, but I did. I went inside like a thousand sixteen-year-olds had before me, asked for a job application and came back out to the van with it.

"Fill it out," he said, and he handed me a pen.

He didn't trust me to fill out an application inside. He thought I would just go through the motions. When I was done, he read it over and made sure that I had filled in every box. When he was satisfied that the application was in good shape, he told me to go back inside and ask for the manager, which I did.

My father stayed in the van, watching as the manager come out from behind the heat tables and I handed him my job application.

"Okay, we'll keep it on file," the manager said to me.

"Thank you," I said.

Next stop: McDonald's.

On the drive my father laid out what my minimum-wage life was going to look like.

"You'll have to take the bus to work and you'll probably get night shifts and weekends to start," he said. "We'll figure out what you're going to pay in rent."

I just nodded and played along.

"I guess you're going to find out what life's like for the rest of the world."

I resisted the temptation to crack wise and say that this might have been what his career prospects looked when he was back in junior hockey, but they weren't mine. There was no sense taking a jab when he was in the middle of this hangdog routine.

Once my father thought that he had made my immediate future look dismal enough, he changed the subject. He talked about the

My father met my mother when he was playing in Winston-Salem.

My father and I at his parents' house in Scarborough, Ontario.

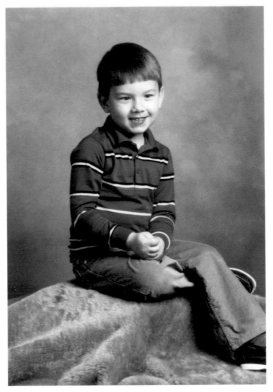

A school photo taken when I was five.

Wearing my father's hockey gloves and holding his stick.

Playing with the Toronto Red Wings. We rolled through the season to a championship, but some people behind the scenes were bothered by my father's coaching.

With the Red Wings. From left to right: Steve Pinizzotto, Brad Bonello and me.

The Toronto Red Wings, with my father standing on the far left. Even though our team had won it all, my father had worn out his welcome in the city league. We moved to Michigan the next year.

Kelley, Shannon and I in our neighborhood in Sterling Heights. Our father pushed Kelley into tennis, but she never picked up a racquet after he was out of our lives.

The pressure intensified when I was fourteen and playing in Strathroy
with the Rockets. I had a few twenty-year-old teammates there.

In Strathroy I was the youngest and smallest player in the league,
but the Rockets named me their rookie of the year.

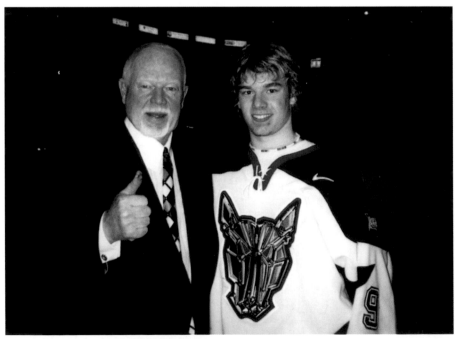

Grapes and I during my rookie year in Mississauga.
Playing for him was quite the experience.

With the Ice Dogs, I wound up being named the Canadian Hockey League rookie of the year in 2002.

I was emotionally drained by the time Minnesota called my name at the 2003 NHL draft.

On the left: Kelley, my mother and Shannon. On the right, my mother's folks.
I had to force a smile for this family photo on draft day.

With my security team at the NHL draft—not your typical draft day photo.

Toronto Red Wings, about Belle Tire, about all the places I had played in my career that was now, according to him, sadly played out. He was, of all things, wistful, or at least what passed for that.

"We had some good times, didn't we?" he said.

Maybe *he* had a good time driving the van with me, age ten, running behind it, trying to catch up. Me, not so much.

I submitted a job application at Mickey D's. And then Burger King. Wendy's. KFC. White Castle. And that's how it went for another three hours. I lost track of how many applications I filled out, but by the end of the afternoon I smelled like a large order of fries. And I sat through my father's nostalgic rewriting of history, all these stories of the places we had gone and fun we had. I sat there thinking: *This sounds like someone else's life.*

When we got back to the house, we had dinner, with my father talking about my moving back and working as a done deal. My mother and sisters didn't register any surprise. They didn't say a word about it. They knew that it was all bullshit, but no sense asking for trouble.

Afterward, I went in the living room to watch TV. My father came in and gave me some sort of buddy-buddy routine.

"Maybe a workout would be good," he said. "Like in the old days. It might be fun, c'mon."

Again, I went along with it. I didn't bother to point out that he had told me two hours before that my career was over. I just went along with it. I lifted weights and shot pucks in the basement. I went for a run. It didn't feel like the not-so-good old days. Over a couple of hours, he didn't try to hit me or kick me. He didn't insult me. He just watched, weirdly supportive. "Buddy," he called me, the only time in my life I ever heard that. Was this really happening? Was this some sort of body double? Maybe other father–son relationships were like this, but he had no practice at it and I had no practice at being the good son. I was just hockey-playing chattel, a high-risk investment that might pay off. Effectively, I was the only potentially valuable property he owned.

The next day, I headed back to Mississauga. I never heard about any job offers pouring in from the fast-food franchises. I missed out on my shot at Employee of the Month. But I did wonder exactly what had happened that day. He might have been trying to scare me straight, to show me exactly what his career prospects had looked like when "Suit-case" O'Sullivan washed out as a player—he had, after all, run a greasy spoon after his last five-game contract ran out in Winston-Salem. But there seemed to be more to it than that. Not about me, but about him: if he wasn't involved on a daily basis, if I wasn't *his*, then successes I called my own didn't matter. He felt like he was losing control. He'd rather have me quit than quit him.

22

THE NIGHT I SAVED MY LIFE

January 2002

In the first chapter of this book, I described what I saw from the back seat of the car on January 4, 2002—what was running through my mind and what I finally did the night I stood my ground against my father, the night I started to turn my life around. But I didn't tell the whole story of that night in the first chapter. A lot more had happened in the hours before that long, awful ride and the fight on the lawn. A lot more happened in the hours after. There were other pieces to the puzzle, other players in the scene. If I had told you the whole story right off the top, it would have been too much for you to sort through. At this point, though, you have a pretty good idea of what my life was like. You have a pretty good idea of the people who were wrapped up in it. What was going on around me will have more meaning now.

It wasn't just my father I was up against.

* * *

Mississauga, Ontario

7 a.m.

For me that day started like every other. I woke up at seven that morning in the bedroom in my uncle's townhouse and got ready for what I figured was going to be a long day: school in the morning, lunch and then the bus to Ottawa for a game at seven in the evening. I figured I'd sleep for a while on the bus to Ottawa and then sleep for most of the trip back. That much was routine. Still, I expected that the day and night were going to be different from usual.

* * *

Ann Arbor, Michigan

7 a.m.

It wasn't long after seven that my father backed the van out of the driveway in Ann Arbor and started on the ten-hour drive to Ottawa. He wasn't about to miss seeing me play, even though he would have come home from work and a few drinks a few hours before, even though he had come out to games four times in the week before.

My sisters were in the back seat, excited to be off school and on their way to stay with my grandparents in Scarborough—my father was going to drop them off at lunchtime on the drive through Toronto.

My mother was sitting beside my father up front. This was going to be the first time since the start of the season that he was bringing my mother along with him. My father preferred going to the games by himself. Any family with him was an unnecessary nuisance, something that could interrupt or interfere with his conversations with team executives, agents or other hockey coaches. I'm sure he told my mother to clear out if he had business to do at the rink, and I'm sure she would have been happy to do that. I'm not sure why she was coming on the trip. It might have been something as simple as my father needing the sleep, and this way he could hand the wheel over to my mother.

My parents had even made a reservation at a Best Western in Ottawa rather than plan to drive back to Toronto or Michigan—again, that was something that just never happened and something that was never explained to me. It couldn't have been a romantic thing, some sort of gift. My father never went in for that. It might have been that, eighteen months away from the NHL draft and my first NHL contract, he saw the promised land—after ten years of moving around and scraping by, they were going to be able to travel to all my games. The Best Western would be a start, but soon they'd be traveling in style to the draft on my agents' dimes, with me picking up their tab when I started making millions.

* * *

Ottawa, Ontario
4:30 p.m.
The team bus pulled up behind the Civic Centre and we started to unload our equipment. Game 36 was just another line, just another date on the Mississauga IceDogs' schedule. It was our fifth game and the fourth on the road in an eight-day stretch since the Christmas break. We were better than the IceDogs' team the previous season, but we were still the worst team in the league, still looking for our seventh win.

Although this was the highest level of the game I had ever played at, it felt like a step down from USA Hockey's program in Ann Arbor. Our under-17 team had been well organized off the ice and we didn't want for anything. The IceDogs weren't exactly a new franchise—they had been around for a few seasons—but it still felt like management was making it up as they went along. The same thing was true on the ice. In Ann Arbor I'd played beside a bunch of kids who would play in the NHL. The OHL had older players and the game was faster, but almost none of my teammates in Mississauga would wind up playing pro hockey.

Still, I was looking forward to getting out on the ice that night. I looked forward to every game. For sixty minutes I had a chance to play—that was the break from school, from practice, from the bus rides and, yeah, from dealing with the father who called Barry's town-house long-distance every night to give my shit about one thing or another that he had picked up the last time he saw me play. Those sixty minutes were the best hour of my day, even against the better teams in the league, like the Ottawa 67's.

* * *

Ottawa, Ontario

7:30 p.m.

Eight thousand five hundred fans packed the Civic Centre for the first Friday-night game of the New Year for the 67's. The game had been sold out months in advance, fans banking on Don Cherry being behind our bench, wearing one of his outrageous suits and putting in a performance. But Cherry didn't make the trip—he wasn't up to the better part of ten hours on the bus when he had to work *Hockey Night in Canada* the next day. Still, fans in Ottawa got some sort of show, at least those who were in the section behind our bench. They got an eyeful and an earful of my father pressed against the Plexiglas, screaming at me for three periods.

Usually my father found a corner of the rink and stood there, strategically positioned so that I could hear his shouting or catch sight of him before face offs. He'd only ever move away if he recognized an agent or a scout—in which case he'd wander by and try to make small talk.

In Ottawa, though, he somehow made his way down to the seats right behind our bench. It wouldn't have been the ticket that I had the team leave him at Will Call, and it wouldn't have been a ticket that he bought off a scalper. I don't know where my mother was sitting, and I'm sure that my father didn't care. Wherever she was, she had to be embarrassed by the scene my father was making and she must have wished that she had never come along on this road trip. He had retired the sad-faced-resignation routine he'd put on while I filled out job applications. He went completely in the other direction, manic, maniacal.

What he was saying was nothing new—calling me a "pussy" or a "fuckin' fag," calling me "useless" or "gutless." Still, this was different from the other times. This time he wasn't a voice in the crowd. He was right in my teammates' ears. They could hear every word and looked at me, shaking their heads, as if to say "WTF." He was just feet away from the coaches. Steve Cherry and Joe Washkurak pretended not to notice him when he started to pound his fists on the Plexiglas. I caught looks from them, looks that said, "We can't believe it either."

There was nothing that I could do during the game, nothing the players could do. Maybe the coaches could have called arena security—even if they couldn't nail him with causing a disturbance or menacing and hoof him out of the building, they could have asked to see his ticket and told him to move back to his seat. Looking back, I'm surprised that the police in the arena didn't step in on their own. They had laid down the law with fans doing a whole lot less. Then again, it was the visiting team that was getting the abuse, and they would have thought my father was just an Ottawa fan venting, dialing the heckling up to 11—a bit extreme but nothing criminal. Maybe they thought he had a couple of beers in him and was a little wild. But I suspect that if he had been drinking, the whole thing would have only escalated in the arena and not waited for later.

One thing for sure: my father's act would have been toned down if Don Cherry had been behind the bench that night. Not that he would have been on his best behavior even if Don had worked the game—that hadn't stopped him from acting out before. Still, he would have dialed it down a notch in the arena, and he would have stayed out of earshot. There was no chance of "Suitcase" winning a battle with Don, little chance that he wanted to get on Cherry's bad side. My father had wanted to be one of "Don's guys," and I was his ticket to the inner circle. He would have been able to go only so crazy but no crazier. And if my father couldn't exercise any self-control at all and shouted and pounded the glass just the same, I'm sure security and the police would have taken my father's sideshow more seriously if he had been doing it within spitting distance of a hockey icon.

Players are supposed to be able to tune out hecklers. They're supposed to not even notice the extraneous stuff in the arena, the world on the other side of the glass, to be in a bubble. I had thought that my father's yelling couldn't affect me, not after all those years of it. But in Ottawa it did. I'll admit I was distracted. I'll admit that it gnawed at me. I was only able to give the game divided attention.

My teammates played really well against the 67's, but I had a brutal game. I screwed up chances. After my teammates came back to tie the game, I took a bad penalty and Ottawa scored to take the lead—for good, as it turned out. It was maybe my worst game of the year. No excuses, it's just something that happens. It didn't happen because of my father, though he didn't help. It was just one of those nights when nothing works for you.

I was frustrated as hell and started to jaw at my father, over my shoulder, not looking back at him. I provoked him. I was practically begging him to come over the glass at me—if he had crossed that line, he'd have been in a hell of a lot of trouble. Really, though, there was no calculation on my part. I mouthed off to my father and goaded him because I was sick and tired of his shit.

"Shut the fuck up," I yelled.

"You fuckin' loser, you're out of your fuckin' mind," I yelled.

I was mad but I was still rational. I made my mind up right there on the bench that this had to end. It might seem like a strange place and time to make a life decision, but really that's how it played out. It was now or never. I had always thought that the day would come when I was going to have to walk away from my father—when I was eighteen, when I made it to the pros, sometime down the line. That night in Ottawa, though, I realized there was no waiting until I had a pro contract and was self-sufficient. I had lived in fear of being physically beaten by my father. Now I was worried that he might take it a step farther. He seemed capable of doing absolutely anything.

* * *

Ottawa, Ontario

10 p.m.

Before the game, it hadn't entered my mind to look for a confrontation with my father in Ottawa. I wasn't looking for a confrontation with my father. Not before the game. Not after. I did everything I could to physically avoid him. I was one of the first to shower, get dressed and head out to the bus with my equipment. My hair was still wet and I didn't comb it. It was a race. I figured that if I could beat him out to the back of the arena, I could get on the bus while he was waiting for me outside the dressing room. I figured if I was on the bus, I was safe.

I did beat my father out to the bus. Only by a few steps.

I was walking toward the bus with my hockey bag over my shoulder and my sticks. My father was yelling at me from behind. I didn't turn around. I tried to ignore him, but I had a sinking feeling that he was going to get physical.

I threw my hockey bag and sticks into the bus's hold. My father grabbed my shoulder.

"You're fuckin' going home," he yelled.

He let me loose for a second and bent over. Then he grabbed my bag out of the hold and threw it on the snow-covered pavement. I didn't say anything, just walked away from him and started up the steps into the bus. He grabbed a handful of my jacket and pulled me backward. I was knocked off balance but managed to stay on my feet.

"What the fuck?" I said. "Just leave alone. Get the fuck out of here."

I got out of his grip and onto the bus. He followed me on and dragged me down the aisle, yelling, "It's fuckin' over! You're going home."

There were only a couple of players on the bus, and they had no idea what the hell was going on. The lights were off. There were no adults in the seats. The driver wasn't on the bus. Neither were the coaches.

It didn't occur to me till later on that the coaches being there might have shut things down. The whole night would have turned out differently if Don Cherry had been there. Don's exit from the arena was always like Elvis leaving the building. Hundreds of people crowded around. Extra security would be outside, pushing back hordes of fans looking for an autograph or a photo with him. Don might have already boarded the bus when my father went for me after the game. If Don didn't or couldn't physically stop him, he would have at least asked him what the hell was going on. He would have said that it was a team rule, that players rode the bus home with the team, no exceptions.

If Steve Cherry or Joe Washkurak had been there, either of them would have given him the same message. Maybe with a bit more of a physical pushback than Cherry, who was almost seventy.

Then again, more people around might not have changed things so dramatically. While my father was dragging and shoving me toward the van, I could see twenty or thirty adults standing around behind the arena. Most if not all of them were family of players or fans who would have been inside earlier. None of them tried to step in. None of them said a word—not one Good Samaritan among them. I have no idea what went through their minds. Did they come up with their own interpretation of events? *Probably a father giving his son some tough discipline ... It's none of our business.* If you had asked them about the first sign of character in a hockey player, they would have said the willingness to stand up for a teammate who was being ambushed. And yet outside the arena, not one of them budged. My father probably physically intimidated most of them, but they didn't have to stand in his way to call the police or security. Nobody tried to help me.

* * *

My father dragged me over to the van and threw me in the back seat. He picked up my equipment and threw it on top of me. My mother was sitting in the front seat whimpering. She had known what my father was going to do. He'd spelled it out to her and told her to wait there. If she'd had her wits about her, she could have left the van and told the coaches. She could have told a cop. She could have asked anyone standing around for help. Instead, she just sat there, did what she was told and said nothing to my father and nothing to me.

You might give her the benefit of a doubt. You might think that she felt threatened with physical abuse herself over the years and again that night, like those people who stood by and watched in back of the arena in Ottawa. I don't see it that way. I don't think she deserves any sympathy.

It's one thing to feel threatened in your marriage if you have no children. Accepting that physical threat from your spouse and trying to soldier on—that's a personal decision. But tolerating your spouse's abuse of a child is unacceptable, even unconscionable. When my mother sat by passively all those years, she enabled my father's abuse. Even though he did a lot of it out of her sight when we were on the road, she had seen the evidence—I was wearing it all over my face and body. And she had seen him punch and kick me hundreds of times. She should have done something the first time it happened, taken my sisters and me out of harm's way, walked out on my father and reported him to law enforcement. Some women in my mother's position might have felt so financially dependent on an abusive husband that they feel they can't leave. That wasn't the case with my mother. In fact, the Martins had always been my parents' safety net, a cash machine that my father had access to because my mother's birthright was their bank card and passcode. A lot of times the Martins were my parents' single biggest source of income. If my mother had taken my sisters and me away from my father, her parents would have been there for her.

By standing by and offering no response, no pushback, no resistance, my mother abandoned her responsibility as a parent: the protection of her children. Her tears in the front seat of the van meant nothing. Her passivity implied approval of or at least resignation to my father's abuse of me. That's how it had been for years, and that's how it was the night of January 4, 2002. She'd had opportunities to save me from those beatings every day all those years when I was growing up. Just one phone call to the authorities would have done it. There were hotlines she could have called. There were friends she could have called who would have offered her any support she needed and a roof over our heads in an emergency. If she had called a guidance counselor at any of the schools I had attended, she could have got help. I'm sure that if she'd reached out to USA Hockey when I was in the program, Moe Mantha and others on the staff would have jumped in. But instead of reaching out to others who could have helped us, my mother kept the family secret. If you were to ask anyone who knew her when I was growing up, you would get the same answer—she "seemed so nice." She kept up appearances. She knew what a monster my father was but gave him cover. People would think such a "nice" woman could never stand beside a husband capable of crimes against his family.

That night was another example of how my mother enabled my father. Once again she passed up the opportunity to get help for us.

* * *

The IceDogs team bus was still sitting in the parking lot and players were still coming out of the arena when my father put the van into gear and took off. He drove over to the Best Western. My parents had checked into the hotel before the game and left their suitcases there. My father pulled the van up to the front doors.

"We're fuckin' going back to Michigan," he said to us. "Get the fuckin' bags and check out."

She said nothing—nothing to him, nothing to me. She and I went into the hotel and up to the room to pack their bags. We were out of the van and away from my father for ten minutes, the perfect opportunity to get help. There was a phone in the room. I had no way of calling the team to let the coaches know what was going on—these were the days before cellphones and texts. Still, my mother could have called 911 and told the dispatcher that she was concerned about her husband's mental state, that I was being held against my will, that she feared for my safety. And if she had done that, I'm sure the police would have arrived in the time that it took her to check out. She could have alerted the front desk at the hotel. She wouldn't even have had to come downstairs to the lobby. She could have deadbolted the door and waited for help.

I didn't call 911 and deadbolt the door myself because I couldn't have counted on my mother to back up my account of the incidents when the police arrived. She would have put on the "nice" act and told them that it was all a family argument that would blow over.

The forgiving take on my mother's inaction is that it didn't occur to her to reach out for help. Fact is, she failed as a parent again.

She dutifully packed up in the hotel room. She stifled her tears while she carried the bags through the lobby, again keeping up appearances and not causing the staff any alarm. Then she put the bags in the back of the van, took her seat in the front and burst into helpless tears, picking up where she'd left off.

When I got into the back seat, my father kept up his crazy, threatening monologue, but for a while at least I tuned him out and thought about my mother.

Dozens of times she had seen my father slap me around and done nothing. She would ask him to stop but couldn't stop him. So many times she had stayed in bed while my father was keeping me up all night, making me do push-ups and sit-ups to exhaustion, punching and kicking me to motivate me. She had to have heard that going on, and sometimes even if she did sleep through it, she saw the evidence. She never questioned my father about the game the night before, never asked the next day why we came home at two in the morning when we should have been back before midnight. Fact is, she had a good idea of what happened after a game.

My father wasn't so much tough as brutal. He headed the family in a reign of terror. My mother was the exact opposite. People mistook her surrender and submission to my father for a happy marriage. They thought someone that "nice" had to be a good mother, had to be the glue in a happy marriage with that crazy, off-the-wall character. A lot of people had suspicions about my father, but he fooled most into thinking he was a decent if driven rough diamond. My mother fooled them all. Everyone thought she was the rock of the family when what I saw was a woman sleepwalking through life.

I know some will defend her and say that she feared for her own safety or maybe that of my sisters, that my father would have assaulted her if she had ever called the police. If that was in fact the case, then she was willing to put her interests ahead of mine. I would have to pay the price for her fear.

After all that had happened over the years, it was on that night that I could finally see my mother's role. She couldn't have done less to protect me over the years. I couldn't even say for sure that she didn't buy into my father's plan to turn me into a pro hockey player—whatever he thought it would take.

* * *

Highway 401 near Kingston, Ontario
10:30 p.m.
Sitting in the back seat, I also realized that there wasn't help waiting for me at our destination, my grandparents' place in Scarborough. Again, like my mother, my grandparents might have feared my father lashing out at them, and that fear might have trumped any objections they had to the abuse.

* * *

Over the next five hours, he kept coming back to one of his go-to threats.

"I brought you into this world and I can take you out," he said.

I took it the way that it sounded: a threat to kill me, a very real threat. When he had said it before, it had just sounded like bragging about his power over me. Now it was sounding like he thought it wasn't just within his power but also within his rights.

134

I had always thought it was hyperbole. I'd taken his threats of hitting me seriously, but killing me … no, I had never taken that seriously. But I had never seen him in the state he was in now, never so extreme for so long. I'd thought he wasn't just capable of "taking me out of this world" but sort of leaning that way. But my hockey career had been his whole life. If I was going to break away from him, he had nothing else to look forward to, just another dead-end job for minimum wage, another plea to his in-laws for a bailout, another day in a loveless marriage and dysfunctional family. Going to jail for killing me or ending his own life might not have looked so bad to him by comparison. I thought I had to fear for my life because of how little value he found in his own.

I had always known that I would break away from my father. I had thought it would be a process, that I was going to have to claw for every inch of independence. I thought my father would have to cede control but that that would come over a long haul. I had played for him all those years, but eventually I was going to be playing for a team that was going to pay me. That was going to become my first loyalty: an NHL team that was going to be paying me for control of my playing career. If there was going to be a single moment of truth, a moment when my life would change in a fundamental way, I thought it was going to be when I signed that contract. After all, that contract had been my father's objective from the very start.

I had never imagined, not until he grabbed me and pulled me off the bus in Ottawa, that my independence from my father would come down to a showdown. I had always thought that breaking away would be for a better life, but now I was thinking that it might be the only way to *save* my life.

* * *

Even though my father had been awake for at least eighteen hours and maybe more than twenty-four (having worked the night before), he was wired. He didn't do drugs, but it seemed like was on amphetamines or cocaine. He was shaking. His eyes were popping. He was talking nonstop. He drove the entire way from Ottawa to Toronto with only the one stop for a piss break. He had the pedal down and was going way over the speed limit. And just like the van, he showed no sign of slowing down. Over the course of hours, his rage only accelerated. A manic episode, a breakdown ... I'm not a psychiatrist, but I'm not sure that a medical specialist could have diagnosed my father if one had been sitting in the front seat next to him.

I was agitated too, but I was aware of everything going on. I knew that there was going to be a confrontation and that it was going to be physical, like so many before. I tried to stay as calm as I could. If I was going to get out of this night alive and in one piece, it *wasn't* over, no matter what he said. If I could break away, I was going to keep playing hockey no matter what he thought, I wasn't going to have to give up the game. And I grew cocky about it, just like I had on the bench earlier when I was chirping back at him. When he ranted and looked in the rearview mirror, he caught me smiling, and that only stoked the fire. I had to be careful, though—I knew I was going to have to stand my ground and confront him when we got to his parents' place. That was going to be me seizing the moment on my own terms.

I couldn't control my father. No one had ever been able to talk him down or reason with him. But I knew how to push his button, and I knew exactly when I was going to do it. That much I could control.

* * *

Scarborough, Ontario

January 5, 2002, 2:30 a.m.

"Get the girls, get their shit packed and get 'em out here. Don't waste any fuckin' time."

Again, my mother got out of the van and went up to the front door. It was locked, so she rang the bell. I could see my grandparents standing in the doorway, my mother explaining that we were going back to Michigan. My father kept the van idling and watched his father and wife talking. I opened the door.

"Stay in the fuckin' car," my father said.

"No, this is it," I said. I got out and stood on the lawn. "I'm not going. I'm staying here."

"Get fuckin' in!"

"I'm not going anywhere. This is it. I'm done with it."

I could have run then. I could have outrun him. I could have run and hid or tried to get help, but in the back seat I had made my decision to make my stand.

He took a run at me and I stood there. He started throwing punches.

"You little fuckin' bastard. You piece of shit."

He put everything he had behind every punch and landed every third one on target. He was looking to knock me stone-cold, lights-out unconscious. If any one headshot caught me wrong, I'd have a concussion that would send me to hospital and to a dark room for weeks at least. I punched back and flushed him a couple of times.

"You wanna take a punch at me, you faggot?"

He got me down, bent over me and punched away. Awful minutes passed. He was hyperventilating. He punched right through a smoker's cough and a gasp for air. And finally he punched himself out, couldn't throw one more shot. He stood up and staggered away.

Lights went on at the neighbors' homes.

"Is that enough?" I said.

I crawled away. My mother was just standing by, weeping, and didn't help me up. I got up to my knees and then my feet. While my father was bent over at the waist, trying to catch his breath, I walked into the house, past my grandparents, who were standing by the door. They looked at my sweatshirt, torn, wet and covered in cold mud. They looked at the cuts and bruises on my face. They said nothing. My father stood on their lawn and told them what had gone on.

"He had it fuckin' comin'," he said.

While he was justifying every last punch, I was on the phone to the police. I can't remember calling 911. I might have. My mother might have. My grandparents might have. I was exhausted and my mind was foggy. Everything was a blur. I spoke to the 911 dispatcher.

The dispatcher had the address from the call display and double-checked it with me. "Is this an emergency?" he asked.

"Yeah, it's an emergency."

My father saw me holding the receiver. In less than a minute, in the time it took me to dial the number and the dispatcher to pick up, it was over. Everything. My father probably couldn't hear me. If he didn't know I was on the phone with the police, he had to have suspected that that was next. He stood there while I stayed on the line.

"My name is Patrick O'Sullivan … I've been beaten up by my father … I'm cut but I think I'm all right … I'm afraid what he's going to do … I'm afraid he's going to kill me."

"Police are on the way. Stay on the line."

He didn't need to hear the dispatcher.

"Fuck," he said. And that was all. He knew it was over.

It was the first time I had ever seen my father back down, the first time I had ever seen him run. No time for goodbyes, not even a last threat. He drove off and a few minutes later a couple of cruisers and four cops were at the house.

* * *

Scarborough, Ontario

3:30 a.m.

A police officer walked out to the cruiser parked in front of the house and got on the radio. John O'Sullivan. February 26, 1960. Six feet. 240 pounds. Black hair. Brown eyes. Michigan plates. Possibly heading to the border.

Inside the house another officer took the lead. He pulled me aside and asked me questions. He tried to calm me down. I was shaking. He probably thought it was just nerves, but it was more than that. I hadn't slept in twenty hours and hadn't eaten since lunch. I was exhausted even before I had to fight for my life. And anyone who has been in a fight knows just how much it takes out of you.

"How did this start?"

I didn't know where to begin. "It's always like this," I said.

"Then how did it start tonight?"

I told him about the beat-down on the lawn.

"He did that?" the officer asked, pointing to fresh cuts and bruises on my face.

139

"Yeah," I said.

And when I answered all of his questions, I had some of my own. What next? Yeah, he'd be caught and questioned. I wanted to know: Could he be charged for those other things? It had been years, I told the officer. Years. And it had been just like this. Lots of times worse. The officer took down everything. He asked and asked again.

"What else did your father do?"

"He would throw me out of the house and lock me out all night in the middle of the winter. From eleven until the morning and I was freezing out there."

"And how old were you?"

"Eleven, twelve. He did it all the time."

The officer told me that the police were going to follow up. I could hear the other officer asking my mother and grandparents questions in another room. I couldn't hear exactly what they were saying.

"Is he going to jail?" I asked.

"Your father is in a lot of trouble," he said.

That only left me one question to ask myself: Why hadn't I tried to get help sooner? If the police had asked me, I wouldn't have had a good answer. I wouldn't have had any answer at all.

I told the officer that I was worried that my father was going to come back, and he did his best to calm me down. Arrangements for me to stay with someone would be made in the morning, they said. Until then a cruiser would stay parked outside, to protect me and nab my father if he tried anything.

He didn't.

* * *

Scarborough, Ontario

8:30 a.m.

Before the cruiser left in the morning, an officer told me that U.S. Customs in Detroit had spotted the van at the border. My father had used one of his fake IDs to cross the river. He was at large, but a warrant was out for his arrest.

I was exhausted. I had been played a game, been beaten to a pulp. I had slept a bit on the bus on the drive up to Ottawa, but I was ready to pass out. I went to one of the upstairs bedrooms and stretched out. I tried to find a way to put my head on the pillow that didn't put any pressure on the welts on my face that were still swelling up. I checked to see if I was leaving any drops of blood on the pillow. I closed my eyes and tried to will myself to sleep. I was still shaking and sweating, just too much adrenaline pumping.

Eventually I managed to drop off for a few minutes at a time, but whenever there was a knock at the door I sat bolt upright—it would seem crazy for my father to come back to his parents' place with a warrant out for his arrest, but he had an established history of doing crazy things. Whenever the phone rang downstairs, I woke up and tried to hear what was going on. I knew there would be a lot of calls back and forth with the police and the team. I knew the story would be out there—not in the newspapers but on the hockey grapevine. I knew that by the time I came downstairs a lot of people who'd had suspicions about my father for years would have had them confirmed. Anybody who had something more than suspicions about my father would be thinking that they'd seen it coming.

* * *

Mississauga, Ontario

6 p.m.

When Joe Washkurak got in touch with me later that day, he told me that he had made arrangements to have me picked up and escorted into my uncle Barry's townhouse to gather my stuff. The police wanted to make sure that my father hadn't shown up at Barry's, but I didn't think he'd be there—he was crazy but not stupid. That would be the first place the police would have looked.

I was glad that I didn't have to go into Barry's alone. Barry would have been the first person my father called, probably not even an hour after he took off the night before. He would have kept Barry updated. If the police caught up with my father, Barry would have instructions for getting him bail.

After gathering up my clothes, Joe Washkurak dropped me off at the home of Matt Tanel, our backup goalie. Matt's father was a police officer, so there probably wasn't a safer place for me to stay on short notice. After a few hours there, my nerves jangled a little less and the adrenaline slowed to a trickle.

Only then did it really sink in. This was my new reality. It wasn't just my father who was going to be out of my life, but his whole side of the family. Just as there was going to be no "patching up" with my father, there was never going to be any way that I could fully trust the rest of them. It would have been tough enough to maintain any connection with them because of their knowledge of the abuse I was put through and their silence. No matter what my father would ever do, they were going to defend him just by reflex—he had emotionally manipulated everyone around him. It was left to me to break away.

23

GETTING BACK ON MY SKATES AND GETTING MY SKATES BACK

Mississauga, Ontario, January 2002

For the four days, my father was at large with a warrant out for his arrest. I don't know where he would have been hiding, or even whether he stayed in Michigan or came back to Toronto. I imagine that he slept in a van or managed to couch-surf at the house of someone he worked with. And I imagine that he came up with his own explanation for his need for a place to stay. *The wife kicked me out of the house, nothing that's real serious, just temporary. We'll get back together, for the kids' sake.* He would have come up with some bullshit line that would make him seem hard-done-by and sympathetic.

I missed a couple of days of school—I didn't want to go in with lumps and cuts all over my face. My teammates had to know, but I didn't want anyone else at school to know.

I missed a couple of practices. It wasn't just that I was beaten up physically and distracted by all the shuffling in and out of offices and the courthouse and the police station. On top of everything else, my father had run off with my equipment in the back of the van, so before I could get back on the ice I was going to have to get fitted for new skates and order a batch of sticks. It doesn't sound like much, but I was like most players at that level: particular about my equipment, attached to it. Sticks and pads—replacing those was just a nuisance, but my skates, well, that was like switching cars on a driver at the Indy 500. It would take a while, maybe even weeks, to feel comfortable in them—pretty much in keeping with everything in my life *off* the ice.

When I made it to practice on Tuesday, most of the players were up to speed on everything that had gone on after the game in Ottawa. The team's staff filled in most of the other blanks and put into place a new protocol: from here on out, I was to go nowhere alone—not to school, not the drive to practice, not in my room at the hotel on the road, not in any other situation that might come up. No matter what, everyone had to assume that my father was just around the corner, waiting to pick up where he had left off on my grandparents' lawn. My teammates supported the rule and bought in, which reassured me but also made me feel claustrophobic. Everyone in the dressing room wants to blend in and be just another player. No one wants to be *that* kid. The other guys understood, especially after the game in Ottawa, that I didn't want to be *that* kid, but it was beyond my control, just my bad luck.

* * *

Mississauga, Ontario, January 9, 2002

We were playing the St. Michael's Majors, one of the league's top teams, on Wednesday night. The IceDogs management was ready to let me sit out the game or maybe even a couple of games if I didn't feel ready. I told the coaching staff that I wanted to be in the lineup. I was anxious and determined to play. Sitting on the sidelines watching the game would have felt too much like my father had won. That was the whole point of the beat-down on my grandparents' lawn—so I couldn't go back and play. I had to show him that it wasn't over.

Even though I wanted to play, I had no idea how I was going to be able to perform against St. Michael's. I was still rattled. My nerves were still jangling and I had spent a lot of nervous energy over five days. My energy level was low—I'd had trouble sleeping and not much of an appetite. I'd had one practice in my new skates. None of those things helped, but any one of them I could get past, at least for a game. It was more than that, though.

On top of everything else, this would be the first game that my father wasn't going to be at.

It was understandable when I was eight or nine years old, what looked like normal stuff. A young kid has to count on a parent for transportation. A parent wants to ensure that the kid is in a good environment and is having fun. Still, you'd have imagined real life would have intruded occasionally, a work conflict or a doctor's appointment or the flu, something that could not be avoided that meant my mother would have to get me to the practice or game instead of my father. But real life never got in the way of my father getting me to the arena.

Time and space didn't get in the way, not even driving thirty hours from Nova Scotia to Chicago to see a lousy game that everyone on the ice forgot about five minutes after the buzzer. It was hockey first and foremost, and whatever else there was in my father's or my family's life could only compete for second place.

Yeah, you'd imagine that his absence should have made things easier, lifted a weight off. Still, it was in the back of my mind. From the second I stepped on the ice to the second I stepped off, he had watched every play I made, every stride I took. I had always played knowing that I was being watched. That hadn't been in the back of my mind—it had always been a lot closer to the front than I liked. It had felt strange in Mississauga back in the fall when he hadn't been there at practice—he had never even missed a practice in all those years. And now it was going to be a game without him. I'd known it was going to come to this someday. It was what I had been working for. Still, it happened so suddenly. It was a shock that I was going to have to deal with.

We had trouble drawing a crowd on a good night in Mississauga, and that Wednesday night in January was not a good night. The league stats show that 1,800 bought tickets and came out to the game against St. Mike's, but it didn't feel like half of that. I skated in the warm-up and looked around the arena. Out of force of habit, I had always tried to spot my father during the warm-up, and he always tried to get my attention.

After the warm-up, we went back to the dressing room. Joe Washkurak came into the room and took me aside. He kept his voice low so that the other players wouldn't hear.

"I just talked to Metro Police," he said. "They arrested your father."

"Where?"

In five days my father could have been a thousand miles away, could have assumed another name. I asked where the manhunt ended, but really I wanted to know how the police chased him down.

"They got him outside. He was trying to come to the game."

Even after putting out an all-points bulletin for my father, the police didn't really have to search for him. If they had wanted to just wait, he would have come right to them. He was so obsessed with seeing me play that he couldn't stay away, not even when he was risking arrest, not even when he couldn't have known for sure that I was going to play. The need to see me play outweighed the potential of landing in jail.

We wound up beating St. Mike's 6–3 that night. We had a great game, maybe our best of the season. It might have been my best game of the season too, the exact opposite of the game in Ottawa. I had a goal and a couple of assists, but it was more how I felt out on the ice. In Ottawa every bounce had gone against me and I'd gotten getting tenser and tenser every shift. Against St. Mike's, the first game of the rest of my life, the game just flowed.

In a Hollywood movie, the fans would have been on their feet, cheering loud enough to make your ears hurt. This wasn't a Hollywood movie, though. It was a small crowd, and at times, in the middle of play, the arena was almost as quiet as at practice. You could hear players calling for the puck on the ice, bodies hitting the boards and skate blades carving the ice. It was the type of night when my father's voice would have been the loudest thing in the building, when I wouldn't have had to look for him because I could just hear where he was. And that game, I heard nothing, and no one else did either.

Like I said, a player just wants to fit in and not be the special kid. That night I wasn't the special kid, the kid with *that* father.

While the game was going on, the police impounded my father's van, but not before going into the back seat and pulling out my equipment bag. I got my skates back.

* * *

A couple of days later I had a short conversation with my grandmother. It would be the last one we would ever have. "Maybe it would be the best thing if you patched things up with your father," she said.

I felt sick to my stomach.

My grandmother had seen what happened on the lawn. She saw the bruises on my face. She knew what my father had put me through. She knew what type of father he was to my sisters, what type of husband he was to my mother. I couldn't imagine why she thought things would be better if I didn't cooperate with the police and the warrant for his arrest was thrown out. Compassion for her son, even if she thought he was mentally ill and not responsible for his actions, wouldn't have explained her seemingly heartfelt plea for some sort of truce. I had no idea how she thought we weren't way past the point of forgiving and forgetting.

And then it came to me in a flash: my father must have gotten to her. He had called the house. Maybe it wasn't compassion. Maybe it wasn't a mother's love. Maybe she feared him enough to do his bidding for him. And to do that, she was basically offering me back up to him for more abuse, sacrificing me so that everyone else remained safe.

24

NOT QUITE A FRESH START

Plymouth, Michigan, January I9, 2002

The Toronto police charged my father with assault. He'd wind up facing three counts: the first for what happened on January 4 in Ottawa and the others dated the next day in Kingston and Toronto. A judge set a date to hear the case and released my father on his own recognizance. The judge attached two conditions of his release. One: My father was "not to be in the province of Ontario except for attending court or counsel's office." Two: He was "not to be within 50 metres of any ice rink in Ontario and not to attend any ice arenas where the Mississauga IceDogs hockey team are [playing]." Even before he'd appear before a judge to enter a plea, he did both.

The IceDogs had a road game against the Whalers in Plymouth, Michigan, just a few minutes from the house where my father was living. I knew he was going to be there—so did the team. The coaches and my teammates were extra cautious with me. My father wasn't worried about being seen. He didn't hide in the shadows or in the back row. He took his usual place in the corner of the rink and yelled like he had at any other game. That night he was able to go through his whole routine with impunity. Although the judge barred my father from any arena where the IceDogs were playing, the conditions of the peace bond didn't carry any weight in the U.S.

Just in case we might have missed him, my father left a calling card. My mother had come out to the game and she had left our border collie in the back of her van. After the game, my mother went back to the van and found that my father had taken the dog. He might have thought the dog needed walking. He still thought all of this was going away. The letters he sent to me care of the team spelled that out—that I was going to drop the charges and we could go back to what he thought were the good old days. He was going to get a wake-up call the next day.

* * *

Windsor, Ontario, January 20, 2002

After the Plymouth game we stayed over in Windsor because we had a game there Sunday afternoon. Everyone with the team knew that there was a risk that my father was going to try to track me down. Even if he didn't go looking for me, it was going to be impossible to stay away. I don't know if my father tripped an alarm at the border or if security at the Windsor Arena spotted him, but police arrested him at the Windsor Arena. He had breached a condition of his peace bond and would be sentenced to fifteen days in jail.

* * *

Toronto, Ontario, February 2002

When my father appeared before a judge in Toronto, he pleaded guilty on the second and third counts of assault, those in Kingston and Toronto. He was given what I thought and still think was a slap on the wrist: five days on Count No. 2 and ten more consecutively on Count No. 3. Of course I thought he should have done more jail time. It seemed unfair: He had put me through years of abuse and he was being punished by days in jail. My mother, the team officials and my agents, all the adults, told me to try to keep it in perspective. A restraining order against my father was going to be issued and the conditions set down to keep him away from me were going to be extended. My mother had retained a divorce lawyer and though my father would try to make things as miserable as possible for her and for my sisters and me, it was going to be finalized in a few months. The message that everyone around me tried to drive home: *Look on the bright side. It's over. It's a fresh start.*

My mother's divorce lawyer talked to her about having me see a psychologist. It's standard stuff for kids going through a much less troubling divorce to get that sort of counseling. I had no interest in it. My father had always said I wasn't tough enough. This was just my first chance to show how tough I was, to prove him wrong—if not to him, to me. I had survived his abuse. I was convinced that I was strong enough to handle anything thrown at me. I was convinced that in any room I walked into I was the strongest willed there. Divorce, the idea that my father was out of my life, was nothing I thought I needed help with. The proof was on the ice.

My game took off those weeks when he was in jail. I was able to go into games free of his advice. Even though the IceDogs were out-manned most nights and other teams could focus on shutting me down with nineteen- and twenty-year-olds bigger than me, I held on to my spot in the league's top ten scorers. And more than that, I could enjoy the game more, for once like everyone else in the dressing room.

It turned out that I wasn't completely free of my father. After he had served his two weeks on the assault charges, I knew he wasn't going to be able to stay away. I looked for him in the stands before games and a lot of nights I'd spot him. So did my teammates and the coaches. As much as I could pick anything out in the crowd noise, I listened for his voice—it wasn't just his voice but his usual instructions, no different from when I was eight years old. Maybe he toned down or cleaned up his act from the game in Ottawa so that he wouldn't attract the attention of security, but still he did what he could to let me know he was out there at games.

When I couldn't find him and couldn't hear him, I was relieved. I could play my game with an uncluttered mind.

Even when I saw or heard him, I could get past it, I thought. It sat in the back of my mind for a while, but then I knew he wouldn't be out there waiting for me after the game, ready to rip me or make me chase the van or beat the shit out of me again. All he could do is annoy me, I thought. There was nothing I had reason to fear, I thought.

25

ALL-AMERICAN AGAIN

Ann Arbor, Michigan, March 2002

It wasn't like I went through life without a care in the world for the rest of the winter and into the spring. I knew my father couldn't bring himself to stay away from IceDogs games, so the team still abided by the same rules: I was never left alone for any stretch of time and my roommate would screen my calls in the hotel on road trips. It might have made some kids feel like I was a bubble boy, but I felt exactly the opposite way. Yeah, he was in the back of my mind, at least that's the way I looked at it. But before I had been completely preoccupied with him. By the spring of 2002 I'd never felt as free in my life. I'd never felt more upbeat about what was ahead for me.

We wound up finishing last in the league that spring, no surprise. In fact, it might have been a surprise that we had been as competitive as we were. My season didn't end there, though. USA Hockey called me and asked if I would be interested in a spot on the team going to the world under-18 championships. I jumped at the opportunity. It wasn't just a chance to keep playing. It was a chance to get back on the ice with everyone I had played with in Ann Arbor, the same team that had won the gold at the under-17 challenge in Truro the year before. Most of all, it was a chance to win.

I wound up staying with the Eaves family in Ann Arbor. It was a perfect fit. Mike was coaching the under-18 program that season and he had always been in my corner. He could be critical of me when it was necessary, but he was always fair and he always let me know that he believed in me as a player. I can say point blank that he was the best coach I'd ever play for. Patrick had been my linemate when I played on the under-17 team and he was my best friend in the program. I loved getting on the ice every day with Mike running practice and skating beside Patrick. They forced me to raise my game. The change wasn't just at the arena, though. No, it continued when we would go back to the Eaves's house after practice.

I had been around "normal" families before, of course: those few times that my father might let me out of his sight for a night and I'd stay over at friends' homes and the months I had billeted with the Tanels. I had seen parents and kids interact with real love and without abuse. With the Eaves family, though, it was different. I liked Mike as a coach but he was demanding. He pushed hard. He showed no favoritism and paid no special attention to Patrick on the ice. And Patrick could give it back when Mike reamed him out at practice. Yet when we drove away from the arena, anything done or said there was left behind. They didn't bring the game home with them. What happened at the rink that day barely came up at dinner or through the evening. It was the exact opposite of my family-life experience. No night workouts. No wake-up calls before dawn. No constant badgering. With Mike and Patrick, we'd watch a game on television but it wasn't a tutorial. The Eaveses weren't slackers, the farthest thing from it, but they kept things in a healthy balance. When Mike pushed Patrick at home it was to get his homework done, same with his other siblings. Mike was an ex-NHLer and had his own ideas about the game, but he didn't impose them on Patrick away from the rink. Patrick had free will and Mike encouraged him to make choices on his own. Mike had played at the University of Wisconsin and his father had attended Denver University and coached at Ohio State—still it was left to Patrick to decide where he was going to college, and he went off the board to Boston College.

My father thought he could *toughen* me into a player. I always had known that there had to be another way, a better way. Living with the Eaves family those weeks I got to see it up close. More than ever I had a sense of what I'd missed out on.

* * *

Piestany, Slovakia, April 2002

When we went to the world under-18s we knew that we had a chance to win a title.

We were facing the same teams that we had beaten at the under-17 tournament in Truro, though Canada's roster was limited to players whose major junior teams, like mine, had missed the playoffs. Still, we weren't the favorites going into the under-18s. The Russians were the team that everyone was talking about and Alexander Ovechkin was the player that everyone was watching. He was an '85 birthday, like me, one of the few in the tournament. In fact he was six months younger than me, so he was eligible for the draft two years down the line. If all the NHL scouts in the stands had had a chance, they would have taken him above anyone else there—maybe over any other teenage player in the world. And if all those scouts had to bet their own money on the winner of the tournament, they would have pushed all in on the Russians.

I had never played better in my life that I did in Piestany those two weeks. I was able to focus on my game more than I ever did before. Officials with the team, including the U.S. Marshal who traveled with us, told me that there'd be no way my father would make it to Slovakia. Despite their reassurances, I couldn't completely rule it out—he did, after all, drive from Nova Scotia to Chicago overnight to see me play a meaningless game, so I'm sure he would have been willing to pay any price to make it to the biggest games in my career, no matter where they were played. After a couple of days on-site, though, I realized that there were only teams, NHL scouts and locals around—he always stood out in a crowd, but there'd be no missing him in Piestany.

It was more than a clear mind that raised my game. I had a comfort level with Mike Eaves, and he was confident in my ability. We had an even more talented roster than the team that had won the under-17 championship. Zach Parise, who had left the under-17 program the year before to open up a spot that I filled, came in like me for the pre-tournament camp. Years later Ryan Suter would be named to the NHL first-all-star team. Ryan Kesler would play for the U.S. at the 2010 and 2014 Olympics. Ten of us would go on to play in the NHL. I skated on the first line with Patrick Eaves and wound up leading the U.S. team in scoring, tied with Russia's Alexander Semin for second place in tournament scoring, behind only Ovechkin.

The way the tournament played out we wound up playing Ovechkin and the Russians in the last game of the tournament. We won lopsided games over Belarus and the Ukraine and we beat Canada 10–3. We just got by the Finns 3–2 and we wound up get stoned by a hot goaltender when we lost to the Czechs 1–0.

The Russians rolled through the tournament unbeaten. In a skills competition, I'm sure that they would have beaten us—they were bigger and faster, they shot harder and they had amazing puck skills. Ovechkin just steamrolled defensemen who were going to be high draft picks and NHL veterans. His teammate Nikolai Zherdev might have been the fastest skater I'd ever seen. They had a defenseman, Anton Babchuk, who had a cannon from the point and would be a first-round pick that June.

If you were going to look for one weakness in the Russians' game, one chance we had to beat them, it was pretty plain: the Russians were all out to impress the scouts and were selfish with the puck. They were players after my own father's heart: they didn't seem to give a damn about their teammates when they were playing to get drafted. We were the exact opposite: Mike Eaves had us all buying into the team concept. That's how it had been when we were playing in the under-17 program, up against older teams over the winter—that was the only way that we could compete with them.

The tournament had a screwy format—it wasn't a winner-take-all final. Going into that game we needed to beat the Russians by two goals to win the gold. Mike Eaves had us ready and we jumped out to a 2–0 lead in the first period on a pair of goals by David Booth, who'd go on to a long NHL career. Ovechkin scored a goal in the second period to pull the Russians within one—all they'd need for a gold if they were able to hold us off the rest of the way. The Russians didn't exactly put it on cruise control, but a lot of them didn't play smart hockey either. They could have played a tight defensive game, taking no chances and sucking the air out of the game. Instead of turning the game into a chess match, though, one forward after another tried to go through our whole team rather than passing the puck and playing a possession game. Still, it looked like they were going to hang on right until the last shift—then with fifty-eight seconds to go, Ryan Suter set up Zach Parise for a goal to make it 3–1. We had beaten the Russians but they'd done their fair share to beat themselves.

26

GOING PUBLIC

Mississauga, Ontario, April 2003

A writer with *ESPN The Magazine* had found out about my father landing in jail and about the judge issuing a restraining order. The writer had contacted the agency at the time and asked about talking to me. He told the agency that he didn't think it was appropriate to report the story without my consent, and that I couldn't make informed consent until I turned eighteen. The writer just asked if the agency would keep the request in mind and mention it to me down the line. He told them he wouldn't try to ambush me and wouldn't try to report the story without me.

Despite my performance as an underage player at the world under-18s the year before, despite making the U.S. team that went to the world junior tournament, despite leading the IceDogs into the playoffs for the first time in the team's history, there was a lot of negative buzz about me among NHL scouts. That had spilled over to the media as well. Supposedly I was trouble, supposedly a problem child. My character was called into question and no one was subtle about it. The agency made a calculation at the end of the season, in the days before the Central Scouting Service's combine—the physical testing and interviews for the top 100 draft prospects: I had to take control of the story.

I wasn't sure about the idea, but a few days later I sat down with the writer from *ESPN The Magazine*. We met in a sandwich shop around the corner from the IceDogs' arena. I didn't feel comfortable about some parts of my story. I didn't really want it out there about the night my father served me Spam and beans and made me eat my vomit. I left that out. I also left out my father butting out cigarettes in my face. It was too hard to talk about—I hadn't told anybody about that, not my friends on the team, not my agents, not anyone. It was too hard to talk about, too embarrassing. It was tough enough to tell the rest of my story, tough enough to know that people would know that part of my life before they'd meet me and would pretend when we'd talk like they had no idea. Still, I laid out a lot of my story, and everything about the game in Ottawa, the ride in the van back to Toronto and the rest of the last night I had anything to do with my father.

After we spoke, the writer managed to track down my father—he contacted the lawyer who had represented him when my mother filed for a divorce the year before. My father was in complete denial. He told the writer he was proud of everything I had done. Though he didn't come out and say it in so many words, he said I couldn't have made it as far as I did without him. "Cathie and I might have done more if we had had more support," he said. "I was totally committed to doing anything for Patrick and my daughters. Kelley is top-ten in the state in tennis. She should get a scholarship."

The writer knew but didn't mention to my father that Kelley hadn't picked up a racquet since the split.

When the writer brought up the fact that I wasn't in contact with him, my father was unrepentant. He said it was just something that the family was going through and that it was bound to pass. "I have no regrets," he said. "I wouldn't do anything different."

When the writer said that he knew about the jail time he had done, my father described it as a misunderstanding. "It wasn't an assault, or even a fight," he said. "We're best friends. We'd always wrestle and scrap a bit, like friends. I only wish Patrick were more like me as a player, a tougher guy."

And when the writer asked my father if he was going to be at the draft and talk to me there, my father broke. "Now you're pushing my button," he said and hung up.

* * *

Mississauga, Ontario, May 2003

The writer showed up at the combine and talked to me before I went through a couple of hours of physical testing and two days of interviews. Twenty-six teams had booked interviews with me. Every team took up the full twenty minutes on the schedule and a few teams went long, one of them an hour. The agency had tried to get the word out in advance of the combine, and NHL executives and scouts had followed up with coaches I had played with in Ann Arbor. In the interviews it seemed like the bad rumors hadn't been completely snuffed out.

I heard a lot of the same questions. *How would you characterize your relationship with your father?* "It's over." *What's the difference between your game now and five years ago? "I always loved the game but I enjoy it more than ever before." Do you drink? "No." Have you ever been in trouble with the law? "No." Ever been in jail? "No."* The questions Boston asked were a bit weird, and it felt like the execs in the room were trying to yank my chain. *If your car broke down, how would you get to the arena—taxi, bus, subway, walk?*

On the second day, by the time I had talked to twenty teams, I was exhausted and my eyes were starting to glaze over. It wasn't the toughest thing that I'd ever had to do—you could probably pick any night at random from when I was ten or twelve or thirteen years old and it would be a lot more ugly. Still, it was just like a slow drumbeat of painful stuff for me to talk about, having just talked about it twenty or forty minutes before and knowing that I was going to have to rehash it all in another twenty or forty minutes' time. I knew that other players at the combine didn't come in with question marks attached and weren't pressed like I was. My bad luck. I was agitated, no doubt, but I also knew that I couldn't let them see me sweat, or at least I had to try not to. Any of these teams might be the one that was going to draft me. I had to try to make the best of it.

The last team that I talked to was the New York Islanders. At the end of the interview, their head scout handed me a fifty-page psychological exam to fill out. The team hadn't asked anyone else at the combine to take the test, and it was obvious that they were trying to figure out if I was in my right mind. I didn't complete it. I wasn't thinking straight. I could have asked the team for more time. I could have asked to take the test home and turn it in later, just to be able to do a good job and give it my full attention. But I'd been blindsided and was tired and just wanted it over. If I had put my best foot forward with twenty-five of the twenty-six teams, then I figured I had done a pretty good job.

* * *

June 2003

The story in *ESPN The Magazine* came out after the combine. It put me in the best possible light, summing up my father's failed pro career, his obsession with making me a player and the years of abuse I survived. It detailed his conviction and jail time. It laid out my father's words, and used them to hang him. It described how my father ignored the restraining order by going to my games and trying to reestablish contact with me through letters and phone calls.

The story seemed to hit the mark with what the agency had wanted to get out there: I came out of it a sympathetic figure, and the media turned around 180 degrees. *Sports Illustrated* said on its website:

> Now that the truth has been revealed, it's hard to come down on O'Sullivan for his "off-ice woes." In an excellent article in its current issue, *ESPN The Magazine* reveals that O'Sullivan is the victim of an abusive, overeager father. While some scouts are apparently still worried that a tough family situation could follow O'Sullivan into the NHL, perhaps noted tough guy and former Broad Street Bully Bobby Clarke is just the type of general manager who would be willing to select the incredibly talented O'Sullivan.

Newspapers started calling the agency after the story came out, but I felt talked out at that point. My mother talked to a few reporters but I declined. I had agreed to the interview with *ESPN The Magazine* with the idea that I was going to speak my piece once, getting out in front of the story so that it wasn't going to be *the* story wherever I went. It was tough enough to talk about once—I didn't really look forward to doing it again. And again.

(The next season I made exception for *The Fifth Estate*, the Canadian television program. I suspected that they were going to go ahead with the story whether I cooperated or not. I knew that they were a serious outfit, and the producers couldn't mess around with me on video the way that some print reporters might have.)

The reception of the ESPN story led me to believe that I had put the fire out. Looking back on it now, I can see that I was looking through rose-colored glasses. I read everything the way that I wanted to read it. That draft preview from *Sports Illustrated* was a perfect example. Seeing the line about it being "hard to come down" on me as a victim of abuse—that suggested that going public had been a winning strategy. I didn't pay enough notice to a line near the end, about how scouts "still worried that a tough situation could follow" me as a pro. And that was dead on, completely prophetic. Psychologically, how much it followed me is open to interpretation, but one thing was sure: NHL scouts and executives were worried about it. They would be worried about it at the draft and wherever I'd play in the league. In that sense it followed me and no amount of truth-telling would ever shake it.

27

DRAFT DAY

Nashville, Tennessee, June 21, 2003

I didn't sleep well the night before the draft, and I didn't feel like break-fast that morning. My agents had brought me and the other clients they represented down to the draft a couple of days early because teams will ask to talk one last time to players they're interested in. We were in the dark about where teams had me on their lists. Everyone who came down to Nashville for my big moment told me not to worry. My agents, my mother, her parents, my friends and teammates from Mississauga, my billet family and others, they all had the same mes-sage: things were going to be all right.

That morning, an hour before we were going to head over to the arena, I put on the same suit I had worn to the combine. I also put on the ring that USA Hockey had given players after the World

Under-18s. I had never worn it before. I had never even taken it out of its case. I don't know if I thought it would be a good-luck charm or maybe some sort of reminder to myself that I belonged near the top of this draft class. I did imagine going up on stage and shaking hands with the GM who drafted me—my ring was going to be my message to him that he had just drafted a winner. The suits and everything else were window dressing. That ring defined who I was and what I had done to get this far. I even imagined that the GM might be wearing a Stanley Cup ring himself.

The draft was on a Saturday, starting at noon. The league had told my agents that security was on the alert for my father. A few people were trying to reassure me, telling me that, even though there was no restraining order against him in Tennessee, he wasn't crazy enough to show up and make a scene. Those who were closer to me and knew the full story were more likely to think the same way as me: he was in Nashville. There was no way he could stay away. He couldn't miss this any more than he could have missed my first junior game. He couldn't miss this any more than he could have not made it out to the under-17s. *Everything he had done for me*, he'd have said. If he had been doing time, I'm sure he would have been plotting a prison break with a getaway car heading to Tennessee.

I was told that the uniformed security officers were going to be watching for him, but it didn't matter what kind of dragnet they had in place—he'd figure out a way to be inside that arena. He knew he was hot, but that had never stopped him before, not even in small rinks in Ontario where his mug shot was posted at the one door all spectators had to walk through. He could lose himself in the crowd of ten thousand or so that would be in the arena in Nashville.

I tried to not let any thoughts of my father ruin the day: this was going to be *my* day, not his. I thought I had a chance to go between ten and twenty. The NHL's Central Scouting Service—scouts who work for the league and provide player assessments for all its teams—had come out with its end-of-season prospects rankings. CSS had me ranked as the fourteenth-best player (not including goalies) in North America. CSS's mid-season rankings back in January had had me in exactly the same slot. I thought that I was more skilled than a bunch of players higher up on the list, but I also understood that at 5-foot-10 and 180 pounds, I was considered undersized for the next level. I knew my size might drop me a few spots, but I couldn't see anything worse than the twenties.

My agents reminded me: just going in the first round would put me in the elite group of players, and the 2003 draft was considered one of the deepest drafts in years, maybe the deepest ever. NHL executives knew the difference, but most fans didn't. And because of the ESPN story and the media coverage in Nashville, I had more ink than 99 percent of players, even those projected to be in the top five picks. In fact, my father had more ink than *all* those players.

* * *

Every top prospect at the draft had a team of family and friends with him. I had twenty-five tickets set aside for mine. Before the first pick, everybody threw in five bucks in a pool to see which team was going to draft me. Everybody was laughing and high-fiving and having a good time. I was as tensed up as I had been at the combine.

The commissioner was booed when he called the draft to order—

that was business as usual. The Pittsburgh Penguins had the first pick, and everyone knew in the arena knew their pick before they announced it: Marc-André Fleury, a goaltender from Quebec who had been Canada's best player at the World Juniors in Halifax.

A few picks in, my sister Kelley spotted my father in the stands on the other side of the arena. He was sitting in section 107 in the upper bowl, the nosebleed seats. He was easy to pick out. He wasn't trying to hide in the crowd. He was sitting by himself—no one in his row, no one behind him, no one in front. He was even waving, trying to get our attention. He held his hands up and shrugged, as if to say, "What's going on?" We told the agents, who then told the NHL security detail that was sitting nearby. There was no ignoring him, no wishing he wasn't here. I had no idea what he was thinking. Was he going to just stay on that side of the arena, or was he going to make a scene when my name was called? Was he thinking that there'd be a reunion on draft day? Was what he'd said to ESPN actually a delusion rather than line of embarrassed bullshit? We tried to keep an eye on him, but it was like he knew he had been spotted. He left his seat, went out to the concourse and didn't come back. He must have figured that he could stay ahead of security if he kept moving. I panned the stands for a while after that, but then I forced myself to stop, to focus on the picks as they were made. I couldn't be looking for him when my name was called—that would just ruin the moment.

The rest of the picks went pretty much as usual through the first ninety minutes—teams taking ten minutes or so to go up on stage, call out the names of their first picks and pose for official photographs. I had hoped to go in that first hour or so, but I wasn't disappointed or surprised that my name hadn't been called through the tenth overall pick.

I started to edge up in my seat at pick No. 11, when the draft entered the range where Central Scouting and the previews thought that I'd fall. One by one the names were called. Jeff Carter, a big forward who had come in to play for the Strathroy Rockets the year after me, went at No. 11 to Philadelphia. Hugh Jessiman, a 6-foot-6 monster right winger they called Huge Specimen, went to the New York Rangers at No. 12. Next pick, Los Angeles took Dustin Brown from Guelph, Ontario, a good player with a couple of inches and 15 pounds on me, but ranked way up at No. 2 on Central Scouting's list. Zach Parise went to New Jersey at No. 17—no surprise, a really good player and the son of a respected former NHLer who became a coach. With every pick, another person on my team saw his five bucks in the pool burn up.

I thought I might go to Minnesota at No. 20, but the Wild took Brent Burns, a winger who had scored fifteen goals for Brampton that year and had been No. 39 on Central Scouting's rankings. Burns was 6-foot-5, and more and more teams were opting to draft size. The picks kept falling in the twenties, players I thought I'd go ahead of. At No. 23, Vancouver took Ryan Kesler, a gritty role player on those under-17 and under-18 teams, a bit of a late bloomer. At 25, Florida took Anthony Stewart, a winger whose numbers weren't close to mine but who had three inches and twenty-five pounds on me.

My best friend and linemate from the under-17s and under-18s, Patrick Eaves, ended up going 29th overall, to Ottawa. I was happy for him, but I was also disappointed—and embarrassed to have been the center of all the attention on my team. Everyone just stared blankly forward, disbelieving, everyone except my mother, who was sobbing uncontrollably and unable to speak. The last pick of the first round, No. 30, was Shawn Belle, a defenseman from the Western Hockey League.

I was ready to walk out of the arena before they made pick No. 31. More names were called, names on the second and third pages of Central Scouting's rankings. By the end of the first round, I just shut down. I didn't talk to anyone. I'm sure that some tried to give me consolation or to reassure me. I didn't want to hear it. I had wanted this to be my day, but it was still *his*. It was *his* day because he was in the minds of executives and scouts who looked at my name on their team's lists. I knew that if I had a father like the fathers of players in the first round, if I had a father who stayed in the background, even if I had a father with some issues but nothing as serious as a criminal conviction and jail time, I would have been called up to the stage in the first thirty picks, probably in the first twenty.

It was early in that second round that the crowd started to chant "O-Sul-livan, O-Sul-livan" between picks. The commentators on the television broadcast of the draft had noted on air a few times that my name hadn't been called, but even the fans in the seats were aware at that point that I was conspicuously undrafted. The story in *ESPN The Magazine* had been picked up by the other media and had made the rounds. So people who had read the stories or heard about it called my name, and not just when Nashville was on the clock and they wanted to let the Predators know who their choice was. They started the chant no matter which team was on the board. I know they had the best of intentions. They were making their emotional plea to the teams to do what they thought was the right thing. They wanted a happy ending to the story. That afternoon, though, it was the exact opposite for me, the farthest thing from a happy ending, unhappier every time I heard the chant start. At a time when I wanted to leave the building or at least fade into the background, I was reminded of the hopes that I had come to Nashville with and all those years I had put in pointing to this day.

It went on for more than an hour. It went on for almost two, as team after team made pick after pick. At one point, I leaned over to one of my friends from the IceDogs and said, "Now they're drafting Tier II players." Kids who played a full level below the OHL.

Finally, at No. 56, almost out of the second round, the Minnesota Wild announced my name. I stood up and shook hands and exchanged hugs with those around me, but I couldn't force a smile. My mother couldn't turn off the tears or say a word to me. Most who were picked celebrated. A few who were disappointed at least made a show of it and appeared relieved. For me it was like a funeral. I went down on the floor and shook the hands of the general manager, Doug Risebrough, and others at the Minnesota table. I took off my jacket and put on a team sweater that they had ready for me—no name on the back, unlike the players in the first round. I'm sure the Wild staff could read my mind.

The Wild's PR man took me to a makeshift office the league had set up to sign some official forms and pose for photos in my team sweater. Then he showed me out to an area the league had set aside for the media to talk to the draftees. I had no place to hide and only a couple of minutes to compose myself. I had to talk. I wouldn't say that it was the worst day of my life, but it was easily the worst day since my father was out of my life, a disappointment that I had never seen coming.

I tried to put a brave face on it. "It was hard sitting there. As soon as you hear your name called, you forget about everything else and you're the happiest person in the world," I said. "To be wanted by someone is a good feeling. I'm really excited that someone stepped up and decided to take me, and now I'm looking forward to working with Minnesota."

Barely a minute in, the reporters asked the inevitable questions about my father. I knew I was going to have to say something but I tried to keep it cut and dried. "I don't talk to him," I said. "No one talks to him in my family. It's tough because I didn't pick my family and I can't control that stuff. I've come a long way in two years. I guess you can say it's turning a page and starting a new chapter."

"I love the game too much to give it up for anything. Now for the first time, I'm not worried about anything. I have no stress. I'm looking forward."

All of it I wanted to believe.

Across the room, other reporters asked Doug Risebrough about drafting a kid with "baggage" and "issues." He pushed back against reporters who set it up in a way that questioned or criticized my character. "This was a really talented kid who is dealing with some issues that weren't really of his design or making," he said. "He was very open about it. We were comfortable. He was driven to be an offensive player. It doesn't discourage me that he isn't a complete player. We'll introduce him to all the possibilities. He's actually a pretty smart tactical player."

It was an interesting choice of words and more accurate than Risebrough even knew: "driven." It never came up in our conversations at the combine or in Nashville before the draft, but that was what my father had done—drive me to be the player he wanted to be and the player he wanted me to be. *Get your goals, get your points and don't give a shit about your teammates until you get to the NHL.* Maybe Risebrough had intuitively figured out that was the message in my ear.

Another Minnesota exec, Tommy Thompson, Risebrough's assistant GM, had the book on me as well. "He's an extremely skilled player who becomes extremely frustrated," Thompson said. "Something is not always clicking there." Again, it was fair criticism at the time—my father had been brutal on me, but with him out of my life I had in turn become tough on myself. I knew enough about the game to be a pro but had never learned to have fun at it.

I was encouraged that they seemed to believe in me, seemed to get me. That said, the draft was the most frustrating few five hours of my life. Other players drafted—even kids who went in the eighth and ninth rounds and would never play a NHL game—wore their sweaters out of the arena, went to dinner with them still on, sat on patios and had a beer to celebrate. They were going to hold on to their sweaters as keepsakes, souvenirs to hang in their basements.

When I left the arena, I took off my Minnesota sweater. I couldn't take if off fast enough. I folded it up and packed it away. I didn't want to be reminded of draft day, the day when everything was supposed to have come together but didn't. I knew that I couldn't feel sorry for myself, that I couldn't send the wrong message.

* * *

I didn't feel like talking to anybody when I went back to the hotel. The phone rang in my room. I didn't know if I should answer it. I hadn't picked up the phone in my room in Nashville unless I knew a call was coming. I didn't pick up the phone in my room on road trips with the IceDogs either, one of the rules we had put in place after my father was arrested and charged. I always let my roommate screen calls, but there was no one around to screen this call for me. It could have been my father—he could have tried phoning around to the hotels that the NHL people had checked into. On impulse I picked up the phone. It was one of my friends from the team who had come down to Nashville—I was still so rattled by the day and by the message that I'm not sure which one of them dialed my room.

"Wayne Gretzky is down in the lobby," he said. "He wants you to come down."

I didn't know if this was legit. It would have been the worst possible time for a prank. I thought maybe there was some other reason that someone wanted me to go down to the lobby. Again, could I put it past my father to try to set up something like that?

When I made it down to the lobby, Wayne Gretzky was standing there. I was surprised that he was standing there alone. I'd always imagined that someone like him would draw a crowd but I guess everyone else in the NHL was busy at official events after the draft.

"Patrick," he said, in case I couldn't pick him out of a lineup. "Wayne Gretzky. How are you doing?"

I can't remember exactly what I said at that point. I'd gone from one state of shock at the draft to another here in the lobby.

"I just want to tell you that my wife read the story about you in *ESPN* and started crying," he said. "She told me, 'You have to read this.' I did and I was crying too. The stuff you went through was awful."

Again, I have no idea exactly what I said. This just came completely out of left field. I thanked him. I told him that I appreciated the gesture. But what can you say to someone in a situation like that even at the best of times?

"Hang in there," he said. "Don't let today get you down too much."

We talked for maybe five minutes, that's all, and it did raise my spirits a bit. Only later did the conversation hit home, the irony of it, the reason that it might have meant enough to Wayne Gretzky to call me and come by my hotel.

Wayne was one half of hockey's greatest father-and-son story. He always talked about the influence that his father, Walter, had on his career. They seemed to go everywhere together. They were best friends—it seemed like they couldn't have been closer. Wayne went on to be the player that my father had always wanted me to become. My father had imagined that he was playing the same role in my career as Walter had played in Wayne's.

My father always figured that the Gretzky's backyard rink made a good story, but he also thought the truth had to be more complicated than that—no one could be as good as 99 without a plan, a program, a coach and trainer there 24/7. Wayne always talked up Walter's teaching, coming up with drills, imparting the fundamentals.

My father knew that Walter Gretzky had played in the minors. In fact, he didn't even make it into a major junior game or the pros. My father was obsessed with me becoming Wayne and he was obsessed with being Walter—and, of course, he was nothing like Walter. He was the opposite of him in every way. I thought about what my life would be like now if I'd had positive reinforcement from my father, the positive reinforcement that Walter gave Wayne. My father could have had that kind of influence on me, but he went to excess in every way. Making me a player didn't have to be inhumane and abusive. It could have been fueled by love and kindness and support.

If I'd had someone like Walter Gretzky as my father, my draft day would have played out differently. Maybe I would have been a first-round pick without what the scouts considered "baggage." Even if I hadn't been, even if I had still dropped in the draft, I'd have felt better about myself and would have had a family at my back. I wouldn't have to count on the kindness of strangers and a legendary player for a pat on the back.

28

SOPHIE

Toronto, Ontario, October 2003

The IceDogs had a new owner in my third year with the team: Mario Forgione, a real-estate developer. Mario had always loved hockey and he had always managed to combine his passions and his business, so it stood to reason that he'd take an interest in the game. He owned a couple of junior teams at a lower level than the OHL and a minor pro franchise in Pensacola, Florida, before he bought the IceDogs. One of his partners was Chris Pronger, the NHL All-Star defenseman. With Mario coming in, Don Cherry wasn't going to be involved in managing or coaching the team. It was a fresh start for the IceDogs, and we really needed it. I didn't imagine that Mario's buying the team was going to have much of an impact on my career. Mario had hired Greg Gilbert to coach, a guy who had experience playing and coaching in the NHL, and I thought he could help me with my game. And Mario was prepared to help me with my off-ice issues rather than judge me, even calling in lawyers he had worked with to go to court with me when I got an extension on the restraining order against my father. As it turned out, though, Mario's buying the team changed my life. I just didn't know it at the time.

That fall, Mario invited all the players and coaches to his house for a dinner—a chance to meet and get to know the boss and his family. At the dinner I talked to Mario's daughter Sophie for a while. She knew nothing about my background, about the draft or really about hockey. In fact, she didn't seem interested in the game at all. Mario and Sophie's mother had divorced when she was young and both had remarried and started new families. Sophie had spent most of her time with her mother, who had moved to Colorado a few years before. Sophie didn't get the same immersion in hockey that her younger stepbrothers did—Adam was our stickboy and Mike was the team mascot at games. Only a couple of months before the school year, Sophie had moved up to Toronto. She'd had some issues at school in Denver and Mario thought that she'd be better prepared for college if she did grade 12 at a private girls' school not far from his home. I put together that even by the high standard of Italian families, Mario was awfully protective of his daughters. She was told to stay away from the players, and we were told to stay away from her. That's the usual rule in hockey or all sports, I guess—the daughter of the coach or manager or owner is off limits. Mario hammered the point home to all of us.

Still, Sophie and I hit it off. I liked talking to her. I had really never talked to a girl I connected with as quickly as I did with Sophie. We didn't make plans or anything like that. It was only at practice a few days later that I gave my email address to Adam to pass on to Sophie and made him promise that he wouldn't say a word to his father. He passed on the note, and he kept his promise. It was a pretty risky move, when I look back on it. It could have given Mario a reason to trade me to another team, and maybe he would have, but the IceDogs were having their best ever season—we were one of the best teams in the league. And if he asked Sophie about it, she would have told him that it was innocent enough. Which it was, then. We exchanged messages by email. We chatted on MSN Messenger. We didn't even really see each other except when Mario brought Sophie out to games and they'd be around the arena afterward, waiting to pick up Adam and Mike. That probably tripped an alarm for Mario, or at least had him watching me closely.

The stakes were raised only at the end of the season, when Sophie invited me over to Casa Forgione … while Mario and his wife and the rest of the family were home. We just hung out in the living room and watched television while Mario watched us—there was no way that Mario was going to let Sophie out of his sight, no way he was going to leave her alone with me or let her take one step out of the house with me around. I didn't take that personally. And I didn't take it personally when I went to the front door to put on my shoes to leave and saw that Sophie's stepmom had left a Bible for me beside them. Any message that Mario and his wife were sending me, I really don't think that it had anything to do with my backstory. I'm sure Mario would have been as suspicious and cautious with any other player who had come along. But it was all pretty new stuff to me. I had met girls when I was in school in Ann Arbor and in Mississauga the first two years. In Ann Arbor and all the years before, my father had me under his thumb and gave me almost no free time to actually socialize with anybody. When

I was able to get away, back when I was a sophomore in high school, players on the team went around in groups together, eight or ten guys and eight or ten girls. It was never like a dating situation at all. And for a lot of my time in Mississauga, I'd never been left alone, a precaution that the team took with me because of my father.

I didn't fit the profile of boys Sophie had known when she was in Colorado. Even though I was the property of the Minnesota Wild, even though I had gone to training camp with them, I had been sent back to junior and hadn't signed a contract. I wasn't making anything more than pocket money playing for the IceDogs. It limited our options for dating. I could take her to Mr. Pita for lunch, or to a movie. Just getting to see her was tough too, limited by the team's schedule. My Friday nights and a lot of Saturdays were spoken for. Road trips meant whole weekends away. Sophie had come up from Colorado to go to school in Oakville and get her marks up, so most weeknights she stayed at home, hitting the books. Because we didn't go to the same school, there'd be stretches of days when we'd only talk on the phone or chat online.

As boyfriends go, I'm sure I didn't qualify as a catch—no money, not around enough, not even a home and family to call my own. And I definitely didn't qualify as someone Mr. Forgione and his wife had hoped that Sophie would wind up in a long-term relationship with. Sophie, though, has always had her own mind about things, and she's no slave to convention. It wasn't that she believed in me as a player— she would tell you that she didn't know enough about hockey to make any judgment like that. But she did believe in me as a person, even with baggage that would scare almost everyone else away. We saw each other as often as we could, as best we could. Mostly I came over to her house—it wasn't like I could take her home to my family.

Just hanging around the Forgiones' house was an experience like the one I had when I moved into the billet's home back in January 2002 or when I stayed at the Eaveses' that week before the World Under-18s. I saw displays of affection and devotion. I heard laughter. I saw how other families lived.

Other players had girlfriends that they'd see in school, girls who would wait for them after games. If Sophie came out to a game, it was nothing much more than a wave. Other players' girlfriends grew up around the game, and a lot had brothers who had played. Sophie didn't know the game at all. My first sense was that she didn't particularly like it or at least didn't find it that interesting. It might sound strange, but I liked that. After all those years of obsessively focusing on hockey, it was a nice change to be around someone who saw more to life.

29

COMEBACK

Helsinki, Finland, January 2004

Not even close to 1 percent of kids who ever play the game will make a nickel at it or play for their country or anything that proves that they've made it. But even if you're in that elite group, there's another fraction, a 1 percent within the 1 percent. If you're in *that* 1 percent, you are going to make it no matter what. If you're part of that 1 percent, you don't need luck—things are going to work out on just your talent alone. If you don't mess up, if you can stay out of your own way, things are going to be fine. It's not true if you're just outside that group—if you're in the 95th percentile, the 97th or anything just short. No, if you're anyone else, if you're not in the 99th percentile, luck is a huge factor. All the clichés apply, but mostly it comes down to being in the right place at the right time. It plays out in a game, it plays out in *the* game.

Scoring the winning goal in the 2003 World Juniors.

In the locker room after winning the 2004 World Juniors. From the left: Brady Murray, Zach Parise, me, Dan Fritsche, Brett Sterling and Ryan Kesler.

After we won the 2004 World Juniors in Helsinki.
With my linemates Ryan Kesler *(left)* and Patrick Eaves.

Zach Parise and I
after winning the 2004 World Juniors

Playing in my third world junior
tournament on home soil was a great
experience.

Rob Blake and I, celebrating one of my goals in LA. Getting to play with him was an
honor, and he was by far the best captain and person I got to play with in my career.

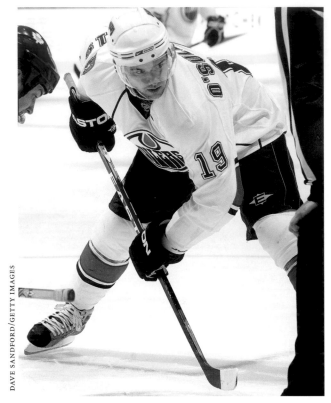

In Edmonton I got mixed messages about my role in the team. I wound up on the checking line and killing penalties, something I hadn't done much in the NHL previously.

Sharing a laugh with an old linemate from LA, Dustin Brown. He would do a lot more laughing in the coming years, winning two Stanley Cups while my career slowly dwindled away in frozen Edmonton.

Sophie and I have been together since we were teenagers.
She has always been in my corner.

The summer of 2009, at my engagement party. From the left: my best man, Dan
Carcillo, me and my father-in-law, Mario. Teeth optional.

My beautiful wife and I on our wedding day, June 19, 2010.

Holding my son Henry. The birth of our two boys made me realize
that there were things much bigger than the game.

My wife and I with our two sons, Henry and Nathan, outside our home in May 2015. If
someone had told me when I was twelve years old that I would someday have a loving
family like this, I would have thought they were crazy.

Putting my son Henry's hands on a golf club for the first time.
If they choose to play sports, I hope it's something other than hockey.

Just how important luck is I realized only after the fact. It played out for me in the biggest game that I ever played.

On my second trip with the U.S. team, to the World Under-20s, we played Canada in the final. We had the same team that we won with at under-17s and under-18s two years before, but we weren't favorites. In fact, against Canada, we were huge underdogs. The Canadian team was stacked. The 2004 World Juniors was the first time Canada's 1985 birthdays had all played together. Going into the tournament in Helsinki, everyone in the game knew that the Canadian '85s were a really strong group—today they're considered the best class in the history of the game in Canada. The Canadians absolutely steamrolled teams in the opening round, outscoring opponents 25 to 4 in four games, and then crushed the Czech Republic 7–1 in the semifinal. The experts ranked the U.S. fifth or sixth before the tournament started, but we won our side of the draw and had a bye into the semifinals, where we beat the home team 2–1.

Even though we made the finals, a lot of people thought the game was just a formality. It looked like Canada had a bunch of guys in that 1 percent. Overconfidence looked like more of a threat than we did, strictly David-and-Goliath stuff.

USA Hockey officials didn't get the news. The higher-ups at headquarters in Colorado Springs, those who would see the team only when they flew in for international tournaments, let it be known that they needed a win badly. Even if this hadn't been such a strong Canadian team, history would have shown that this was a big ask. We were only the second American team to make the final—the team in '97 was shut out by Canada in the gold-medal game, and that predated USA Hockey launching the Ann Arbor project. But we didn't really need more motivation. Though I had another year of eligibility, most of our key players were 1984 **birth**days, my teammates from my year in Ann Arbor, and they weren't going to be back together. This was our last shot at it as a team.

In the final, the Canadians came out and tried to run us out of the rink. They were the bigger team and they took runs at us, trying to knock our heads off. That was always what the Canadians did in the tournament. European kids had never seen that stuff before—they just play a different game—and usually the Canadians just knocked the will out of them in first five or ten minutes. We didn't back down like the other teams in Helsinki did. Our game was no different from theirs. We hung around and we had our chances. Still, at the end of two periods we were down 3–1, maybe a little unlucky not to have at least one more goal to show for the way we played. It was a game that Canadian teams in this tournament just don't lose—somehow, Canadian teams find a way to get out of jams most of the time, but given any advantage, they had never let go. We could see it in the faces of the Canadian kids when they were skating off the ice: they thought this game was done, and the last twenty minutes were going to be their victory lap.

In our dressing room, Mike Eaves set the tone. He didn't panic or yell or raise the stakes. He didn't say that we had to play better. He told us that if we just kept playing the way we were, things were going to come. "One goal and it's a whole new game," he said.

I had been playing the best hockey of my life before leaving for Helsinki—I had 28 goals and 23 assists in 29 games in Mississauga. I had thought I had played pretty well in Helsinki, but through five games and the first two periods of the final, I didn't have much to show for it, just one goal. Early in the third period, though, I had an opening—the Canadian forwards were caught deep in our end, and we had a long three-on-two break. Patrick Eaves got the puck over to me on the wing and my snapshot beat the goaltender, Marc-André Fleury. That made it 3–2 with a lot of time left, and for the Canadians, the goal sucked the air out of the room.

We started to take control of the game on the next shift, and Ryan Kesler tied the game about two minutes later. For the next five minutes or so, it looked like the game was going to head to overtime. Even if we owned the puck, we still had to beat Fleury, and he had been the best Canadian player in the under-20 tournament in Halifax the year before. NHL people considered him the best goaltender to come along in five years, maybe more. He was going to raise his game and not give up anything cheap, or at least that's what they figured.

Then with about five minutes to go in regulation, Drew Stafford picked up the puck in our end and saw that I had slipped behind the Canadian defense on the right wing. He threw the puck up the ice and I controlled it, cleanly behind Brent Seabrook, the defenseman on that side. There was nothing but open ice between Fleury and me, but Seabrook put a hook on me and wasn't going to let go. I was still trying to break free, still skating toward the net, when Fleury came out of his crease to clear the puck—or at least try to. I was almost on top of Fleury, and he should have just dropped on the puck and covered up. Instead he tried to clear the puck and ended up firing it off the back of the other defenseman, Braydon Coburn, who was coming back on the play. Fleury tried to dive back into his net but he was too late. The puck crossed the line and we had a one-goal lead. My teammates skated up the ice to celebrate but I didn't know how the puck had crossed the line—I thought it had gone in off me. I was the last American player to touch the puck so I wound up credited with the goal.

The Canadian guys couldn't believe it. This was the first time they had trailed all tournament. They were rattled. That Canadian team had a bunch of guys who are in the 1 percent: Crosby, Getzlaf, Perry, Carter, Richards and Weber—guys who would win Olympic gold and make $8 and $10 million a season down the line. Though a player might be in that 1 percent, no team is, not as a group. The Canadians had tons more talent than we did, but we played better as a team, and in those last five minutes we might have played our best hockey.

Because I scored the winning goal, I was one of the American players the reporters went to after the game. One reporter asked me about the Canadian players saying they'd lost on a "lucky" goal. It felt like the word was robbing us of credit I thought we earned. "It doesn't matter," I said. "If he didn't hook me I would have scored on the breakaway."

It wasn't an arrogant line, just a jab for a jab. There was no way we were losing that game. We ended up outshooting Canada 10–1 in the last ten minutes of the gold-medal game.

Inevitably, I was asked about the story that had come out at the draft. I didn't want to get into it, and I made a point of not mentioning my father. I didn't want to ruin this moment, but if I refused to answer the question I'd just be adding to fuel to the fire. "I've had some tough times, no doubt about that," I said. "But that stuff's in the past and I'm just excited about playing hockey. Obviously winning this tournament is the highlight of my career so far. Winning is part of the healing."

And winning with that team—completing the cycle with wins in the three major international tournaments—was, like I said, the best moment of my career. That was the best team that I ever played with, and I had been an important player with that group. It ended up that a couple of guys on our team would be 1 percent players themselves, Zach Parise and Ryan Suter. And with the way that we played in the third period, those two goals, those three gold medals, I came away thinking that I had a chance to be part of the 1 percent, someone who'd walk out of the wreckage and still make the moment mine.

That would pass.

I had no idea when I came off the ice that night that I'd never again play a game that mattered as much.

* * *

Mississauga, Ontario, January 2004

The fans booed me in my own rink. I was standing at center ice and I didn't know how to react. I tried to laugh it off. Here I was, the team's leading scorer, the captain, the one top player who'd stuck around through tough years without asking to get traded, and I was getting booed. All I had done was play for the wrong team. I didn't take it personally. It's just the way Canadians feel about the tournament. All you can do is laugh at things beyond your control and move on. Having a gold medal to show for it made it easy to laugh off.

When things would be beyond my control later in my career, it would be impossible to laugh off.

30

LONG DISTANCE

Mississauga, Ontario, October 2004

Sophie stayed a part of my life, but circumstances forced us to be physically apart. It was more than just a hockey schedule. That was really the least of it. Sophie worked in her father's office that summer, but she had only come to Toronto so that she could get herself ready for college. She had set her mind on going to the University of Denver. Given that, we knew that she was going back to Colorado eventually and that we were probably going back to the relationship we had in the beginning—phone calls, chats online, visits when possible. That was always in the cards. Circumstances took a serious and eventually tragic turn when, back in Colorado, her mother was diagnosed with cancer. It turned out to be an aggressive form of cancer, and she was put on a schedule of radiation and chemotherapy. Sophie had been accepted to DU's business school and was ready to start classes but deferred so that she could stay home with her mother and help out with her brother and sister—looking after them by himself would have spread her stepfather too thin. It was a sacrifice Sophie had little choice but to make. I called every day, but at my end of the telephone I felt powerless to help most of the time. Words of encouragement really don't pack a lot of weight in that situation. She needed me there and I couldn't get away. I know now that it would have been easy for her to think that I wasn't just geographically remote but emotionally remote too—even when I do care about someone, I know it doesn't always show and doesn't show as much as it should. It was a strain on our relationship, but really Sophie had far bigger things to worry about than me. I told her that I would find a way to come down to Denver as soon as our season was over. I wanted to believe that our relationship could last through something like this, but I had to be realistic: serious relationships and even marriages have broken up over a lot of things less significant than what we faced. And we were still teenagers who had not even known each other for two years. Just as statistics, we shouldn't have lasted, never mind the awful complicating issues—my history and the most emotional strain she was under.

* * *

Denver, Colorado, September 2005

I had spent more than a month with Sophie that summer. Her mother was in failing health. Doctors had told her that further treatment wasn't going to help her. It was clear that she had weeks to live. Her mother had one wish for Sophie: she told her not to defer another year. Sophie pushed back at first. She wanted to be there to the end for her mother. Her mother, though, recognized that Sophie was emotionally spent. She also knew that she was going to need professional help to stay at home in her last weeks of her life and that her husband was going to put everything aside when the end came near. Sophie's half-brothers were a year older than they had been when the diagnosis was down and they were better prepared for the inevitable. Sophie's mother wanted to see her daughter moving on with her life. So at the start of the school year, Sophie enrolled in Denver University. For some people it would have been a burden lifted off them, but Sophie didn't feel that way—it was tough for her to head off to school each day, seeing her mother so weak, worrying about her. It wasn't quite the fresh beginning that her mother hoped for, but Sophie appreciated her mother's selflessness and let her know that.

A boyfriend or a husband in a situation like that can feel like a fifth wheel, and I did a lot of the time. I was still just a teenager and I wasn't equipped to be "a rock" through all of this. I had lived through a lot, but this was all new ground for me. I could only do my best for as long as I was there, and I could only be there until I had to head to training camp for what would be my first season as a pro, which would start in Houston. I struggled to help before at times while I was in Denver, but once I headed off to training camp I felt completely powerless. Sophie told me that she understood, but she had to resent the fact that, again, I was just a voice on the phone. We weren't married and I was barely a professional—she was like a hockey wife but with none of the benefits and a lot of emotional weight to carry.

I had hoped that I would make the Wild lineup that year, but management wanted to me to put in a full season in Houston. I let the team know about Sophie's mother's health and asked if I was going to be able to go to Denver for the funeral, whenever it would come. The people in the front office told me that they understood and that they could give me a couple of days' leave on short notice. I told Sophie that and she said she understood, but I'd have understood if she didn't really. And when the day would finally come a few weeks later, I would fly in one morning and be gone not even forty-eight hours later. Even saints wouldn't understand.

31

OLD SCHOOL

Minneapolis, Minnesota, September 2005

"Understand, you are not going to play center in this league. And you're not going to play here this season, no matter how well you or what you do."

Less than two minutes before, I had sat down across from Jacques Lemaire in his office. I figured it was going to be basic stuff, a coach-to-rookie speech like all the others. I had separated my shoulder in training camp and had spent a few weeks rehabbing. Now I was ready to go. I figured Lemaire was going to give me the standard work-hard-and-you'll-get-rewarded line or something like that. I figured I'd get told what my season *could* be if I held up my end and the stars lined up right, no guarantees, no promises, just reason to keep the faith. Instead, Lemaire was telling me what my season *wasn't* going to be, what my career *was never* going to be.

There was no pushing back, not with his position and mine. He had played for eight Stanley Cup winners with Montreal in the sixties and seventies and coached the New Jersey Devils to a championship in '95. He was a Hockey Hall of Famer. It wasn't just that he had credibility. He was old school. The Wild management were all old school. The GM was Lemaire's teammate from the Canadiens teams in the seventies, Doug Risebrough. Other people on the staff were their friends and contemporaries. Risebrough and Lemaire aimed to build an organization in the image of those glory days.

I was just twenty. I'd always considered myself a student of the game. I read about the NHL's history. I respected the hell out of these guys for what they had done as players and as executives—just the last season (before the lockout), the franchise's third in the league, the Wild had made the Western Conference final. I had to believe Lemaire knew what he was talking about. I wasn't about to question what he was telling me. I wasn't even going to ask him why I wasn't going to play center or make it into games with the Wild that season. I knew that if he was telling me this, then he was speaking on behalf of the entire organization, not just giving me his personal opinion. Still, I was disappointed. I tried to hide it. I probably didn't pull it off.

I had hoped to play that season with the Wild. I thought I had a good chance. In their first three seasons in the league, the team had a history of playing kids straight out of the draft. The Wild's first pick in my draft year, Brent Burns, went straight to the NHL at eighteen. It seemed like Risebrough and Lemaire's philosophy was to keep their best young players close and under their direct control, develop them with the big club rather than trust them to find their way in the major junior leagues. I had put in two more years with Mississauga. I had done the work needed to take the next step, at least by spring. Instead I was being told before training camp started that I was going to spend the full year with the minor-league affiliate in Houston.

Going back to draft day two years before, I'd had a good feeling about being drafted by the Wild. I had talked to twenty-six teams at the combine, and my interview with Minnesota had gone well, one of the best that I had there. They didn't dig deep with questions about my father. They seemed to be satisfied with the background work they had done.

I guess it came down to my expectations of how an NHL team would operate—I'm sure that it's what a lot of people would expect.

The Wild had used a second-round draft pick to acquire my rights. It didn't carry the prestige of a first-round pick, and the money that they'd commit to a second-rounder was about half the amount they'd be looking at with a top pick. Still, the Minnesota staff had picked me ahead of hundreds of others—they had thought there was something I could offer. It seemed like it would have been in their best interests, not just mine, to put me in a position to be the best player I could possibly be. The Wild had all kinds of knowledge and experience on their staff that I could learn from. And yet the message that I took away from my meeting with Lemaire and all my dealings with the club was straightforward: come back when you've figured it all out, and you have to figure it out on your own.

In the years since, people have asked me what teams did with me in terms of psychological work, either general sports-psychology stuff that all players are expected to go through or support that they wanted for me specifically because of my background. And people are always surprised to find out that the teams I played for did nothing. People presume that these organizations, with all the money they have and all the money at stake in salaries, would have a vested interest in their players' psychological and emotional well-being, and in my case, reasonable questions and concerns too. I can't speak for most organizations from personal experience—I'd end up playing with five of the thirty NHL teams. Still, from my time with those teams, not one of them ever wanted me to sit down with a psychologist who worked for them—not for an assessment, not for therapy. In Minnesota, it seemed like that would have been the last thing that team executives had in mind—it's not like the Canadiens teams they played for had ever given special consideration to anyone. Montreal's management hadn't given any extra attention to Guy Lafleur when he had been a first overall pick back in the seventies—in fact, they might have actually gone out of their way to make things difficult for him. That was the old-school culture—it was all about independence and self-reliance, you working for the team, not the team working with or for you. Come in as boys and become men and Canadiens … or don't. It's all up to you.

At some level, I was okay with that. Although I expected them to want to do *something* about my issues, I didn't want to feel or look like a special-needs case. What's true for you as a ten-year-old kid—nobody wants to be *that* player, the one who isn't like everyone else in the room, the one who is separated from everyone else—remains the same ten years later. Wherever I was going to play, whether it was with their big club or, as Lemaire was telling me in no uncertain terms, in Houston, I really didn't want to be *that* player. Teammates in any dressing room I'd walk into would know my story on day one, and a lot of them wouldn't appreciate any special attention that I'd get. And I get that.

I was determined to figure it out on my own. I took it as a challenge. And I'd challenge them to stick to their guns about keeping me down in Houston all year.

* * *

Years later I heard what Doug Risebrough had told someone about me.

"When I met him at the combine and at the draft, I had an idea of what he'd been through," he said. "And I thought, 'He's going to be all right. He's a strong kid and he knows what he wants. I like him.'"

Risebrough also said something about pulling for me to make it.

What Risebrough had said was good to hear, but it's also where an old-school organization fell down. Risebrough's willingness to go just on his gut about my character isn't his belief in infallibility or anything like that—it's just a resistance to any idea that clinical help might have helped me to "be all right."

I'm not suggesting that a sports psychologist or any other professional would have helped me—no one will ever know. But it might have helped me, or it might help someone else who comes into the game after surviving trauma. The old-school thinking is that players look after themselves and that teammates look after each other. At best, the old school is just unaware of the help that might be out there. At worst, the old school is indifferent to it—the we-don't-do-social-work approach. It's hard to imagine that any outfit would be indifferent to the mental and emotional health of employees who have issues and have endured trauma, but it's even harder to imagine that any organization that invests millions in those employees wouldn't do everything it could to maximize the return on its investments, including trying to get help for those who might need it.

I don't know if most organizations in the NHL or other pro sports operate the way that the Wild did with me—Risebrough, Lemaire and the other old-school guys in Minnesota are almost all gone, and management there might look at things differently now. Still, I'll bet that there are more old-school guys still working in hockey. Generations change, but the culture of the game changes a lot more slowly.

* * *

Houston, Texas, April 2006

The call that I had expected, the call from Minnesota, never came. I had struggled at the start of the season, scoring only six goals by late December. Then I took off. I scored 41 goals in the next 38 games. I had five hat tricks, won all kinds of awards as the league's rookie of the month and player of the month. Half that number of goals would have been a ticket to Minnesota the next season, but scoring more than a goal a game for a stretch of months should have guaranteed a call-up. Whenever the phone rang, I thought it was going to be Minnesota telling me to pack my bags, my plane was leaving in the morning. That call never came. It came for five or six of my teammates, other forwards who'd get a few games in with the big club, a chance to show their stuff. Every time there was an injury or trade that seemed to open things up for me, it was someone else who got his ticket to the big club. I was going to have to wait—47 goals would have tested management's resolve to keep me in the minors.

But the morning after our season ended in Houston, I did get a call. It was USA Hockey, phoning to invite me to play for the national team at the world championships in Latvia. I wasn't ready to play for the Wild, in the opinion of management, but I was ready to skate with an all-star team of NHLers in international competition.

32

CROW

Columbus, Ohio, March 7, 2007

I felt a shoe dig into my ass. I wasn't looking over my shoulder, but I knew who it was. I couldn't believe that he did it. He had come up to the line before that but stopped short. Here, in the middle of a game, with me sitting beside my teammates, he'd crossed it.

I turned around and said, "Do that again and I'm going to fuckin' drive you."

You know at some point you're going to have to take a hit coming out on the ice. If everybody's doing his job, someone is going to take a shot at you. You come to the bench, catch your breath and get back out there. With the Kings, I knew there would always be a shot waiting for me on the bench. This time it was an actual physical shot, which was hard to believe. All the other times it had been a verbal dig.

Marc Crawford was coaching Los Angeles, and in my rookie season he gave me more grief on the bench than I had to go through on the ice. It was that way from day one. I could do nothing right, and he dumped more shit on me than on the rest of the team combined.

The Kings had traded Pavol Demitra for me in the off-season and L.A. should have been the best situation I could have landed in. The Kings had a bunch of young players ready to break through. They had veteran leadership in guys like Rob Blake, who would end up in the Hockey Hall of Fame. They had young guns like Anže Kopitar, who within three or four years would be on anyone's list of the top ten players in the game. They had a great room—everyone got along, everyone had fun and everyone had each other's back. And it was a team year-round off the ice too. Everyone on the Kings considered L.A. home.

I had all kinds of reasons to love L.A., and just one reason to hate coming to the arena: Crow.

Looking back, Marc Crawford, more than anybody else I met in the game, reminds me of my father. He made it farther than my father did: he played in the NHL for a brief stretch. And he landed coaching jobs in the game after his playing days: he won a Cup with Colorado in his second year with the team, which is something you can dine out on for a long career. A couple of years later he was behind the bench of the Canadian Olympic team—that Canada finished out of the medals didn't land in his lap, though he'll always be the guy who kept Wayne Gretzky on the bench during a shoot-out with an Olympic medal on the line.

Any fan who knows Crawford could easily guess what he had in common with my father. It was what he would be best known for, at least after the Cup win and the crash at the Olympics: anger. Crawford would go completely irrational. Supposedly it runs in his family. I once read a story about Crawford and his father, who put in a thousand games in the minors. Crawford said his father, Lloyd, had a "mutant Irish gene" and, given half a reason, would just blow up. His old man didn't deny it. "I don't know where all that fanatical stuff comes from but it's inside me," Lloyd Crawford said. "Marc has some of it too."

As much as Marc Crawford will be remembered for coaching a team with four first-ballot Hall of Famers to a Stanley Cup, he'll always be remembered for two uglier incidents. One was harmless: back in the '97 playoffs, when he was with the defending Stanley Cup champions in Colorado, he went apeshit in a game against Detroit, eyes bugging out, screaming and looking like he was ready to go over the Plexiglas to strangle Detroit coach Scotty Bowman, who just watched him with a poker face. The other was anything but harmless: Crawford was coaching Vancouver when Todd Bertuzzi ended up breaking a bone in Steve Moore's neck, ending his career and basically wrecking his life. Crawford distanced himself from the incident—said Bertuzzi was operating on his own and against coach's orders—but then a lawyer told him to clam up and he never spoke about it again. Bertuzzi filed a claim against Crawford but dropped it in 2012 and a couple of years later Moore's lawsuit against Bertuzzi was settled out of court. Some would find it hard to believe that Crow sent Bertuzzi, with a three-inch and forty-pound advantage, over the boards to jump Moore, but then some people would find it hard to believe that a father would send a nine-year-old out to punch his friend and teammate. Hockey does some weird things and has some warped values.

The public perception of Crawford as a hothead has stuck since then, and it isn't wrong. It's just not complete. It's more complicated from the perspective of a player. And from my perspective, being son of one and a rookie player for the other, it was spooky how similar my father and Crow were in some ways.

Like my father, Crow had no time for positive reinforcement. Like my father, he believed in the complete opposite: he emphasized the negative. He was the bad cop.

Unlike my father, he coached an entire team in L.A.'s practices, but like my father, he singled me out for special attention. I was the guy he ran. I was the guy he made of an example of. It might have been the way he had coached at other stops. It might have been the way his father coached. And, yeah, it *was* the way that *my* father coached.

When Crow signed on with the Kings, he claimed that he had calmed down—a couple of stories even said that he had "reformed." He claimed that he picked his spots. I was his spot. I was coming off my season in Houston, looking to break into the NHL. Crow put the emphasis on "break."

At one point that season, he made all my teammates stand to one side on the ice while he bag-skated me, had me skating lines for twenty minutes straight. It was supposed to be punishment for screwing up a drill, a misdemeanor that would usually just get a bark out of a coach and nothing more. Instead I was singled out and humiliated in front of all my teammates. It was a power trip—he had the most power of anyone on the ice, and he singled out me, a rookie, the guy with the least amount of influence. The Kings' other rookie, Anže Kopitar, my room-mate, was a first-round draft pick—an important asset, according to the organization—and he was a couple of years younger, so Crawford cut him slack that he wouldn't give to me. "It was hard to watch that bag skate," Anže said. "It really wasn't fair. It would be hard for anyone to see a friend and a teammate go through that type of thing."

The bag skate was an extreme example, a one-off. The most painful one came in Colorado when I took a slapshot in the mouth. I lost three teeth at the root and had my jaw broken. I didn't even go to the hospital for X-rays that night. I just got stitched up at the rink, about forty stitches all through my mouth and face, and went to hospital when we got back to L.A., to get my jaw wired. I showed up at the arena for practice—I thought if I missed a practice, Crow was going to send me down. Even with my face purple and stitched up like a baseball, Crow rode me, said I was soft for wearing a face shield screwed onto my helmet and told the trainers to take it off. Thankfully, they told him they wouldn't. Team doctors told them I had to wear the mask.

More typical was the bench minor—whenever the team was handed a too-many-men penalty or a referee hit him with a minor, Crow would send me over to serve the penalty. It got so predictable that I'd have one leg over the boards whenever I thought they were calling a bench minor before Crow even told me to go. And when I'd be skating over, he'd heckle me, the way a fan dumps on the visiting team. *While you're sitting over there, think about your trip down to the minors.*

I did get hurt that season, and Crow did send me down. Even when I was called up, Crow gave me no reprieve. My teammates talked to me about it, and the veterans told me that Crow's running me was the worst they had ever seen. They would have told me different or wouldn't have bothered if they'd thought I brought it on myself. They also said they didn't know how I could take it. And I did. I didn't laugh at it, but I did always brush it off.

"My standard for bad stuff is different than yours," I told them.

My standard for bad stuff changed when it became physical. Crow kicked me in the ass in Columbus, but it hit close to home. It wasn't the worst, but it did cross the line. Bag-skate me, rip me, do whatever you're going to do, but you're not going to be physical with me. I've lived that already.

Crow blinked. He didn't change that season, but he never kicked me in the ass again.

* * *

I can't know exactly why Crow treated me the way he did, any more than I can get inside my father's mind.

Maybe he thought focusing his anger on one player got his point across to the team, and I was the one easiest to sacrifice. I wasn't struggling and didn't deserve all the shit he put me through, but I was a rookie. He could make an example of me. His message: shape up, get with the program or this can be you. That could have been the case, though it wasn't a message that needed to be sent to a team that bought into the program, a team that worked hard almost every night. And it's a message that a coach in his first year in the league might feel like he has to send, not a guy with a Stanley Cup ring and fifteen years of NHL experience.

Maybe it was strictly personal. Maybe he just didn't like me. I could tell that I provoked him by my reaction, or at least my lack of reaction. He'd shout at me and I would just take it when a lot of guys would shout back. He'd center me out and I wouldn't even change my expression. My teammates asked me how I could take it. "My standards for bad are different than yours," I said. Those who knew my story understood. My threshold was a lot higher than almost anybody's.

Eventually, though, Crow crossed the line in Columbus. That was just too much like my father. If he could have made it over the glass in Ottawa that night back in 2002, that would have been my father's shoe kicking me in the ass. It didn't matter if Crow knew my story or not, if he had a message for me or for the team—I wasn't taking his shit.

Maybe the saddest thing is that by the end of my rookie season, I was playing really well, so well, in fact, that Crawford would have lost credibility with my teammates and the confidence of management if he didn't play me. In the end I won a spot on the first line. I put up a point a game through the last twenty games.

* * *

Los Angeles, California, September 2007

Going into training camp in my second season, I thought I was in for more of the same from Crow. I thought that all I could do was cross days off the calendar until he was fired—like all coaches in the league, management would eventually cash him in. A strange thing happened, though. Crow was different to me.

He treated me no different from the rest of the guys. I wasn't one of his favorites—I'm not sure he had any. Still, he gave me a fair shake

No young player took my place as Crow's personal punching bag. We added a couple of European players, Ladislav Nagy and Michal Handzuš, and they had bad years, but Crow didn't target them. He gave shit to Alexander Frolov, a Russian guy who once fell asleep in the dressing room in uniform after the warm-up, five minutes before we stepped on the ice, but it wasn't a season-long deal like mine had been.

All I could take away from my experience with Crow was that he could turn his act on and off, again like my father. For appearances, for effect, whatever the case, he could put the anger away, no matter if the "mutant Irish gene" was lurking underneath.

Even in Crow's good graces I couldn't trust him at all, no more than I could trust my father. I find it hard at the best of times to trust people, but I can usually work past it. With Crow there was no working past it, just like there was no working past it with my father. Crow had kicked my ass all season, but actually kicking me in the ass, he crossed the line. My father had crossed it a thousand times and Crow just once, but once was enough. Once was too much.

* * *

Los Angeles, California, March 3, 2009

Crow was gone the next year, and I thought I would get a fresh start with a clean slate when Terry Murray was hired to replace him. I thought my career was ready to take off and I could see that the Kings were putting together a lot of talented young players. But the team traded me that spring to Edmonton.

It had started with something small: my agent had kept me out of L.A.'s training camp, fighting over a pay raise. It boiled down to be a hundred grand, as it turned out. That seemed to poison the well with the Kings—I don't know if he held it against me, my agents and all of us, but Dean Lombardi, L.A.'s general manager, traded me—it was a three-team deal that sent the Kings Justin Williams and Carolina Erik Cole. I understand the trade—Justin is a heck of an asset and would be a huge part of two teams that would win the Cup in L.A., the most valuable player on the second championship team. Still, Lombardi might have been able to get Justin for another player than me.

I knew Edmonton was a franchise in the middle of a rebuilding plan—but then again, the Oilers had been saying that for years and, though they made a run to the Cup final in 2006, there was no breakthrough in sight. When I checked in with the team at a morning skate, management gave me all kinds of mixed messages about my role. The GM told me that he wanted me to do X. The coach told me he'd like me to do Y. Five-on-three penalty kill? I hadn't played a shift in that situation since I'd turned pro. It's not my game. Five minutes after leaving their offices, I wished I had asked them if they had ever watched me play or if they had mistaken me for another player.

I had landed in the worst organization in the league, the most dysfunctional on just about every count. The Oilers had acquired me when they had maybe six NHLers exactly like me before the trade—smaller, skilled forwards who didn't offer much of a physical presence up front. And not surprisingly, they all struggled in Edmonton.

33

WEDDING INVITATIONS AND CHRISTMAS GIFTS UNOPENED AND RETURNED

Edmonton, Alberta, October 2009

After I called 911 that night in '02, after the restraining order was in place, after the divorce was final, my break from my father was, with the exception of occasional sightings at junior games and pro games, for all intents and purposes complete. You might presume that his court-ordered absence from our lives would bring my mother, my sisters and me closer—we had been through an awful time and we had survived it. Free of him, we could move forward and find a positive direction.

It didn't work out that way, though. A long way from it.

Yes, my father was the obvious villain in the story, but there was a lot of dysfunction to go around, by no means limited to him. It wasn't like we were a close-knit family. My father had effectively separated me from my mother and my sisters. We shared a roof but really not much else. My mother was at some level relieved when my father was out of the house with me for days and nights at a time. She didn't have to put up with his foul mouth and his rages like I did. She made half-hearted attempts to get between my father and me when he went after me right in front of her, but eventually walked away. Though a lot of the physical abuse was out of her sight, she knew the hell that he put me through. She could pretend that what she didn't witness didn't happen. She didn't have to worry about the impact that it would have on my sisters. So long as it was the men in the family on one side, the women on the other, she seemed prepared to live with it.

The most time that he spent around my mother or my sisters came when we were in Michigan—my father was trying to groom my older sister, Kelley, as a tennis player. He imagined that he could take the formula he used for turning me into a hockey player and work his magic with her. I'm sure that my hockey still meant more to him—that turning Kelley into a pro was probably a longer shot given a later start than other top players. Still, she advanced all the way to the top ten in her age group in Michigan and was probably on track to land an athletic scholarship if she stuck with it. In fact, the reason he wanted to stay on in Ann Arbor after I landed with Mississauga was that he thought Kelley could get more court time and better coaching there.

It sounds strange to say, but I feel like I never had a chance to get to know my younger sister, Shannon, at all. By the time she was starting school, I was already off playing in Mississauga. I was just never around—my father left my mother all of my little sister's child-care responsibilities. She would have had every reason to feel like an afterthought in the family. She was too young to understand—but might now—that being an afterthought to my father was a blessing, not a curse.

That's one price of my father's obsession that's easy to miss: I never really developed relationships with my siblings. And that didn't change after our father's conviction and our parents' divorce.

Fact is, by the time I made major junior hockey, I was used to being on my own.

That was true from my first season in Mississauga. I lived a very separate life from my mother and sisters. I was more like a relation than any part of the family.

My mother took my sisters back to North Carolina to be close to her parents after the divorce. I went back to North Carolina for a couple of weeks in the summer of 2002, but Winston-Salem really wasn't a great place for a young pro trying to land in the NHL someday. There weren't other players to train with. There wasn't quality ice time. After a couple of weeks in Winston-Salem with my mother and sisters, I was restless. I was afraid of getting out of shape and falling behind other players—my father's mindset, no doubt, but an obsession that is fairly common among athletes in all sports. So I went back to Toronto, where I could get to the gym and find ice for a pickup game with other juniors and some pros.

And that's how it played out the summer of the draft and the summers after that. Over the years it was never longer than a couple of weeks in North Carolina in the off-season and sometimes less, because I would spend some time visiting Sophie when she was living in Colorado. Other than that, I saw my mother and sisters only when the NHL schedule brought my team through North Carolina. Given that I had played my entire career to that point in the Western Conference, my teams would play only one game in Raleigh each season. It never worked out that the mother and sisters would come to see me during the season—even though Kelley was through high school, my younger sister, Shannon, hadn't graduated yet, so that kept my mother home-bound.

* * *

My father being out of our lives should have meant a fresh start for all of us. It was for me. It wasn't for my mother.

Living with my father was hell, and so was going to court to get a restraining order and a divorce. Having to tell your young daughters that their father is going to jail would be some sort of hellish experience as well. I appreciate that's a lot of weight to carry, but if that's what you have to do to get out of a dangerous marriage, it's a trade that you have to make, every day, no questions. And if you watch your husband beat up your son, your marriage is dangerous simply by definition. To think otherwise is pure denial.

I don't know what a reasonable time is to get back on your feet, to start healing and getting on with the rest of your life. Nobody could give you a hard and fast answer on that. You'd have to judge it on a case-by-case basis. I didn't expect it to be overnight. How many months or how many years, I really didn't know. Fact is, though, more than five years after my mother first filed for divorce, she showed no signs of pulling her life together. She didn't even seem motivated to try. She'd checked out emotionally. She stayed at home, never trying to find work, never even looking to train for a profession that would support her and my sisters. She saw herself as a full-time mother, someone who would stay at home and see her daughters through. That would have been acceptable in other circumstances, but her judgment was questionable and her commitment less than wholehearted. Kelley had dropped out of high school not long after the divorce. My mother let that pass and didn't put any demands on my little sister as far as school went either.

I don't know if my father ever sent her any support payments. Even if he did, based on an income that was never much above the poverty line, the court couldn't have demanded enough for my mother to make ends meet. My mother needed some help until she could get her life straight. First that came from her parents, just as it had before the divorce. They bought her a house. They covered bills and expenses as they came in. And then, after I signed my first contract, the money came from me.

I sent her money regularly. She didn't work from a monthly budget. She would ask, and I would wire her money. I knew her account number by heart. I never sat down to add up the dollar figures. She never sent me any accounting of it. Everything was on a piecemeal basis. And in time, her requests went from basic bills or unexpected expenses to big-ticket items. A bathroom that needed new fixtures, a kitchen that needed updating, a landscaping job—based on what I was cutting checks for, they could have shot a season's worth of a Home and Garden Television series at my mother's house. The strange thing was that when I would come to visit during the summer, the work I paid for wouldn't have been done—my mother would tell me that she had dropped a deposit with a contractor who was backed up on his schedule. For good reason, the requests for money for work on her home started to leave a bad taste in my mouth when I signed a check, especially if it wasn't an essential repair. I felt like my trust had been violated, like I was getting played.

My mother also put in requests for money for my sisters. Some things they needed, and I had no issue helping out. But then I realized that they weren't going to school and that my mother was letting them hang around the house. I understood that Kelley was troubled—she never picked up a tennis racquet after our parents' divorce. My mother could have tried to help her get in better shape emotionally but settled for letting her be. Likewise, my younger sister, Shannon, was basically left to her own devices—my mother had no demands or expectations about her going to school and no concern about her friends.

What had been a pressure cooker with my father was now a weightless environment. Other than asking her parents or me to help provide for my sisters, my mother seemed to do precious little parenting, and for a full-time stay-at-home parent, that's not a good thing.

It wasn't something that I concerned myself with too much when I was in Los Angeles or on the move to Edmonton. I had my life and work to worry about three time zones away, and I was just in my early twenties, not emotionally equipped to fill the role of father to my sisters and lifeline to mother.

* * *

Sophie did not want to be a girlfriend of a NHL player. Just like a lot of players are content to live within the bubble of the league, removed from real life, a lot of women are happy just to be a "hanger-on" and enjoy the lifestyle their boyfriends' work affords. Not Sophie, though. She wanted to know if I was serious about her. She wanted commitment. She wanted to start a family, and she didn't want to wait. We had practically grown up together. I couldn't imagine my life without her—she was pretty much what I had for family. And so, the summer before my first full season in Edmonton, I proposed to her and she accepted.

It was only after that, when my finances really became *our* finances, that Sophie and I sat down and went through the books. She had been aware that I had been helping my mother and sisters, but she wasn't aware of the extent of that help. I had effectively been paying my mother a living wage, even when I was a rookie trying to establish myself as a NHL player. Across not even four full NHL seasons, I had given her upward of $400,000.

If you're looking at the number and comparing it to the biggest contracts in the game, then $400,000 might not seem like a lot. You might think the same if you look at the numbers on the deal I was playing under in Edmonton: a three-year deal at $2.9 million per—a very good salary, twice the league average. When I scored twenty goals in Los Angeles, I wanted to believe that I hadn't just earned that contract but had also won a place in the league and would have a long career—I thought I was smart enough to figure out what it was going to take to stick. That's to say, I was guilty of a conceit that infects 99 percent of the league when they break in. If you didn't believe in yourself along the way, you'd have never got there in the first place.

After I was traded to Edmonton, though, I lost a lot of those illusions. I had no real security. I had beaten the odds just making as far as I had in the league: four out of five second-round draft picks don't stick. The reality gets even colder than that—more than half the players who make the league play less than a hundred games across their careers and don't make close to $2 million in their lifetime as players. If I had been the player that my father had planned to make me, an all-star, one of the league's 1 percent, someone who plays a thousand games and makes $80 million in his career, then giving away $100,000 a year would have been sustainable. That wasn't me, though.

When I sat down with Sophie, with her finance degree and the work she'd done in her father's company, she was able to put it into context. Blindly giving my mother money was no longer acceptable. And I realized that it was no longer just my money but *our* money. It was just common sense.

I was going to have to have "the talk" with my mother.

* * *

I didn't go into it angry when I picked up the phone, but I was going to be plainspoken. I was going to give her a financial facts-of-life speech: I can't foot the bill for your new kitchen or an extension on your house or anything like that. I was going to give her a pep talk too: if there's something that you'd like to do, a line of work that requires training or school of some kind, I'd be ready to help out. I'd think of that as an investment and an incentive. I didn't flatly come out and say that the indefinite period of mourning had to end. I tried to keep the message positive.

She basically said nothing. She seemed surprised that money was an issue. She cut off the call, got off the line.

There was another message I intended to get across. I wasn't shutting her out of my life. I still wanted to have a relationship with her. I still wanted to have a relationship with my sisters. I just didn't want that relationship to be founded on nothing other than my providing financially. I was prepared to be supportive. I wasn't prepared to be the sole means of financial support or the main means of the same. I didn't want to go from my father's retirement plan to hers.

I didn't know that it would be the last time that I'd talk with her.

* * *

That conversation with my mother didn't really enter my mind a couple of weeks later when Sophie and I were putting together the guest list for our wedding. The date was months off. By that time, I figured, things would have been sorted out and settled. Between the invitations being sent out and the ceremony, we'd hash it all out, I figured. In the days leading up to the wedding, we could talk face to face, I figured. Maybe it would be awkward, but we'd move past it—we had moved past a lot worse already.

My mother sent her invitation back unopened.

A couple of weeks later, Sophie and I sent off our Christmas gifts to my mother and my sisters. We were both filled with dread, and it turned out the way we feared: a couple of weeks later, the gifts too came back to us unopened.

I called her and left messages a few times. The calls I made weren't returned. After a few weeks I got the message and stopped trying. I was going through a difficult time with the team. It was stressful enough. I had to focus on my job, and I couldn't afford any stressful distractions.

My mother never tried to contact me by phone, by email or by letter. If she wanted to reach me, she could have easily—my email address hasn't changed in ten years. People I know have mentioned that they've seen her and that she asked about me, about Sophie and my sons. That's as far as it went, though.

Nothing has changed in the years since. Radio silence.

I never thought when I made that call to her that it was going to work out this way. I thought that she might be upset at first, but I was sure that she was smart enough to understand my situation once she sat down and looked at the big picture. My sisters needed a self-sufficient and ambitious role model as a parent, especially given that they had no positive role model from my father.

For now it's not a matter of curiosity for my sons: they're not really old enough to ask why they only have one set of grandparents or why they only have aunts and uncles on one side of the family. When they're old enough, I'm going to have to fill in a lot of details about my life. I don't know which absence in their lives will be harder for me to explain: their grandfather or their grandmother. I suspect it will be the latter. They'll get why my father had to be shut out of our lives, just as a matter of safety. They'll have a tough time understanding how my mother could walk away from Sophie and me without any explanation, without a single word since that phone call in 2009. I know I did. Only one thing had changed when she stopped picking up the phone or replying to messages: I had stopped writing checks. I can only conclude that money mattered more than anything else.

34

SCRATCHED

Edmonton, Alberta, January 2010

"You're going to be a healthy scratch," Tom Renney said.

"What?"

"You're going to be a healthy scratch," he said. "We're going to have a bunch of you in and out of the lineup for the rest of the season."

"Why are *you* telling me? Why isn't it Pat telling me this?"

Pat was Pat Quinn, the Oilers' head coach. Renney was his assistant.

"I'm speaking for Pat," Renney said.

"I think this is bullshit," I said.

I went off. It wasn't quite like my father going off on Tom Watt at the University of Toronto, but it was salty and to the point.

I could go into more detail, but ever since I had been traded to Edmonton, it felt like this moment had been coming. Eighteen months earlier, I had been a first-line winger with a team that was on the rise.

I had been happy in L.A., certainly when Crow was pink-slipped and Terry Murray came in to take his place. But it seemed I'd lost a grip on my career in just a few months. It was like a long, deep cut with a razor blade—just one stroke, you might not even see it at first, might barely feel it coming, but there's no stopping the bleeding.

I didn't get a honeymoon in Edmonton. I was put in a role that couldn't have given me a greater opportunity to fail: the third line, with the assignment of slowing down and stopping opponents' star players. At the end of the season, my center, Shawn Horcoff, a longtime Oiler, one of the fan favorites, had the second-worst plus–minus in the league, a minus-35, the basic measure of defensive effectiveness. Only one player in the league had a worse number: me.

Sophie was with me at my career's low point. We had spent time together in the off-season the past few years, but during the winters we'd had pretty separate lives—while I was playing, she was in business school in Denver. The previous summer, after the trade, we'd had the big talk: she would come up and spend the season with me in Edmonton if we set a wedding date. And so we did.

A year or two earlier she would have come away with a very different picture of the life that NHL players lead. If she had been in L.A. with me, there might have been ups and downs across the season, a player's mood swinging with the way he and his team are playing. In Edmonton there were only downs, and my downs were, like my plus–minus number, at the bottom of the league.

After games where I'd been on the ice for four goals against, which happened a few times, I would come home with her and she would want to talk. I'd tell her that I couldn't. I felt physically ill. I would have five or six beers to try to steady my nerves, but the mood would last six, even eight hours, without sleep. I know guys who might take an hour or two after they get home after a bad game, but losing and losing the way we were was digging down deeper in me. We were a bad team, and I was failing as badly as if not worse than anyone else on the team—whether or not I was being used right, I had to accept responsibility for that. I was losing my grip on a career in the NHL. Sophie had known me for five years. She was engaged to me but not engaged in the game. There wasn't really much we could talk about—or, at least, having to explain it would just dig the hole deeper and put me in a worse mood.

* * *

There's nothing worse in hockey than being a healthy scratch. If you have a shred of pride, if you give a shit, you don't want to be told that you're not good enough. As a rookie you can take it, you understand that your turn will come, but I wasn't a rookie in Edmonton. As a call-up from the minors, as a depth player in case of injury, you get it, but I wasn't a call-up. I had a contract that was paying me $2.9 million a season. It was the second year of a three-year deal. A player making $2.9 million isn't supposed to be the healthy scratch.

Getting scratched would have been hard to take anywhere, but nowhere would it be harder than Edmonton. For one thing, everyone in Edmonton recognized Oilers on the street. For another, everyone there knew everything about the team's business. In L.A. if you walked out in the street, no one recognized you. And people in L.A. are used to star culture—no one in L.A. is such a big deal. Wayne Gretzky can walk around there without getting hassled. In Edmonton, though, there was no escaping public attention. Players were known wherever they went and people had no filter—they'd ask you right up front what's going on with the team, without any hi's or how are you's. And when the team was going badly, you got no relief. People pressed you. Things were definitely going badly that season. The Oilers were heading to a last-overall finish. I felt like Sophie and I couldn't go out for dinner. The waitress was likely to say, "Hi, my name is Meghan and I'll be your server. Why are you a healthy scratch?"

Still, the worst part of being a healthy scratch was going to home games. Healthy scratches sit up in the press box during games. In every other arena in the league, the scratches can take the elevator that takes the media and people in the luxury suites up to the top level. In Edmonton, though, there is no private elevator to the press box. Scratches have to walk through the arena concourse to take escalators upstairs. It's like a public-shaming exercise. Fans will heckle you, and you have to not make eye contact or engage them or you're just asking for trouble. One time I just stayed down in the dressing room when the team went out on the ice for the game, but then management set down a rule that barred healthy scratches from the room on game nights. The team wanted you to parade in front of the fans on the worst nights of your career.

As a healthy scratch, the love I had for the game was getting sucked right out of me. Worse, a healthy scratch showing up on the box score was a black mark on a player's resumé. Memories are short in the game. Two years before I had been a twenty-goal scorer playing on a second line for an emerging team. But no one remembered that after the season in Edmonton. The team was a mess, the worst in the league, and I was a healthy scratch. People would put it together: if he can't play for Edmonton, who *can* he play for?

* * *

Edmonton, Alberta, April 13, 2010

When I went into Steve Tambellini's office, I didn't know that our end-of-season meeting would turn out to be a bookend to those few minutes I had spent with Jacques Lemaire. After all, I had been just a kid all those years back in Minnesota, hadn't played a NHL game outside of exhibition season. Back then I couldn't have seen what was coming. Going into Tambellini's office, I was an established player with almost three hundred career games, and I knew how the league works. I thought I knew how bad it was.

Tambellini let me do the talking, and I wasn't going to try to write a fantasy when it came to my self-evaluation. I wasn't going to try to explain or defend my season. I didn't say anything about being used on the checking line—Tambellini had been in the NHL a long time, so I figured he knew what a bad fit it was for me to skate there. I didn't say that the lines of communication with our coach and his staff were an issue—the Oilers were going to fire Pat Quinn after one year of his three-year deal, so I would have just been piling on top of their mistake. I stuck to the subject of my play and I said that I was really disappointed in my season. I owned it. Tambellini nodded but said nothing.

I told Tambellini that I knew that my body language was bad, that I acted out on my frustrations too much, that I could have handled bad situations better. And I told Tambellini that I wanted to play better for the Oilers, that I was willing to work in the off-season harder than ever.

I had planned to say all of this. It didn't make any impression on Tambellini. Then I went off the script, or at least said something that came to me while I was sitting there.

"I think it might help if I saw someone," I said.

I spelled it out. With the team going bad, just like I had laid it out and just like we both knew; with other things in my life going bad, though I didn't get into the split between my mother and me. I told Tambellini that I could be better for the team if I were in a better place emotionally. And that some outside professional help might get me to that place.

Tambellini said nothing. He didn't pick up his pen and make a note of it. He let it go right by.

About five minutes later, the meeting was over.

* * *

Sophie and I were on our honeymoon in Bora Bora when I got the news from my agent: the Oilers had traded me to Phoenix and were buying me out of my contract. I hated the timing but I wasn't surprised.

I don't know why Tambellini brushed off my suggestion about getting help. Maybe I wasn't his type of player, even if he had traded for me and taken on my contract. Maybe he didn't believe that type of work can help a player—no one on the team was seeing a sports psychologist so far as I knew. Plus I wasn't the only one on the team who felt like we were playing in a cloud of poisonous gas in our rink. A few of their young players had to walk through the concourse as healthy scratches and were taking it at least as hard as I was.

Tambellini might not have reacted to me floating the idea of psychological help because he didn't believe in me as a player. That would have been him changing his mind over a bit more than a year—when he had traded for me, he had handed L.A. a useful second-line player and knew exactly what my salary was.

Why Tambellini did any of this didn't matter. Things had gone bad, and fast, in just over a season. How bad I didn't know, though.

I didn't know it at the time, but I'd never have a one-way NHL deal again. The 1 percent players, the very top guys, leave the game on their own terms. The average player doesn't. For him it happens fast. I might have had a different story than anyone else, and I think I had more skill than most. But at the end of the day I had turned out to be an average NHL player.

35

THE LAST TIME

There is no curtain dropping at the end of my career. It's not like *Rudy*. For a pro athlete it's almost never like a movie, almost never a dramatic finish that plays out in front of a packed arena. It's usually something small and private, not a last game but something near the end. That's how it was for me.

I asked my agents to try to find me a one-way deal after Phoenix bought me out—a one-way contract that would guarantee me an NHL wage and give me a real shot at making a team. After a few weeks my agents told me there weren't any one-way offers out there but ten teams had interest in me if I'd sign a two-way contract. Offers ranged but I'd make the NHL minimum for as long as I stuck with a team and then, if I was sent down to the minors, I'd be looking at making about a fifth of the NHL minimum.

I wound up signing with the Carolina Hurricanes. It seemed like a fit. The team was rebuilding, and though I'd never lived in Raleigh, I knew and liked the state where I had spent a lot of my youth. That my father had wasted all those years in North Carolina playing in the Atlantic Coast league didn't weigh on my mind—maybe he would turn up at a Hurricanes game, but then again it had been a few years since he had shown up on the radar and he could have shown up anywhere. That my mother was living with my sisters just down the road didn't weigh on my mind either—maybe she would reach out, but then again I didn't need to be within driving distance for her to do that, not when she could have just picked up a phone or even sent an email.

In the end, it didn't matter.

It didn't work out for me with the Hurricanes. There was one spot open on their roster and my competition was an eighteen-year-old straight out of the draft, Jeff Skinner, who would be the league's best rookie that season. That was all she wrote in Carolina. After I played in ten games and was a healthy scratch for ten more, the Hurricanes traded me to Minnesota. I finally played for the team that had originally drafted me, but that only lasted a couple of months. I didn't get to play much and didn't make much of an impression.

The Wild ended up assigning me to their minor-league team in Houston, where I had played as a first-year pro. Minnesota might have thought and hoped I wouldn't report—especially because at this point Sophie was pregnant and we had set up house in Minneapolis. In fact, right before the Wild sent me down, Sophie's father had driven from Toronto to Minneapolis with a trailer full of furniture. Moving to Houston would be a whole new set of headaches—getting out of a lease, finding a new place and a new obstetrician. If I didn't report, Minnesota would have been off the hook for the balance of my contract. Even Mike Yeo, the coach in Houston, told reporters that he doubted I'd stick it out. "You don't know if the buy-in factor is going to be all there and if he was going to be completely committed to the team concept," Yeo said.

I did stick it out. At that point I hadn't given up hope of getting back in the game. Hope was fading fast, but not gone completely.

It turned out that I would never have as much fun as a pro as I did playing for Houston that spring. We had a great bunch of guys. Only a few had played in the NHL. Most were rookies or second-year pros who were going through this for the first time. They didn't look at veterans just as obstacles on their climb to stardom. If my teammates had heard any bad buzz about me after Edmonton, it meant nothing to them. And over time they got to know my story. My roommate and best friend Jed Ortmeyer is the person I told the most to.

In Houston I never felt like I had the weight of the world on my shoulders. We just went out and played. The team had been struggling before I got there, but we wound up making a long playoff run that spring.

Still, a long way from the NHL, my past revisited me and gave me a couple of bad memories that were never going to fade.

* * *

Peoria, Illinois, April 19, 2011
We had won the first three games of our first-round series against the Peoria Rivermen—that didn't make game 4 a desperate situation for the Aeros, but it was for me. Sophie was with her father and stepmother

in Florida and ready to give birth to our son. I was going to miss games 5, 6 and 7 if the series went that far because of the birth—there was no way that I was going to be away from Sophie and our newborn for a game in the minors, and to the credit of Mike Yeo, the team didn't expect me to come out to those games if it played out like that. If Yeo and management questioned my buy-in when I arrived in Houston, I had proven to them that I was committed to giving my best.

Midway through the second period of game 4, I picked up the puck on a turnover at our blue line and had a breakaway. Peoria's goaltender was Ben Bishop, who'd end up being one of the top goaltenders in the NHL a few seasons later. I fired a puck past Bishop and put Houston in front 2–1. Peoria came at us the rest of the game, but that wound up being the final score. We were through to the second round and I was going to be able to be with Sophie in Florida the next day, and with our newborn the day after that. It was a huge relief and as satisfying a goal as any I had scored since the gold-medal game at the World Juniors all those years before.

After the game Jed and I walked out of our dressing room together and headed down the hallway to the back door of the arena and to the bus that was going to take us back to the hotel. We planned on getting a few guys on the team together that night and having a few beers to celebrate the win and toast my first son.

My father was standing in the hallway, smiling.

It registered but it didn't register. Or at least, I didn't let on that I saw him or recognized him. I hadn't seen him this close since I appeared before a judge for a restraining order when I was with the IceDogs. Still, there was no mistaking him. He looked the same, sounded the same.

Why now? And of all the places, why Peoria?

It made sense, though. My father couldn't get that close to me or any other player at an NHL rink. Arena security keeps everyone at a distance from the teams. In the minors, though, security is nonexistent and autograph seekers can pretty much walk right up and knock on the dressing-room door after a game. In Peoria my father was just a face in the crowd. In this case, he was a face in the crowd that I wasn't going to acknowledge.

I gritted my teeth, stared straight ahead and kept on walking. Jed didn't know that anything was going on. He just thought my father was another fan and ignored him.

"Hey, Patrick," my father said.

He actually thought that I was going to stop to talk to him. He made it sound all buddy-buddy, like nothing happened over all those years, like nothing had happened eleven years before on his parents' lawn, like he had never gone to jail.

I tried to hold it together. I tried not to be mad. I tried to ignore the knot in my gut. I tried to keep composed. *Don't do anything stupid. Don't say anything. Don't do anything.* All these thoughts were other ways of saying: Don't be impulsive, like he always had been.

A small part of me wanted to finish the fight he'd started when he jumped me at sixteen, but that could only lead to trouble and I couldn't afford anything like that with Sophie back in Houston.

"You had your kid yet?" my father said.

For a second I thought that this was his way of telling me that he had been keeping tabs on me, stalking me, all these years. But then I remembered that a newspaper story that day had mentioned how I would miss the rest of the series if Peoria won game 4.

I wanted to lip off to my father like I would have years back. I could have said that I was bringing my son into the world and that I'd never look at him as a retirement plan. But again, I didn't want things to escalate. I just wanted to be away from him and back in Houston. I walked right by him.

"The least you could do is get a haircut," he said.

I went through the doors and got on the bus without a word.

"Patrick just shut himself down and right then I knew something was up," Jed says today. "I knew something had gone on back there in the hallway and I had some idea what it was."

I walked past my seat and into the washroom in the back, locking the door. I stood there for about ten or fifteen minutes, until the bus started to pull away. There was a mirror in the bathroom but I didn't look in it. I didn't want to see anything that looked even a little bit like my father.

When the bus pulled away, I was sitting on the other side of the aisle from Jed. The bus was noisy and my teammates were still buzzing after the win. Jed was watching me.

"You know who that was?" I said.

"Yeah," he said. "Are you okay?"

I told him I was.

I was angrier than I let Jed or anyone else know. I had a few beers with my teammates that night, but I wasn't happy the way I should have been. I felt like my father had come back from being dead-to-me to steal what should have been a good moment, the last good one I'd have in the game.

* * *

Houston, Texas, April 20, 2011

I drove Sophie to the hospital the next day. On the drive she asked about the game and I gave her a blow-by-blow of what happened on the ice. I didn't tell her about seeing my father. I wasn't going to let him ruin a great moment in my wife's life. It wasn't hard to keep the incident on the down low. Sophie was obviously preoccupied, and over the years I'd had a lot of practice at holding the worst stuff back. I tried not to think of the implications or what he might do next. Clearly, he still wanted to get back into my life. He might have thought that he was all that was missing in my career—that with him in the picture, I'd be back in the NHL and be an all-star in no time.

I wouldn't tell Sophie about seeing my father in Peoria until I thought the time was right and she was ready for it. That time wouldn't come until months after, maybe even close to a year. I knew it would ruin her day, but she had a right to know.

* * *

Binghamton, New York, June 3, 2011

I was stretched out on my bed in the hotel room, trying to grab a nap after lunch and before we had to go to the arena for a game against the Binghamton Senators in the league finals.

The phone rang and Jed answered it.

I just heard Jed's side of the conversation.

"Hello … Who's this? … He's not here."

Jed hung up without saying goodbye.

I didn't think anything of it. I figured it had been a fan—a lot of times the shit disturbers who pull for the home team will make prank calls, trying to wake up the other teams' players when they're trying to sleep. I didn't bother asking Jed who it was who called.

A few minutes passed and Jed checked to see if I was asleep. I wasn't.

"That was your father," Jed said. "He said he wanted to talk to you. When I told him that you weren't here, he told me to ask you to leave tickets for him at Will Call. I didn't know if I should tell you, but I think you'd want to know."

He knew it would gnaw at me, but it was something he had to do. It would be worse if I just spotted my father when we stepped on the ice or if he tried to do what he had in Peoria.

I didn't bother alerting arena security. There was no restraining order against him, nothing to prevent him from buying a ticket and walking through the door, but still, if he did show I had no idea what might happen. I was annoyed, not worried, by the prospect of him showing up. On the ice that night, I looked into the stands like I had back in junior, like I had on my draft day. I hadn't done it in five years or so. I looked for him and I thought I spotted him, but I didn't stop and stare and tip him off. I tried to be discreet. I didn't want him to know that I'd got the message he left with Jed.

I didn't see him after the game. I don't know if he tried to see me and arena security headed him off. If he had managed to get past security, it might have been the worst thing to ever happen to him. All my teammates had my back and they would have been in a bad mood after a tough loss on the road and just looking for any reason to take it out on him. It didn't come to that.

* * *

Since that night in Binghamton, I haven't had a phone call from my father. Not a letter. Not an email. I haven't seen him. I don't know if he has tried to find me, and I don't know if he's still looking for me or not.

In the years since, I've heard only one story, just a few weeks before I sat down to write. Someone back in Michigan said that he bumped into my father a couple of times in bars there. My father still tells people he's in touch with me. He says he still talks to me and that we're on good terms.

"I don't know if he had a load on or if he's too embarrassed to say that you two don't talk," the guy who saw him told me.

It's hard to imagine how trying to fabricate a story of our relationship is any less embarrassing and shameful than what's already public knowledge, including his criminal record.

It might be that he really believed what he said—that he is on good terms with me. Maybe that ambush of me in Peoria passes for a father–son moment for him. Maybe he thinks I left tickets for him in Bingo but they just couldn't find them at the Will Call window. It might be that he is that deeply delusional.

People ask me all the time if I know where he is or what he is doing.

I don't know, and I don't care to find out.

36

WHEN IT WAS GONE

Gothenburg, Sweden, October 22, 2012

I had made my decision to walk away from the game a few days before, but I didn't tell anybody. Not management, not my teammates, not even Sophie.

I love the game—the playing of the game on the ice, the game in its purest form. The business of the game had worn me out. The way things had gone down in Edmonton, Carolina and Minnesota was bad, and the 2011–12 season with Phoenix was tougher—the Coyotes told me to move Sophie and Henry to Phoenix because I was going to spend the season there, but as soon as they arrived with the dogs in tow I was assigned to their minor-league team in Portland, Maine. I'd see them when I was called up to Phoenix for a few days every month. It was a mess. If the team had been straight with me and told me that I was going to spend the season in the minors, I could have planned around it. I wanted certainty for Sophie, Henry and my second son, who was on his way the next winter.

I thought Europe would give us some certainty. I could make a decent living over there like a lot of other players had. I could play the game. It would be an adventure.

I had switched agents the season before, and my new agent looked for a deal for me in Europe. Big-money was out there, something like NHL dollars, in Russia and Switzerland. That was out because it meant training camp in August. He came back to me in the fall with a deal that HIFK, in Helsinki, was offering, and I jumped at it.

About three weeks in I realized that I had made a mistake.

I liked the game in North America, whether it was the NHL or the minors. I liked getting out on the ice and competing. In Europe you play fewer games and the emphasis is on practices—*long* practices, a grind that leaves you with long waits until the next game. It was all the work of hockey with none of the play. I thought Helsinki was great—it brought back memories of the World Juniors in '04, and it's a world-class city. I was at the wrong time of my life for it, though. Not with a wife, a young son and another on the way. We needed to be in a stable situation. I wanted to spend more time with my son and help Sophie out with the newborn.

To me the choice was clear.

I was going to tell management about wanting to walk away after a game against Frölunda, a Swedish Elite League team that HIFK was meeting in a European club-team tournament. HIFK had been good to me, and I felt like I couldn't leave the organization or my teammates hung out to dry, a man short with an important game coming up and without enough time to find a replacement as an import player.

When I stepped out on the ice in Gothenburg, I felt a sensation that I had never felt before and won't ever again: emptiness. I never had trouble motivating myself to play. I had never stepped on the ice when I felt I had nothing on the line—even though the NHL teams I played for never made the playoffs, I always felt that I had to prove myself, earn my salary and hold on to my job. I tried to do more than go through the motions. I have no idea if it looked that way. We wound up shelling Frölunda that night, 8–0, but the score meant nothing to me. The feeling that I had that night—the lack of feeling, really—confirmed to me that I was making the right choice.

* * *

When I came back from Gothenburg, I phoned Sophie in Florida and told her I was going home. It was time to get on with the rest of our lives. She didn't really see it coming. She had been thinking about coming to Helsinki in December once I was settled, and she'd thought that I was going to play another five seasons or more. She was prepared to stand by me no matter where the game would take me. She didn't try to talk me out of it—she just didn't want me to make a spur-of-the-moment decision that I'd regret later. She also knew that the average professional doesn't walk away from the game healthy at twenty-seven, especially when only three years before he was earning almost $3 million a season.

But even at twenty-seven, I had been dominated by the game for two decades. There were more important things that I had to do. And now I had the time to focus on them.

37

HELP

Santa Monica, California, November 2012

I sat down, picked up a pen and wrote for more than two hours, almost three, the first day. I would do it every day I was out in California. That first day, in those first two hours, I wrote down stuff that I had gone through that had taken me years to talk to Sophie about. Even in the first two or three days, I wrote out in awful detail stories about growing up that I had never told anyone but my wife. In days after that, I wrote about times that I couldn't even tell her, memories I'd tried to bury, memories that I would have found impossible to talk about at all. It wasn't just all pouring out, though. I wrote about the recent past, what happened to me as a player, as a boyfriend and then a husband and then a father. I wrote about the here and now, what happened in my average day as an adult, what made me happy and what made me sad. I put it all down on paper. I was in Santa Monica for thirty days, and every day I sat down and poured it all out—not just every incident, but everything that I remembered about every incident. And I have a memory that's pretty much photographic and not selective. My life was laid out on stacks of paper—*pounds* of paper. I wrote up to thirty pages a day for those thirty days. I wrote right through writer's cramp.

I didn't try to make it a journal or diary that I was trying reconstruct after the fact, not year by year and blow by blow. Each day I tried to write about an event or time that was important to me. These were the stories that I told myself. Not secrets—it's not a case that I try to conceal. Just the stories that I'd think of first if you were to ask me what made me the person that I am.

It's a strange thing, something that I didn't know going in: I thought it was going to be so much harder to write it all down. I can sit across from you and for a couple of hours I can tell you about awful things that my father put me through and about my mother's neglect. I can do that, and even if it makes you uncomfortable, I'll feel nothing, or at least nothing that doesn't pass after a few minutes. It's like I'm just rewinding and playing back the tape. I'm reciting fact from memory, like the multiplication tables. I thought writing it down was going to be so much tougher, just the physical act of it. I was wrong, though.

It turned out that I could write about things that I could never talk about, not with my best friends, not with Sophie, not with an analyst who's expert in getting people to open up. I thought it was just because I was doing this alone, but that turned out to be only a part of the story.

Writing it down was different. Just the act of writing takes more time, and the effort forces you to think harder about each and every word. And the way that I was writing it out—not just what happened but everything that was around me, everything I was thinking and feeling at the time—made my past come alive again like it never did when I told anyone stories about my past, not even when I told Sophie.

For thirty days I wrote without stop, probably because if I stopped, I might have trouble starting again. I wanted to avoid any temptation to put this off until later or until tomorrow. I had to do it, I thought, and I had to do it now, otherwise I might never do it. I needed to take stock of my life so I could have a life worth living. I needed to understand trauma to understand how trauma affected me and how to move past it.

* * *

I had been looking at seeking out psychological help for a couple of years. Early on in my NHL career, I had come around to understanding that I had never addressed the damage done when I was growing up. And I knew I was going to have to do that at some point if I wanted to have a shot at a happy, productive life.

I'd had brushes with it before, but nothing had worked out before Santa Monica.

When I was sixteen, just weeks after my father's arrest, my agents had set me up to talk to a sports psychologist who did some work with them and for NHL clubs—Dr. Scot McFadden. We met just once. Maybe it was an impulsive reaction, but I didn't get a good feeling about the session. That was completely predictable, when I look back at it. At sixteen I didn't feel the need: I had been through hell, and with my father's arrest and the restraining order, I had made it past the worst. I had survived all the abuse and was still making it on inner strength and toughness—at least that's what I thought, and nobody was going to tell me different. I was too stubborn, and everyone was walking on eggshells around me. My mother was too busy sorting out her life to spend any time and energy on mine. My agents had set up the meeting with McFadden but weren't going to push me to seek help I didn't want, not if that was going to piss me off and lead me to fire them as my reps. I hadn't hit the age of majority, but I felt I was ready to make the big decisions for myself. I was old for my age—that was my image of myself. In grade school I couldn't understand how kids would get so upset or even burst into tears if things went wrong, if they failed a test or something like that. I thought they were weak and I wasn't. The same at sixteen: I didn't want to be treated like a child, not after what I had been through, and not as far I had made it in the game.

I had looked at getting psychological help while I was still in the game, but that hadn't worked out either. Again, I met with a couple of specialists but never moved past a single session. One psychiatrist wanted to prescribe me drugs right off the top, but I didn't want any part of that. Sophie and I had met with a psychologist in Edmonton—we understood then that I needed help, that *we* needed help if we were going to be a successful couple, if we were going to make it. She shouldn't have to live with someone who is inconsolable for six hours after loss. The psychologist lost me in the first five minutes when he started talking to me about the Oilers and asking me if I could get him tickets. I wanted to be treated like someone other than an NHL player. I wanted to be able to separate the game and my life away from the arena. He wasn't going to help. He'd only make it worse, like being treated for claustrophobia by a psychologist who wants to hold sessions in his hall closet.

Those were learning experiences, though. I learned that you need to have complete trust in the specialist you're working with, which is a problem when you're like me and you have trust issues with a lot of people. I learned that you have to go into any work in the right frame of mind, feeling good about the process and the person you're working with. And I learned that your mindset and circumstances have to be exactly right or you have no chance of success—when I was living the life of a pro athlete in L.A. and making $2.9 million a year in my early twenties, exactly what was I supposed to think I needed help with? I wasn't a victim, I thought. I was a success story.

I went to Santa Monica with low expectations based on my past experiences, but still I was committed. I was told upfront that it was a thirty-day program and that the days were long. Twelve hours sometimes, sometimes more. I had talked it over with Sophie and she'd told me to go and take all the time I needed. It wasn't anything close to a holiday. I didn't tell any of my friends that I was going to L.A. It wasn't a matter of stigma or embarrassment—I just didn't want to have any distractions. I wanted to be able to focus on the treatment, and I thought having to talk about it or even acknowledge it to friends wouldn't help and could hurt.

And really, I was only ever going to be able to focus on treatment like this when my hockey career was over. I knew that treatment was going to require reliving a lot of awful moments and that all of those things would leave me in no state to play the game professionally, or even to train. All of them were going to leave me in a bad place and make it tough to be around other people. I needed isolation, for however long. To jump out of a session and into a crowded dressing room, to go back over all those years of my life and then land right back in the pressure cooker of pro hockey, just wasn't going to work.

But even on day one I had a good feeling about Santa Monica. Based on what I had heard about the program, I was sort of surprised by the location. The psychologist's offices weren't in a clinic. He worked out of an office building that he shared with law firms and investment outfits in a high-end business district. It was not the place where you expect the wounded to show up—and his patients were the wounded.

To be clear, I was the only pro athlete that the psychologist was seeing. I was going to be the only one he'd ever treated up to that point. I knew going in who his patients were: veterans of the wars in Iraq and Afghanistan. A lot of them had Purple Hearts for wounds that they suffered on the front lines. A lot of them had lost limbs. They had all been diagnosed with post-traumatic stress disorder. And on the first day at the office, so was I.

* * *

Looking back now, it's not a surprise that I wound up being treated by a psychologist who worked with military veterans. One hundred years ago people talked about vets coming back from the front lines with shell shock. What they had was PTSD; it's just that no one had given the condition a name or thought of it as a clinical, psychological condition. That didn't happen really until the seventies, when thousands of American soldiers were coming back from Vietnam and having difficulty or finding it impossible to get by. For many, it seemed like they couldn't return at all to the life that they used to lead. The U.S. Veterans Administration poured millions into clinical studies of the vets. Forty years and millions of soldiers later, the VA still drives research into and treatment of PTSD—its budget for mental health is $7 billion a year.

The work the VA has done on PTSD helps more than the veterans and their families, though: 28 million people in the U.S. suffer from PTSD, most of them never having been in the service.

My psychologist focused almost exclusively on veterans. I never saw one of his other patients in the waiting room, but he told me about them and he made it clear that my trauma was different from theirs. Not that one is worse than another—though it's impossible for me to even imagine what it's like to go through life missing an arm or a leg or with a body that's covered in scar tissue from severe burns. I'm not about to minimize that. But the fact that so many veterans were working on their PTSD motivated me and inspired me. From where I was sitting, their sacrifice and courage made it impossible to feel the least bit sorry for myself. But my case was different from theirs down at the basics.

For many of the veterans, the traumas were isolated, one-off incidents: a single *something* that happened to them during the service. For me, my father traumatized me daily.

For those veterans whose traumas were suffered over the course of time, it would have been over the course of a tour of service or two. For me, those traumas came over the course of ten years.

For most of the veterans on my psychologist's patient list, their first treatments for trauma came within a year or two of their return from action. For me, my traumas dated as far back as twenty years.

And finally, and most importantly, the veterans were enlisted men and women, all adults when they suffered their traumas. I had been a kid and then an adolescent when my father had been beating me. My emotions were still being shaped. My brain wasn't physically matured.

On a lot of counts I wasn't an average patient in his practice, but my psychologist made it clear—I had what they had, and I needed treatment just like they did. He also made it clear that this wasn't something that he could fix in thirty days or over the course of months or even years of treatment. This was work that I'd have to commit to for the rest of my life. This wasn't anything that I'd ever move past and leave behind. PTSD wasn't like that.

* * *

When the psychologist went through the symptoms of PTSD with me, I realized that I fit the profile. One symptom really hit home: sleep. My problems with sleep were a red flag so obvious that other specialists I'd seen should have picked up on it.

As far back as I could remember I had been a bad sleeper. My sleep was disrupted when my father was waking me up at three or four in the morning to work out. Even when he didn't wake me up like that, it was on my mind when I went to bed. Growing up, I would try to grab sleep wherever and whenever I could. As I've mentioned before, I regularly fell asleep in class in grade school and middle school. I'd drift off on the late-night drives back from Alvinston or Strathroy, at least until my father shook me or pushed me because he thought it was unfair that I could sleep and he couldn't. I basically grew up sleep deprived.

Yet after I moved to Mississauga, and later when my father was out of my life, my nights were just as bad. Three times a week, when I was in my early teens or even as an adult, I would have awful nightmares— what psychologists treating PTSD patients categorize as "night terrors." For me they were recurring flashbacks. There wasn't a story, just a flood of images that would shock me awake and leave me trembling.

It was something that my roommates on the road were used to and something that Sophie knew about better than anyone.

When the psychologist listed other symptoms associated with PTSD, I checked off just about every one of them. I recognized myself. I recognized how every symptom played out in my life.

Near the top was a numbing of emotions. I had always been a flat line in that way—most of the time I didn't react emotionally to things like the majority of people. On what should have been a good day, I would be stuck, not allowing myself to be happy. I could turn irritable almost instantly and for no good reason. But sometimes when I was in a shitty situation, like my worst times with Marc Crawford in Los Angeles, I'd surprise people by my ability to shrug it off—with Crawford, I did that right up until he kicked me on the bench. When I told my teammates that "my standards for bad" were different from theirs, it was just another way of saying that I didn't feel things like them. My standard *reactions* for bad were what really differed.

A sense of isolation was another symptom, and it should be obvious by now that I felt for years like I was in this alone, really up until Sophie came into my life. My father isolated me physically and socially. I could never say that I had a best friend or a circle of friends growing up. By the time I landed with the under-18 program in Ann Arbor or with the IceDogs in Mississauga, I might have been able to spend more time with my teammates or with people I met in school, but I also felt *separate* from them, like we had so little in common in our lives that they could never really know me. I don't want to say that I felt lonely, because that only sounds like self-pity or pleading for sympathy. Still, when my father would try to frame our lives as Us against the World, I felt like he was going into the battle on his own and I was doing the same.

The psychologist also told me that people with PTSD struggle to feel for other people in any sort of empathetic or sympathetic way. That again rang true for me. I didn't understand what people went through, going right back to grade school when I'd see kids crying over failing a test or some other disappointment. It was still a problem with Sophie—as much as she knew what I had gone through growing up, she would become frustrated when I didn't feel other people's pain. There's no easy way to say what is at the root of the lack of empathy on the part of people with PTSD—it might be that everyone else's pain seems so small by comparison to theirs, or that so much energy and attention is spent on their own traumas that they have nothing left to give to another's. For me, my attitude might have been "You're on your own." That by itself is cold and not going to win you friends, but it's a lot more dangerous in a partner, a spouse or a parent.

Looking at it on those terms, I understood even better the stakes of healing: as much as I was in this for my own emotional and psychological well-being, I was also doing it for Sophie's and for our sons'.

* * *

Although writing everything down was hard, there was more to the treatment. The psychologist had me go through a bunch of different exercises. In one I had to talk through traumatic incidents blow by blow and we'd work through them in reverse order—like slowly rewinding scenes in a film, back to the first frame. Talking to me in an almost hypnotic cadence, he had me doing relaxation exercises. In doing that, I had to think through my father's abuse in painful detail. I realized after doing it awhile that this backward history was a way of simulating the undoing of the trauma—starting out as the wounded and working your way back to the person you were before, the person you would have been if you had managed to avoid the abuse and violation. And when I did this I found a different Patrick O'Sullivan. In a way, I was able to reclaim a childhood I had been denied by my parents.

I don't take much away from talk-therapy sessions, which might be part of the reason that I'd resisted the attempts at counseling before and which was definitely a major reason why I liked the work in Santa Monica. Talk feels empty to me. It feels weightless. I know that some people like it and even swear by it. I felt that it was a question of personal preference for me. I don't like to talk about the incidents from my youth with anyone, even Sophie, because I don't see how anything in words really helps a relationship—I don't see how anyone can really understand that way. It might be that over the years I used words to cover up the abuse I suffered and my father was able to talk his way past any suspicions. Words had failed to help before. Words are easy to miss. And in the end, talk therapy is based on the idea that the person you are talking can help you. That wasn't what I needed. I needed to be able to help myself—to arm myself with an awareness and a method for helping myself when there wasn't someone there to talk to.

I knew that talk therapy worked for some people who have psychological issues, and I assumed that it didn't work for me because of personal preference. I didn't like the process and didn't feel I was going to make any progress out of it. As it turns out, it wasn't necessarily personal at all: the numbers show that talk therapy doesn't work for a lot of people with PTSD, maybe most. It's not considered one of the more effective treatments. That makes a lot of sense when you step back and look at it—especially when you know research findings about traumatic memory. Experts say that traumatic memories are stored in different areas of the brain than other personal memories, a part of the brain that isn't connected to speech. There's no sure reason why it happens that way, but experts have some theories that make sense: traumatic memories take shape when fear for your safety has kicked in, when adrenaline is rushing, when you're focused on surviving, so they take a different shape. For whatever reason, traumatic memories aren't there to be reached and to be pulled out—they're not consciously recallable, not controllable. They're spontaneous, bubbling up involuntarily, falling out when you don't expect them to—flashbacks triggered by something experienced in the moment. In my case, my flashbacks didn't go to a moment but to hundreds or even thousands of them.

I knew that there was going to be no way that I was going to be able to work my way through a checklist of everything that I had been through, a checklist of every issue that came out of my youth, a checklist of every situation that I was going to find myself in. That might work for some people who have some other sort of specific traumatic event, but not in my case. It had just been too many things over too much time to narrow it down like that—it wasn't like a bull seeing a cape in the ring or the bell ringing for Pavlov's dog. It was going to be a lot of things, and many of them weren't obvious in any way. I'd have to be able to recognize when I was reacting and work backward to a cause. Recognizing when I was upset and irritated was the easiest part—for me, it had always actually been a physical feeling, something that might only start with a knot in the gut and an anxious state. Identifying the root causes, though, was like trying to sort out a thousand-piece jigsaw puzzle of your life complicated by the fact that some of the pieces are missing. Just the ability to identify them, however, neutralizes their effect—you can see each piece for what it is and nothing more.

Some specific things set people with PTSD on edge—the psychologist called them "triggers." I had to be able to identify them or, more importantly, I had to learn how to identify them. If I laid out all my triggers here, this book would run more than a thousand pages. But a couple of them are enough to give you an idea of the process.

One example is the smell of grass. In keeping notes of what looks like dull, everyday routine, I could see that I often had a bad day after doing some chores around the house. I dug down deeper and saw that it didn't happen on rainy days. I dug deeper still and picked out a very specific trend: things went bad for me every time I smelled freshly cut grass. It was no big jump to make a connection with my past. My father had been particular about keeping up appearances of the places we had rented, and he had made me cut the grass to his specific demands. If my lawn cutting didn't satisfy him—and it rarely did—he would beat me. He had effectively conditioned me to be prepared for a physical beating every time I mowed the lawn. Knowing this, the next time I was able to neutralize the reaction. It still takes a bit of a conscious effort, and it might for a long time. It might never be automatic. But awareness of history is the closest thing that I can have to erasing it.

Another example is interrupted sleep. In keeping notes, I noticed that I was really irritable whenever I woke up during the night. I also noticed that it didn't matter what the cause was—it could be the sound of thunder or anything else outside the house, it could be getting up to change a diaper or to go to the bathroom. Any sort of interruption would leave me too agitated to fall back asleep easily. This would have been easy to write off as a sleep disorder. But again, with some work, going back to see the patterns in my life, I was able to get at the root cause: those times when I was in grade school and my father would come home from work or the bar at three in the morning, wake me up for a workout and lock me out of the house in my pajamas. Again, when I wasn't able to sleep through the night, I had been subconsciously and even physically conditioned by abuse. Just knowing what was behind the feeling made getting back to sleep easier or at least possible.

To say that there are dozens more triggers like this is no exaggeration. It would be on the low side. Of course, some things were more obvious than these. It was no big jump to figure out the source of nausea and anger when I'd be around someone heating up baked beans. And I'm sure that over the rest of my life, I'll be identifying still more triggers. The key is to recognize the feeling triggered and then put the pieces of the puzzle together as much as I can.

I know that I'm going to have good days and bad days. I have to enjoy the good days as much as I can and blunt the impact of the bad ones, dial them back. Sometimes I'll have that feeling of being triggered but not be able to make a connection—still, just knowing that it was *something* can help. I try to remember everything from that day so if the feeling and the situation come up again, I'm halfway to the point of piecing together another trigger.

* * *

Fact is, given my history, I have to count myself as one of the lucky ones. The odds are long against a survivor of abuse having a happy and productive life as an adult. Abuse in youth raises the incidence of a slew of problems in adult life. You are more likely to have alcohol and drug issues. You are more likely to suffer from depression and other mental issues. You are more likely to land in jail. You are more likely to end your own life. That I even have the prospect of a happy life means that I'm beating those odds. I'm lucky to be able to afford the help that I found in Santa Monica. I'm also lucky that I'm able to afford maintenance help from a psychologist I see every few months near my home in Florida. I'm lucky that I have been able to cut the night terrors down to one or two a month since I've been in therapy. I'm lucky that the work in therapy has helped me so far, because some do all the work and see no benefit—in the worst cases, revisiting their traumas in therapy hurts them, deepening their despair. I'm lucky that I found something that works for me—it might not work for all others with PTSD, but they might find other effective treatments. I only hope that everyone who suffers from PTSD seeks out help and finds something that works.

part three

38

HOW IT HAPPENED

When I tell my story, people come away thinking, *How could his father do such things to him?* At some level you might presume that his motives are clear and uncomplicated. Clearly, he wanted me to play in the NHL and thought that, left to my own devices, my own desire to make it wasn't enough. Clearly, he thought the ends justified any means. Clearly, he was fueled by desperation and lacked the skills to build any sort of life for himself, never mind provide for a family.

You might make a few jumps when you get below the pragmatic and into his psyche. You can make his motives as complicated as you want. That he wanted payback. That he wanted to win in a game that had chewed him up and spit him out. That he wanted to be in the spotlight in a game that had exiled him to its deep, dark minors.

For years, questions from people exhausted me and angered me. These weren't questions that I asked myself. To be polite, I offered the bare minimum of answers. I'm inured to it. For one thing, it happened, and thankfully, it's over. For another, I think that my father is mentally ill. That he was in some sort of denial or delusion was clear in his interviews in *ESPN The Magazine* and on *The Fifth Estate*, in the letters he wrote to me, in the accounts of people who have talked to him in the years since and in his attitude when I saw him in Peoria or when Jed Ortmeyer spoke to him on the phone in Binghamton.

These, though, explain *why* my father did these things. Not *how*. That's the question I've spent more time thinking about, and it's a question that's easy to answer, at least on its face. How could he do all those things to me, getting away with it for years? He could abuse me because no one stopped him.

It had always been a puzzle to me: even when I was young, as young as eight or nine years old, I understood that my father was unstable. Looking back on it as an adult, I have to presume that his instability had to be plain to others. *Crazy* was the word that people who knew him threw around, whether it was those who played with him in the minors or at University of Toronto, where he was called Crazy John by his teammates. My father could be a stealthy operator—he could work a con like the birth certificate deal at the U.S. Under-15 Festival. He might be able to fool people on first impression, but they were able to figure out who he was before too long. Eventually, they could get a better read of him.

And they could get a clear read of his son.

I was his hostage. That's how it is with a lot of abuse victims. But unlike others, I was a hostage who was out in public. I wasn't locked away and unseen. I played with hundreds of kids and for dozens of coaches. Over the years, hundreds of parents and officials were on the other side of the glass. A lot of people watched me, and watched me more closely than the average kid. That's just the case for any exceptional athlete. My father moved me from one team to the next, from one city or town to another every season. Still, I was around a group of kids and adults three or four times a week, often more. I was around them over the course of months. I was around them for hours at a time. If I had an acne breakout, they would have noticed. If I had a haircut, they'd have noticed. If I came to the arena with new equipment, they'd notice. How could they not have known something was wrong? Even if my abuse wasn't in plain sight, what signs could they have picked up on? And why didn't they follow up?

That my father abused me couldn't have gone unsuspected. It isn't *if* people knew, but rather *how much* they knew. And knowing what they did, it's also why these people did not act.

For years, I thought that breaking away from my father freed me for a journey in hockey. That was how I saw myself, as a hockey player. There's not a lot of introspection on retrospection in the game, not for a player. You play a game and when it's over you look ahead to the next game; one season over goes on to the next one. After hockey, though, I realized that I had to dedicate myself to being a husband and then a father. At that point I started to think of my life experiences in a bigger context. I still had one question that stood in the way of a greater peace of mind: How did nothing stop my father's abuse from happening to me?

I set out to answer that question.

39

SCHNURR

I tracked down Mike Schnurr, our coach with the Falcons back when I was ten playing with twelve-year-old kids. Schnurr wasn't hard to find. He had worked for a food company back when he coached us and was still there all these years later, now as the chief executive. I cold-called him, and when he picked up he seemed distracted, blindsided for sure. I told him that I was working on a memoir, doing some research, calling up teammates and coaches from my time in youth programs. He told me his day was full of meetings and scheduled calls and he didn't have fifteen minutes to spare. He asked if any questions could wait until the next day, so we set up a time in the afternoon. He said that it would give him time to think through his "reservoir of memories." It seemed like he was opting for executive caution, figuring out in advance where he would tread and where he wouldn't.

When I called back the next day, Schnurr had not only considered what he was comfortable saying but also tried to game out my motives for calling him. He had thought through what had happened all those years before and what he wanted to say. He didn't have a prepared list but seemed to work from notes that he had set down. He started out by preparing me for disappointment. "I don't think you're going to like what I have to say," he told me. "I know the story that came out after, but to me, your father was a good guy."

"I knew you'd say that," I said.

True. Schnurr and my father got along, maybe as well as my father got along with anyone at any arena. Schnurr seemed to like the character my father presented, the rough diamond, the hard-ass who looked at everything as Us against the World and wouldn't back down. Schnurr also seemed to like my father because he wasn't like the other players' parents, parents who came to him only when they had problems with his coaching. "I got to know John better than most parents," Schnurr said. "He would hang around the dressing room and talk to me. He had ideas about what we could do on the ice, good ideas. He had a background in hockey, and that set him apart from 99 percent of the parents who never played the game."

Schnurr vividly recalled the first time he talked to my father. "John called up when we were having tryouts late that summer. He said he recently moved into the area from Toronto and he had a son he wanted to bring [to the tryouts]. I said that was okay. Then he said that his son was ten years old and I told him, 'Sure, you can bring him out, but we don't really have kids that young making the team.' Two years up. We didn't have players like that, but John seemed confident that his son could make the team. Very confident."

Schnurr stopped to laugh, his way of acknowledging that my father never lacked for confidence. He seemed to like that in my father.

"I didn't think that there was anything unusual about John … just how he'd take it to the next level," Schnurr said. "I remember there was a rink over in Mount Clemens under construction, about 80 percent along the way, but before the lights and fixtures were installed. I went there one day at lunchtime to meet the arena manager, about arranging some ice time when the building was finished, and I saw John and you. I said, 'What the hell are you doing here?' And he said, 'I brought Patrick up here during his lunch hour from school to shoot some pucks.' I was just laughing inside. That's really taking it to the next level. After a while [we realized] he had an obsession with you making the NHL. That was his motivation. I didn't see anything out of line. He was going to do whatever it took, legally or illegally, to give you the best chance to get to that level. And you know what? He did. He did a good job of making you a player, didn't he?"

I didn't really appreciate Schnurr's version of history—my father enabling me to make the NHL, my father somehow having succeeded because I played almost four hundred games in the league. In spite of my father, not because of him. But listening to the audio recording again, one word jumped out at me: *obsession.* Another phrase grabbed my attention: "whatever it took, legally or illegally." The way Schnurr saw it, my father's obsession had been a healthy one, even if he was prepared to commit a crime. Schnurr made it sound as if I had reason to be grateful to my father for everything the game gave me.

"John's actions in the rink bothered a lot of people," he said, "because he was very loud, aggressive … Well, not aggressive, but very loud. When you were on the ice he'd bang on the glass. He'd make comments to you. I didn't say anything to him because, one thing, it was his kid and he didn't bother the rest of the team. He bothered the parents but they didn't come and register complaints with me. It was a kind of a joke. It was like, 'Look at this guy being a lunatic.'

"Besides, John wasn't bothering the rest of the team. I kind of rationalized in my mind, the fact that the stuff he was telling you to do was the right stuff. He was yelling the right things. He knew hockey. He wasn't telling you to take the puck and try to go the length of the ice, don't pass it and try to score a goal. John would be telling you to make the right plays. He wasn't abusive to other kids. So I accepted it. He wasn't the first parent to tell his kid what to do on the ice. I rationalized it because he was telling his kid to do the right thing, unlike some other parents."

I told Schnurr that I could imagine that his opinion of my father had to be different from other parents'.

"Look, the other parents were uncomfortable around John," Schnurr said. "The other parents talked about him—everybody had a Johnny O. story. He was an interesting study as far as his approach to raising you—it was a lot different. John didn't socialize with them. John would typically stand over by the glass. He was loud. It just bothered some people that he was as loud as he was. As far as the physical abuse goes with you, I'm sure it happened but I didn't see any of that. I heard a lot of stories, but I didn't know if they were true or not. I heard stories, but that's all hearsay."

I listened and listened again to the audio recording of this part of the conversation: Schnurr had "heard stories" but decided on his own that they were "hearsay," suggesting that they weren't credible enough to follow up. Though he said he didn't know if the "stories ... were true or not," Schnurr's actions or his decision not to act made it seem that he gave them little chance of being true. And of course, Schnurr's friendship with my father—they "socialized"—gave him more insight into his character than the other parents who were "uncomfortable around him" had.

I pressed Schnurr. "Who were those parents?" I asked.

"Just other parents," Schnurr said. Though so much was vivid in his memory, he couldn't think of a single player's parents who were bothered by my father and had a story—even though, as he said, "everyone had a Johnny O. story."

It seemed that Schnurr was making this a dead end strategically. He had no problem recalling something as insignificant as the day he had seen my father and me at a rink under construction in Mount Clemens but remembered nothing at all about a parent coming to him to express concern about the way my father treated me. Schnurr's failure of memory was just too convenient a fit for his rationalization of inaction. There were two possibilities. One: Schnurr didn't want to refer me to any of those parents if there would be any chance that they'd think he threw them under the bus, impugning them for their own inaction. Two: Schnurr didn't want to refer me to any of those parents if they might tell me about damning complaints about my father that Schnurr chose to ignore, more damning than Schnurr was painting them, more credible than "hearsay."

Schnurr then took it one step further, suggesting that he was not only right to have done nothing but *had* to keep his distance. "It was none of my business," Schnurr said. "I'm not a psychotherapist. I'm not a family psychologist. There were other people out there that took it to an extreme … not as far as John, but still, it wasn't uncommon for parents to be loud in the stands. John wanted what they wanted, the best for their kids. I'm coaching a team. I had all the duties of trying to keep the team going forward. Obviously, I want what's best for the kids. If John's actions were hurting the team or the other kids, I would have done something. But obviously it wasn't like that. Whatever went on with John, it wasn't bothering sixteen other kids."

That is, even if those stories had been credible rather than hearsay, even if Schnurr had seen a red flag himself, he wasn't an expert. Intervening to protect a kid wasn't part of his job description. Schnurr basically says that the nanny-state approach to child rearing has no place in the game of hockey.

Schnurr claimed what he must have considered a victory at this point of the conversation. "I know that's not what you're looking for," he said.

Schnurr was a prime example of the culture of the game that protected and enabled my father. And like Schnurr, the values at the arena have been slow to change if they've changed at all. They haven't changed for Schnurr, apparently. Schnurr gave up coaching a few years ago, but when I asked if he would do anything different if he saw a father "going to the extreme" or "taking it to another level" today, he said he wouldn't.

"I have my own moral compass, my sense of what's right and wrong," he said. "I wouldn't do anything different today than I did with John and you. If I saw someone who I thought was taking it too far, I might go up to him and say, 'Let me tell you a story.'"

Maybe he would. Maybe he'd think that this was just another parent who wants the best for his kid, and so long as it doesn't bother the other kids, and so long as the team moves forward, there's no harm in it. He sees no real threat in parents being obsessed with their kids' success.

Schnurr had it half right. It wasn't what I wanted to hear, but it was exactly what I *expected* to hear from a friend of my father, someone who thought he was one of the good guys.

40

FOSTER

Dwight Foster was anything but a friend to my father. Though he brought me in as an underage player and brought in my father as an assistant coach with the team in Dearborn, he was the coach who pushed back harder against my father than anyone else. And while Schnurr said he had no regrets, Foster, who's a partner in a venture-capital group in Detroit, has no problem admitting that he wished he had done more to help me.

"I guess there were warning signs of some trouble coming that I didn't pick up," Foster says. "It probably goes right back to when he told me that he'd like to get a tryout for you and then he explained that you were double underage. I told him that's pretty ambitious, putting a boy that young against players two years older. I had a picture of you sort of, based on your father asking for a tryout. I could have seen it if you had a kid who was unusually big for his age, physically advanced.

But the fact was you weren't big for your age. You were average, if that. I played with a lot of guys who went on to play pro, and while a lot of them had played against kids a year older than them, I suppose those who played against kids two years older were really rare. I asked myself, what was the point of having you skate against kids that much older and bigger? … If it was really worth the risk. You could do it, but I don't know that you really *needed* it. It was something John wanted more than anything you needed. That should have been a red flag."

For all his NHL experience, Foster was in his first year of coaching the year I played for him, and he admits that he was on a learning curve when it came to dealing with hockey parents. My father and I came along when he was just at the base of that curve. "You assume that the way that you feel about your kids is the way everyone else feels about his," Foster says. "You figure that if anyone is going to go too much one way, then it's going to be on the side of being overprotective. You can't imagine that a parent who is bringing a kid out to play organized sport, putting in a lot of time and money, is the type of parent who would let their kid get in harm's way—never mind actually go out and put their kid in any sort of danger."

To be fair to Foster, he actually did pick up on the red flag. "[Your father] told me that he had played in the minors, though I can't remember exactly where," he says. "I didn't see much of a way to check out whatever he said. Now you could go online and find out exactly when and where he played, but back then I wasn't able to do much, and that didn't seem the biggest worry—if he claimed to have played in the minors and he was exaggerating what he was a player, that didn't seem to be a big deal. It just meant that there wasn't anyone who played with him that I could call."

If Foster had been able to call Dave Herbst from the Skipjacks in the ACHL or anyone on the University of Toronto championship team, he might have come away with a different picture of my father. Still, Foster didn't like his first impression of him as an *involved* parent, someone who might be wanting too much for his son. That he felt obliged to follow up was in a way a red flag—if intuitively something doesn't feel right, odds are pretty good that something at the root is wrong.

"I made calls to some people," he says. "I tried to check things out. It wasn't so easy with your family moving around the way that you did. I heard from people in Toronto that your father was a real piece of work, high maintenance. Well, there are lots of those. Some of those top teams would have trouble [finding] six players whose parents weren't really demanding. I didn't hear anything that made it sound like he could be a danger to you or anyone else."

Going into that season, Foster was expecting my father to be some sort of headache, but he hoped it would be more of an annoyance than a full-blown migraine. I asked him why he didn't just avoid dealing with my father completely and tell him he didn't have a spot on the team for me.

"I'll give someone a fair shot," Foster says. "You don't know what agendas people have when they're critical of another parent. You have to do your homework, but I was taking it with a grain of salt. It's not like a workplace with professional references or anything like that. I don't want to punish a kid—deny him an opportunity—based on what I have second- or third-hand about a parent."

Foster admitted that he let my father help out as an assistant coach in part because he felt overwhelmed. "I was just happy to have some-one help out, and your father seemed to know the game," he says. "It was my first year coaching. I signed up because my sons were playing and it was a new team, looking for a coach. With my background, I didn't feel like I could turn my back on them. I didn't know exactly what I was getting into, [it was] a lot to run a practice with little kids."

On the ice, all the worst that Foster had heard about my father rang true. Even from the first practice, he started second-guessing his decision to let my father work with the team. "It's one thing to be serious about coaching, but he just went at it with an intensity that was over the top right from the start," Foster says. "It was inappropriate. Almost all of it was directed at you. I gave him a lot of latitude that way—too much, now that I look back at it. If he had treated anybody else's son the way he treated you, I don't think he would have lasted a practice. In retrospect, I realize that sounds bad. It shouldn't matter if it's somebody else's son or your own. There's a right way to work with kids and a wrong way. If he was okay with everybody else but wrong with you, then he's 100 percent wrong ... not mostly right."

Teams accommodated my father wherever I played. He made demands of them and cut special deals, getting registration fees cut or tossed aside completely. Every time teams did that, it only encouraged my father to ask for more and to push me harder to play better so that he could ask for even more. Foster was the one coach or organizer who didn't accommodate my father. When he kicked the two of us out of practice, he was trying to lay down ground rules. Other coaches had felt physically intimidated by my father, who looked and carried himself like a bouncer, but Foster didn't rattle. "I thought that maybe kicking him off the ice and telling him he was done as a coach with the team might shock him," Foster says. "I thought he'd ask to come back behind the bench and that it might make him pull back a bit. I knew how important being able to coach you was to him, and I thought having that taken away would straighten him out some. It didn't work. It seemed to make him that much more intense."

Foster also told me that he wouldn't have hesitated to act if he had thought I was in any immediate danger. "I met your mother and your sisters—they didn't come out as a family as often as the families of other kids did," he says. "Still, your mother seemed like a nice lady who cared for you and wouldn't let anything happen to you. I was thinking she was there to strike a balance. As over the top as your father was, she wouldn't let it get too far, at least that's what I figured."

Foster told me that he had gone back through his own reservoir of memory after he had heard the reports about my father going to jail for assaulting me. He wasn't surprised when the story of the history of abuse surfaced, though he said the "physical stuff" blindsided him. "Your father seemed to have some real issues," he says. "You hope people get over them, but they probably don't more often than they do, I guess."

Nobody I played for knew the game better than Dwight Foster, and no one took less shit from my father. And yet even though he wasn't intimidated or conned by my father, even though he intuitively sensed that my father had "real issues," even though he had seen my father go wild-eyed and out of control when he ripped into his eleven-year-old son in practice, Dwight Foster didn't have any idea about the O'Sullivan family secret. He couldn't see it, he said, because it was so unlike his own experience in hockey. "Your father wanted you to be the best player in the world," he says. "I was never the best player [on my teams] coming up. I just kept playing. I never even thought about the draft until my draft year. My father was supportive, but he wasn't overly

265

involved at all. I was the farthest thing from pressured about playing. I think that's why I was able to keep playing. I had no expectations, never mind demands. I enjoyed the game and I just kept playing. There were guys who were way ahead of me and they gave up the game the first time they had a bit of adversity. I found out that isn't how things in the game are anymore … not how parents are. Your father was the first one like that I dealt with, but I coached for a while and came across others."

Again, in contrast to Schnurr, Foster told me that he felt conflicted when my story came out years after. "I do think sometimes if I could have done something different," he says. "I wondered if I missed something, or if your father was just extra careful not to slip up around me that year. If there had been anything concrete as far as physical abuse goes, I really wouldn't have had any trouble calling a cop. And he knew that too."

41

ALVINSTON

I have to admit that when I sat down to write this book, the season I played in Alvinston was a blur. That year, with all the driving across the border to games and practices, the game was just taking up so much time and energy, more than ever before. A lot of the time I felt like I was asleep on my feet. I have a vague recollection of games but can hardly remember any names at all. The only contact I had with anyone from that season came a few years back when I was playing for L.A. and I got a call from Alvinston—the team wanted to know if I could donate a signed sweater for a charity auction. That was it.

The season was a mess. It had looked like I was going to spend another winter with Belle Tire, and I skated with them for a few games, but my father decided that I was done with the program and started to look at teams in the Great Lakes Junior C league. I recalled my father getting me into practices with a couple of teams, but I wasn't sure which teams those were—it was only when I looked at the league's website that I remembered skating at practices in Blenheim and on the reserve in Walpole Island. I have to believe that my father had told them that I was fourteen or fifteen to get a tryout and that both teams chased us off when they found out I was only thirteen. My memories of making Alvinston were only a little clearer—I do remember the Flyers being such a weak club that they let me stay on. I couldn't remember who had been Alvinston's coach or the manager that season until I called the team. It turned out that Ed Wagner had been the coach and Paul Moffatt the manager.

Because I remembered so little about the season, I could only ask them the obvious question point blank.

"Did you ever have any suspicions about my father abusing me?" I ask.

"Just that one time we pulled you out of the dressing room and asked you about the bruises on your ribs," Wagner says.

I had no memory of anything like that—not of bruises, not of a conversation—but Moffatt confirmed it.

"One of the players came to us before a practice and said, 'Patrick has bruises all 'round his ribs.' It didn't look like normal stuff, nothing you'd see from a game or anything. We hadn't had a game recently, and the last time we had, it wasn't like you had taken a big hit or anything—you probably hadn't taken a big hit like that, something that would leave bruises all over your ribs, all that season. So we definitely had suspicions about that. So I said, 'Patrick, where'd you get those?' I didn't ask if your father hit you or if someone else did. And you said, 'Happened in a pickup game.' Or maybe you said it was skating with another team. But you said it was hockey, nothing other than that.

268

I don't think anybody believed that those bruises came in a hockey game. They were on both sides of your ribs. They didn't look like you took one bad check or fall. We weren't sure that you should even be playing, the way they looked, but you said you were good to go."

"We thought there was more to the story," Wagner said, "but if you were just going to say that you got hurt playing hockey, there wasn't anything that we could really do."

I didn't remember anything like this, but it all fit. I tried to put myself in my default psychological mode back at that time. My only concern had been getting through the day, one hour at a time. My concern then wasn't getting out of an abusive relationship. It wasn't saving my life. It was getting home without getting beaten. Getting home without getting left on the side of the road. I know the calculations that I must have made: telling Ed Wagner and the others in the Flyers office about being beaten by my father wasn't going to help me get through that night. Telling them could only lead to some sort of confrontation with my father, and that would have led to two things: a blanket denial, and a beating when we had left the arena and I was unsafely out of sight.

So I lied.

Then I made myself forget. It was tough enough to live with the secret. I wouldn't want to remember being complicit in the abuse I was suffering. I wouldn't want to remember the missed opportunity to escape.

"Really, it couldn't go much farther than that," Moffatt said. "We thought that we should tell the police, but if you weren't going to tell us what happened ... if you just told the police that it was from playing hockey ... then there really wasn't any point to it. If there's nothing other than bruises—no witnesses or anything like that—our hands were tied at that point. Looking back, we should still have told some-one—it should be up to us to make that call about following it up. We didn't tell the police, but we should have. If it was innocent, then it wouldn't have been a problem."

I believed Wagner and Moffat when they said that had been their thinking. They didn't seem to consider options out there. They could have pushed me harder, could have still called in law enforcement that night, either with me there or after the fact. Hypothetically, if they hadn't believed me, they had options. They could have made a call to Children's Aid—it wouldn't have had to have been authorities in Michigan. Any call to an official with a child-protection service in the Alvinston area would have been followed up and a message would have been passed on to authorities in Michigan.

My father dodged a bullet in Alvinston and almost certainly didn't know anything about it.

I asked Wagner if anyone with the team had said anything to my father.

"I don't remember if I did," Wagner said. "Probably not. He really didn't have much to do with us at the arena. I don't think there would have been much of a point. We know what he would have said."

That would have been true.

I asked Wagner and Moffatt if my father spoke to anyone at the arena. They had only one suggestion.

"Pat Stapleton came out to a lot of our games, almost weekly," Wagner said. "We've always been an affiliate team for Strathroy for years, and Pat would come down to see the players. For sure you were our best prospect, and Pat talked to your father about moving up to play for the Rockets."

"Pat asked us about you and your father," Moffatt said. "We would have told him what we thought. We wouldn't have held back. We'd have told him that we thought you were a good kid, mature for your age. And we'd have said that we thought your father was a strange character ... that he might be an issue."

42

STRATHROY

It's a lot to expect teenagers to have picked up on any signs of abuse or even to have sensed any trouble between my father and me. You'd consider very few teens worldly and wise, and you'd have found nothing to change your opinion in Strathroy's dressing room back when I played there. Still, the Rockets might have seen the behavior of a teammate more clearly than any adult involved with the team would have. Teams benefit from the wisdom of a crowd—they know who fits in and who doesn't. Maybe some kids fly under the radar, but I wouldn't have in Strathroy. I was the new kid, the youngest in the room, the kid who was going to play major junior, maybe even pro. And the players in Strathroy were older than any I had played with in youth leagues, some in university, others a year away. They were almost adults.

I didn't really *know* any of them. I never saw any of them away from the arena. I never had a conversation with any of them outside the dressing room, never rode the bus with them to road games, never went to team functions except the end of the year banquet. The play-ers' way of including me and making me feel included was by at least acting like I was one of the guys, receiving no special attention.

The teammate I knew best of all was Steve Benedetti. Steve was a three years older than me—not the oldest on the team, but a sharp guy, heading to the University of Western Ontario. He played a little minor pro hockey, and these days coaches a Junior B team in London.

Steve said that he and the rest of the team sensed that there might be a shadow that fell across the scene. As much as I tried to conceal everything, there were telltale signs.

"There would be times when you were really upset after games," Steve says. "It seemed like you didn't want to leave the room. You were so much younger than everyone, we just thought it was your age. Some of our guys were seven years older than you. We really couldn't know what was going on in a mind of a kid that young. You were on our team, but we only really knew you in the dressing room and on ice. If you were older and had been billeting or going to school with us, something would have come out. But you were pretty well isolated from us. But we heard stories—about how your father made you do push-ups in the van or run after games. We even heard a story that John had a stationary bike built into the back of the van."

I told Steve that he could believe just about everything except the stationary bike, though I would have preferred it to running down the 402 in a blizzard at midnight.

"We would see him pushing you—there was no question how talented you were, how hard you worked," Steve told me. "It seemed extreme. We would say to each other, 'Geez, his father has got to tone it down a little.' But we never said it to him.

"I remember pulling up to a game in Chatham one time. You and your father were there early and he had you running and working out in the parking lot. I thought then that was crossing the line … That was obvious. Coming up in minor hockey, I had never seen anything like it, not even close, but then you were the most talented kid that I had played with at that point. That was probably why we didn't think anything of it. It was working. It seemed like he knew what it took for you to play at that level."

I didn't prompt Steve about what Wagner and Moffatt told me about the bruises on my ribcage in Alvinston, but he had noticed the same thing in Strathroy a few times. "You would come into the dressing room and we'd see that you had a lot of bruises," he said. "We wondered if John actually had you signed up in another league and you were getting banged up there. But as far as it being something worse than that, I don't think anyone would question it if a hockey player had bruises."

Maybe *someone* would question it, but another teenager probably wouldn't. Neither would another player. Or at least none did in Strathroy.

The bruises were in plain sight in the dressing room, but it would have had to have been a player who spoke to the coach or manager or trainer. No adults were around when we were getting dressed or undressed. In fact, I usually didn't dress before or undress after a game. I'd be in my equipment by the time we pulled into the parking lot. After a practice or game, I wouldn't shower. I'd change into my sweats and pile straight into the van for the drive back to Michigan.

Still, Benedetti thought the adults around the team in Strathroy should have had at least a suspicion that there was something seriously wrong with my father. "I don't know what the coaches and the officials saw or didn't see," Benedetti says. "I don't know how hard they looked. We saw stuff that maybe they didn't or at least didn't pick up on. But they couldn't have missed everything. Just the way John carried on, screaming, someone should have stepped in and taken a long, hard look."

I told Steve that the Rockets staff had had more than suspicion to act on.

* * *

Strathroy, Ontario, November 2014

I drove out to Strathroy. It had been more than half my lifetime since I had been in that town. I pulled up to the arena and passed the back door where my father used to park his van in a tow-away fire zone. After games he used to rush me out of the arena, never hanging around, never talking to parents or team officials, always rushing to get on the drive back to the border and always yelling. A few minutes later I'd be chasing the van out on the highway.

The arena has been updated a little. They've replaced the glass at the end of rink that my father used to stand behind, shouting at me. Still, it's old-school—no seats, just benches, three rows up from ice level, spots on the bench reserved for local fans, mostly farm folks and retirees. On a Saturday night when the NHL is Canada's game, the Rockets are Strathroy's. Things don't change. The stickboy when I was a player is now in his mid-twenties and still volunteering as an assistant trainer. The equipment manager then is the equipment manager now. The president of the team when I was with the Rockets, David Honsberger, has stepped down but still comes to the arena to do play-by-play on the local radio broadcast.

Honsberger was easy to pick out in the crowd. He was still wearing a bow tie on game nights, still wearing a loud suit and probably still hadn't cut his hair since I played there. He had just climbed down a ladder from the booth up in the rafters and didn't recognize me when I walked up to him. No surprise—when he last saw me, I was five inches shorter and had never shaved.

Honsberger seemed happy to see me. "I was just talking about you the other day …"

And he went on for ten minutes, talking about the playoffs back in 2000. It seemed like he could rattle of every goal and every game that spring, in detail. He talked about a point streak I had through the playoffs. He remembered every name. Again, no surprise: he puts together the team's website, and it has a registry of every player who has ever played for the Rockets.

"It was strange," he says. "It didn't feel like you were part of the team in a way. There were at least a couple of times when we had back-to-back games, Friday and Saturday night, away and home. I think one was Mount St. Bridges. And we suggested to your father that maybe you could stay over with one of the other players and his billet families. We thought you were going back with us to Strathroy on the bus. Then we saw your father pulling away with you in his van.

"The last conversation that we had with your father. End of the season, after the awards dinner, and he said, 'Thanks a lot.' Said it with a sort of finality that I didn't expect. He said something like, 'We got everything we're going to get here.' I thought you were going to be back with the Rockets the next year and be a real leader on the team. I was surprised that you ended up with [Ann Arbor]."

I had to interrupt Honsberger's reminiscences to tell him that I was looking to do a book. I mentioned that I had heard that there was a report that someone had seen my father kicking me in the parking lot after a game that season. It registered with him as clearly as the first goal I scored on the first shift in my first game with the team. "We heard about that. We wondered about it, and we watched things after that," he says. "It was an awful thing."

Honsberger's voice trailed off. His discomfort was plain.

I walked around the arena after the Rockets game that night. I hadn't been back in years. My father never parked in the main lot before games. I walked around to the back door, where the Zamboni dumps off scraped snow. Often we had been pressed for time just to make it to the game and I had to start getting into my equipment in the van, so instead of pulling up to the main door, my father would park at the back of the arena by the players' entrances. The same was true after the game. The back door made a quick getaway easy after a game. The back door also put that getaway out of the sight of most of the people at the arena. It sits at the far side of the arena from the main entrance, blocked off from view. It was just the two of us alone there. That would have given my father confidence to hit me without witnesses around. I thought about the times that I'd walked through that back door. It hadn't been *one* time that my father had kicked me or done worse out there. There had been dozens of times, after most games, after most practices.

The report was a fit—where my father would have been confident that he wasn't going to be seen, that it was a kick, his favorite move.

* * *

I contacted Honsberger a few weeks later. We had cut our conversation at the arena short—he had a game to get ready for, and in fairness he could have been a bit distracted. I hoped that our conversation at the rink might have stirred memories, that details would have come flooding back to him. That wasn't the case, though—in fact, it was the dead opposite, at least when it came to the report of the kicking incident behind the arena.

"The more I thought about it, and I talked it over with Pat Stapleton, and we couldn't remember when we heard about it. I couldn't tell you if we heard about it at the time. It might have been after you left Strathroy … might have been only after all those awful things had come out already. A lot of years probably passed."

It seemed weird—a guy whose memory was photographic when it came to my first goal losing grasp of a detail like that.

I asked who would have told him about the kicking incident, and again he struggled.

"Pat and I talked about that and we couldn't remember who it is. He mentioned LM [name withheld by authors], a scout. It's a shame. Can't really know because LM died a few years back."

Again, it seemed weird that someone who could remember a casual conversation with my father at the end-of-season banquet, word for word, would struggle to remember something that would seem a lot more disturbing. It also seemed an unlucky coincidence that the possible witness he held out there was impossible to reach.

As Honsberger laid it out after he had time to reflect after talking to Stapleton, all the dead ends made it hard to find fault with anyone involved with the team—at least anyone who was still alive. What might have seemed messy seemed to have been cleaned up by failures of memory and the passing of the likeliest witness.

I was more than a little suspicious about the holes in Honsberger's memory.

I was able to help him fill in the blanks.

When I met Honsberger at the arena in Strathroy, I hadn't mentioned how I had heard about someone seeing my father kicking me in the parking lot that season with the Rockets. I hadn't known about it when I was playing there. I had found out about it some three years after the fact. And the person who recalled the moment was, in fact, David Honsberger.

I had the notes from the ESPN reporter I had spoken to in 2003. I read them for the first time more than eleven years afterward, when I started kicking around the idea for this book. The original story the reporter filed with the magazine on May 19, 2003, said:

> If Patrick missed a breakaway, John told others at the rink that he'd have Patrick doing push-ups when they got home. "We assumed he was joking but then after players talked with Patrick we realized he wasn't," said David Honsberger, the Strathroy team manager. "Then we had a report that someone saw John kick Patrick after a game. We didn't know what to do about it other than watch Patrick and John a little more closely."

Though it didn't make it into the original story, the reporter did remember that Honsberger had an explanation of why he and the Rockets hadn't done more than just put my father on watch: Honsberger said that the team didn't know which authorities to call because my family was living in Michigan. The reporter also remembered that Honsberger had expressed regret that he and the team hadn't done more to follow up the report.

If Honsberger's version of events as he told ESPN in 2003 was correct, the timing seems clear cut. The sequence: (1) My father said he was going to punish me for missing a breakaway. (2) I told my teammates that it was true, and Honsberger and other adults running the team had an idea of what my relationship with my father was like. (3) Then Honsberger and the team had the report of my father kicking me after a game. (4) The team mulled over what to do and decided that watching my father more closely was the way to approach things.

In 2015 Honsberger was saying that he couldn't remember when he had heard about my father kicking me, and even suggested that it might have been after my story went public. In 2003, before my story went public, he told the ESPN reporter that the team had started to watch my father more closely—which wouldn't make any sense if the "report" came years after the fact. There would be no way "to watch Patrick and John a little more closely" if we had already gone.

Let's say that the incident happened in mid-season. The next two years were the worst of my life. There had been a chance there to head off my father, a chance for a real, meaningful intervention.

The inaction or indecision by Honsberger or others is in retrospect hard to accept.

* * *

Pat Stapleton has been out of the game for a few years now. He also has a reputation for screwing around the media over the years. For four decades he has given reporters the runaround when they call about the 1972 Summit Series—at the end of the final game, he picked up the puck, hockey's ultimate talisman, something that should be in the Hall of Fame, something that might someday yield a fortune when put up for private auction. Stapleton consistently denied having the puck and sometimes claimed one of his teammates came away with it.

In 2003, when my story was first reported, Stapleton took a defiant position with the media, blew off questions about my father.

"Patrick was our rookie of the year," he told the reporter from *ESPN The Magazine.* "John didn't push him into anything he couldn't handle. John was very involved in his son's game but it didn't seem to be anything more than that."

Stapleton also said that he didn't know anything about my father's conviction for assaulting me.

When I contacted him all these years later, he took a sympathetic tone. Then again, according to David Honsberger, they had recently talked about my year in Strathroy and Honsberger would have mentioned that I'd talked to him about working on a memoir.

"It was pretty disturbing stuff, what I heard about it," Stapleton said. "If we only could have known we would have done something.

"We didn't have any contact with anyone from Michigan or Toronto, so we didn't know anything that had gone on there ... nothing about John O'Sullivan."

Stapleton did admit he knew a bit about me from my time in Alvinston, "but not much." It would seem a little odd to view a thirteen-year-old on the ice in a league with players seven and eight years older as business as usual, even if I came in after the season started and led the team in scoring.

About whether the Alvinston Flyers' coaches had talked to him about my father, Stapleton maintained that he did no background check. "I only went to one of [your] games down in Alvinston," he said. "That's all I needed to see when it came down to making the team next year."

That sounds quite different from Ed Wagner and Paul Moffatt's account of Stapleton's attendance at games on a weekly basis over the years as well as of his contact with the Flyers' management about players who could be recruited to play for his Strathroy team. It's hard to believe that Stapleton wouldn't have asked questions about such an "involved" father. Wagner and Moffatt also said that Stapleton and my father talked regularly in the stands at games in Alvinston, that they were laying out the plans for me to play for the Rockets in the 1999–2000 season.

Stapleton maintained that he didn't have a lot of contact with my father even when I played for the Rockets that next season. "I didn't have that much to do with him," Stapleton said. "He kept to himself … stood off down at the one end of the rink, shouting. We didn't talk on a regular basis."

According to Stapleton, I wasn't around enough for anyone to get a read on. "It's one thing if it's a boy who's from the town or nearby … if he's billeting with a family that we know here and gets on the bus with the rest of the team. That's a player we know something about. But if you have someone coming in just for the game, it's hard to know anything much about him."

I asked him if he considered it strange that I wouldn't stay over in Strathroy with a billet family on weekends when we had games on back-to-back nights. "If it was true, it would be a father caring about his kid," he says.

I described what Benedetti had said about my out-of-the-ordinary behavior: that I didn't want to leave the dressing room, that I seemed stressed, that I didn't celebrate goals, that I was concerned with what my father said. Again, a dead end. "I didn't see anything like that," he said.

Finally, I asked him about the report of my father kicking me in the parking lot. "I never heard anything like that," he said. Suddenly the Strathroy Rockets seemed like such a big organization that one division didn't know the other one was doing. When he had a hand in everything to do with the team, and when everyone involved in the operation reported directly to him, it's hard to believe that any report of one his players being kicked by an adult didn't reach his ear ... especially if the source of the report was Stapleton's own longtime friend and scout for the team—that is, a very credible witness.

Stapleton was claiming that he "never heard anything like that" even though Honsberger had told me that he and Stapleton had talked about the report and had tried to remember who had made the report and when it happened. They would have talked only days before I reached Stapleton. If Honsberger has it right, their conversation slipped Stapleton's mind.

Conversation worked its way around to the present day, to the therapy I was undergoing. Stapleton registered no surprise that I hadn't received treatment under the direction of any of the NHL teams that I played with.

"Teams don't do social-work stuff," he says. "That's not what the game is about. Players have to look after themselves."

Again, this was the old school. Stapleton sounded nostalgic about a time long gone, what were better days, he thought. "I didn't really see that with the parents I met twenty or thirty years ago, back when I was first involved with the Rockets. That's changed. Maybe it was the money that had something to do with it."

Stapleton presented it like my father was a harbinger. It was time to get out of the game if he had to deal with people like him. Not worth the hassle. Fact is, however, *I* was the harbinger—the moral imperative that a coach has to have more than the game on his mind, to be aware of and concerned with his players' well-being.

Stapleton had a story and he was sticking to it, no matter how the record worked against it, no matter how strained his version of events seemed.

I hate to think that anyone would expect abused kids "to look after themselves," but I don't doubt that a lot of coaches and teams believe that "social work" isn't part of their mandate. It's an attitude he'd probably share with Schnurr. I can understand how Stapleton would come by that mindset, honestly or not. It would be a generational thing. When he was a kid playing the game back in the fifties, playing in a small town like Strathroy, it might have seemed like there weren't a lot of kids in trouble, like every family was made of a dutiful father, a loving wife and happy kids. If there were others, they were the unseen, the cursed, those to be avoided like the stigma was infectious.

43

MANTHA

Flint, Michigan, November 2014

The dressing room was quiet. Moe Mantha wasn't peeling the paint off the walls. He didn't have that much to say to his team, the Michigan Warriors, a Junior A team in the North American Hockey League. He had given them a couple of days off for Thanksgiving and thought that the boys would come out hard and fast playing at home. Instead his team had flatlined and wound up losing 5–4 to the Coulee Ridge Chill. The players were already dreading the bag skate that was coming. The coach and the owner of the team, Moe, was looking down at his shoes when he left the room and didn't give me more than a quick glance.

"Can I help you?" he said.

Moe didn't recognize me. The last time he had seen me I was sixteen, and since then he had coached hundreds of teenagers, so I wasn't surprised.

"I'm Patrick O'Sullivan."

It's like his world came into focus.

"Jesus," he said. "I'm sorry. Patrick, how are you doing?"

We exchanged a bit of small talk—he asked how my mother was doing and I told him that we were estranged and I had been out of contact with her for years.

Then I explained to him that I was out of hockey and had come to Flint to talk to him for the memoir I was writing.

That caught him off guard. Moe's a plain-spoken, stand-up guy. He had been out of the USA Hockey program for more than ten years. He'd worked in the Ontario Hockey League, but his job in Windsor blew up because of a team-hazing incident and his career had stalled since. At this point of his life he would be fine flying under the radar. He was worried more about saying something that would reflect badly on others and sound like he was bitter rather than about looking bad himself.

"I guess I know what you want to talk to me about," he said.

I asked Moe about USA Hockey deciding to offer me a spot in the under-17 category even after the birth certificate forgery.

"Would they have considered doing it if that spot hadn't opened up when Zach Parise went back to Minnesota?" I asked him.

Moe said the decision wasn't made of necessity—it had been discussed months before. "All of us in the program knew all about you," he said. "Fact is, we had talked to your father and to the agency back when you were playing in Strathroy and just after that season. We were prepared to have a place on the [under-17] team for you as an underager from the start of that season. We were ready to bring you in in September. Your father and the agency said that wasn't their first choice. Their first choice was you going to the O [the OHL] and play-ing in the league as a fifteen-year-old. I don't know if you know that."

I didn't. It had never been mentioned to me. I was never asked about what I wanted, and my input wouldn't have been welcomed anyway. It did seem like my father and the agency were willing to crawl out on the very thin branch of exceptional status, even if it meant passing on a guaranteed opportunity in a positive situation, USA Hockey's program.

I asked Moe if the coaches and staff had concerns about my father. "Did you ever talk about it?" I asked. "Did you have any idea about the level of abuse that was going on?"

"We had a lot of meetings about you," Moe said. "We really were trying to figure out what to do. We came close to going to the author-ities—if you had stayed on another year in the program and he didn't change, then I think we would have had to. Something had to give. We made some decisions about what we had to do. You probably weren't even aware of it, but when we would travel and stay in a hotel, we always made sure that your room was next to the coaches or across the hall. We thought that if there was going to be something going on with your father, we wanted to be around just in case that it went over the top."

This was the first that I heard about it.

Moe went to say that he took my father aside a few times and that Mike Eaves did the same thing, trying the heart-to-heart approach, as if a one-player-to-another talk might have had an impact on him, flattering him by treating him as an equal and making him see reason. That went nowhere, Moe said. My father let him know that he thought *he* was the only reason that I had made it this far—that *his* program mattered more than the program in Ann Arbor. Effectively, he said to their faces that he knew more about the game than all of them did combined.

Moe said that he and Mike Eaves also tried a more direct approach, telling my father to back off or risk pushing me away. "I told him, 'You're going to get the bad end of the deal if you keep acting this way,'" Moe said. "I told him, 'You're going to lose your retirement plan.' But he wasn't listening. Mike went after him when he heard that he made you run home after we lost a game and it was about 10 degrees [Fahrenheit]."

"I didn't hear anything about that," I said. "My father wouldn't have shared that with me."

"I'm sure there was lots he didn't tell you … That game that we played in Illinois after the under-17s in Nova Scotia, when he drove all the way there and back … Right then we knew that we were dealing with a guy who wasn't normal. And that game in Danville, he was worse than he had ever been. In the intermission you guys came off the ice and went to the dressing room. I didn't bother even going in to talk to you guys. I told him, 'This has got to stop. Shut the fuck up. This is a national program … not just a local team. You're not going to do this. And Patrick is riding home with us on the bus after the game.'"

That stood out in my memory: it was one of the few times all year that I actually rode with the team. I'd never put it together that it was Moe standing up to my father, trying to draw a line with him in a futile exercise.

"What did you know about the physical abuse?" I asked.

"That something was happening," Moe said. "We'd see you come into the dressing room with marks on your face. A couple of times it was really bad. A couple of times players came to us and said that there was something going on. The one time I saw your father pull up in the parking lot from our offices. I went out in the lobby of the arena, grabbed him and pinned him. I said to him, 'If you want to hit some-body, hit me. Hit a man. Don't hit your kid.'"

I had known that my father pushed Moe's buttons, but also that my father would have gone only so far with someone in Moe's position. He wasn't going to do anything that was going to hurt my stock in the draft—at least he thought he wasn't doing anything that would. If he hauled off and hit Moe and there were charges laid, I'd be gone from the program—either he'd pull me out or USA Hockey would throw me out or both.

No, my father would come up to the line and not cross it—with everyone else but me.

"When I heard what had happened, I wasn't surprised," Moe says. "It was easy to believe what they were saying about him and him going to jail. I honestly thought it was going to happen sooner or later."

But that's the inconsistency. It wasn't just that he thought it was going to happen. He *knew* it was happening. If he thought it was going to reach the level of it being criminal assault, why didn't he try to stop it from going that far? Moe wasn't afraid of my father physically. He would call out my father. He did what should have been the hardest thing—confronting my father.

"Why didn't you call authorities, even if you couldn't be sure?" I asked.

"Honestly, we were really close to doing something," Moe said. He sounded sheepish, apologetic. "If it had been another season that you were back in the program, I'm pretty sure that it was going to come to that. We thought he would come around ..."

Like Schnurr, Moe Mantha said that times and values have altered in the years since I played for him. "I think now times have changed and we'd be a lot more aware of stuff," he said. "Things that you could get away with then you couldn't get away. I know that I would handle a situation like yours differently."

So *now* a kid who is coming to the arena with black eyes and bruises will trip alarms; coaches and other adults involved with a team will get law enforcement involved. *Now* they'll intervene and try to protect the interests of someone who is as obviously being abused by a parent. Maybe *now* Moe would handle things differently—just saying that he would felt like an admission that he *should* have made the call.

Moe said that my experience changed how he looks at the kids he's coaching now. That all the people he worked with at USA Hockey were changed by what they saw when I was in the under-17 program and what they heard happened to me less than a year after I left Ann Arbor for the IceDogs. I think people would reexamine their attitudes about kids at risk of abuse if they could hear the regret and remorse in Moe Mantha's voice when he said that.

44

WASHKURAK

Toronto, Ontario, November 2014

You'd presume that a professional who had worked with victims of abuse would have recognized the red flags in my case. And you'd presume it was my bad luck that my path never crossed with someone who fit that profile. Yet I saw just that sort of professional on an almost daily basis when I was in Mississauga.

Joe Washkurak was an assistant coach for Don Cherry. At the same time, he held down a day job as a social worker specializing in crisis intervention. Eighty percent of his caseload focused on victims of domestic violence, hundreds of them over his career.

I'll be forever grateful for the role he filled back in January 2002 and during the months after. He helped me clear out of the townhouse I shared with Barry and get settled with the Tanel family. He took charge of security with the team and at the arenas that season. Most of all, he was the best sounding board that I had with the IceDogs' management. He understood at some level, better than others, better than me, that even my father's conviction and restraining order didn't put an end to everything—nothing was fixed. He knew better than anyone I saw on a daily basis back then that I had a chance to heal but only over time.

Joe was behind the bench only that one season with the IceDogs. He was always an energetic, constantly positive guy—in a brutal year for the team, we needed someone like that around. I hadn't talked to him in about five years, and while he was in a different line of work, he hadn't changed in that time.

"I remember on draft day John brought in four funky ties, passed them around and gave Don one," Washkurak said. "He seemed like a good guy. That first day we all thought that. Maybe Don and Trevor knew more about him, but he made a pretty good impression. He wanted to talk hockey and clearly knew the game. I had a sense that he was really proud of you. I remember your mom was there and she seemed supportive, and your little sisters were quiet but well behaved."

Washkurak said that a lot went into the IceDogs' decision to draft me, one of those things being that they considered parents of some other top prospects even more involved than my father. "Some of them were real nutshows," he said and rattled off names. Washkurak said that one prospect's father laid out his demands for money, a car and a leased home, all off the books, none of it guaranteeing that demands were going to stop there or that his son would stick with the team for the long haul or even until Christmas.

"We looked into all of the family situations of the top players," Washkurak said. "You have to when you're looking at having a relationship to a player for years. And your family issues might not have been the norm, but they weren't rare either. Don's brother Richard had gone out to see you a bunch of times and spoke to your father there. Don had gone to games too, went with Pat Morris and Mark Guy. We wanted to see you for sure, but also we wanted to get a sense of him. We were more concerned with him [than we were concerned with you], really. We knew that he didn't really have grounding, an education or a good job. We knew that part was rocky. What did your father do? A super in a building? Maintenance worker? Clearly, you were the best thing he had going, and your prospects were a helluva lot brighter than his. All that plus we had heard from around the Ann Arbor program that John was really hard on you. I remember that you could hear him in the crowd. It was crazy, but still, the physical stuff we never dreamt about."

If the IceDogs management couldn't have imagined the physical stuff, then there had to be a breakdown in their communication with USA Hockey—they couldn't have heard that Moe Mantha had confronted my father about him hitting me. And the IceDogs might have taken any other negative feedback about my father as sour grapes— USA Hockey officials had hoped I'd be back for another year in the program or move on to college hockey rather than major junior. Don Cherry and the rest of his management team could really have bought the Suitcase Sully act.

"Early, things were going maybe even better than we hoped," Wash- kurak said. "I don't know what set John off. Maybe it was that the team couldn't keep it up and started losing. Still, you were playing really well even if the team was struggling. Maybe some fathers get set off when their sons aren't getting played, when the coach isn't giving them ice time. But you were getting a ton of time—we depended on you right from the get-go. The way he was acting ... the way he was mad ... just didn't seem normal. Every now and again you could hear John from the stands. I think as the season went on I had a sense that John was getting louder and yelling at you more often. And it wasn't the team, wasn't the refs or the other team. It was always you. I would have been more concerned, but then after games he seemed fine, at least with me. He never came up to complain. He actually came off pretty decent to me. It was like he had a toggle switch that he flipped after the game."

I can see how Joe Washkurak and the rest of the IceDogs staff could miss it for a while, imagine that the face my father put on before and after games was the real one. Without real hard physical evidence of abuse and any admission on my part, it would have been easy to miss when the coaches' attention was split his attention twenty-two ways, besides keeping up a day job. But in fact Washkurak had reason to act.

"I remember coming to practice one day in December," Washkurak said. "It would have been early in the week, Tuesday, with Monday off after games that weekend. John would have been up for those games. That day you came in you had a black eye. I said, 'What the fuck happened to you?' And you said, 'You know exactly what happened.' I'll never forget that. That's all you said. I didn't ask for any more explanations and I should have. But you didn't want to talk about it, did you, Sully?"

"No, I didn't bring it up with anybody," I told him.

"And nobody else ever asked you about it," Washkurak said. "You just walked away and you went out there and practiced. I didn't know whether to tell people or go to [your father] or Don. I didn't mention it to them. I didn't know what to do. I was pretty torn about that. You were just a minor at the time. You were living with John's brother and I knew it was a bad situation. I don't whether if I had done something at that time I could have prevented all this shit."

"Maybe," I told him, "or maybe it turns out even worse. There's no knowing."

To his credit, Washkurak isn't passing the buck. He puts it squarely on himself. A few others have declined blame that things had gone this far. Washkurak thinks it nobody's fault but his own that it went any farther. He was at that point in a better position to know what was going on, what had happened and even what to do. He knew all about the dynamics of family dysfunction, and in his working life he would have acted right away—his professional obligation. But in the dressing room, in the arena, he had to suppress a Samaritan's instinct to act. Washkurak had always been good to me, and he'd be a great help later on, but he's an example of how a moment's hesitation makes it so much harder to budge later.

epilogue

REAL LIFE

Florida, April 2015

Whenever I drive past the sports complex near my house, I see kids playing Little League baseball, Pop Warner football, soccer and basketball on the outdoor courts. We're living in what all my neighbors think of as a good place, a good community, and they would consider the scene at the sports complex evidence of that. If traffic slows to a crawl or a stop, I'll watch a game being played on a Little League diamond, where parents sit on aluminum benches on the other side of the cage. A strikeout or a pop-up will end the game and the kids will celebrate. They will exchange high fives and shoulder bumps and then go to the other side of the backstop to accept the congratulations of their parents—hugs from their mothers, backslaps and roughed-up baseball caps from their fathers.

For years, seeing parents show any special affection toward their kids triggered an awful feeling for me. I didn't need to think deeply about it to figure out why. The sight bothered me because I wanted the same thing, but I knew it only from watching other families interact. For all my father's pushing, he made a point of never congratulating me for a win, a goal or an award I'd won. Everything I ever did could have been improved upon, at least in his mind. I craved his approval—I wanted a "normal" relationship with my father, a relationship like the ones my teammates and those kids coming off of the Little League diamond had with their dads. My father was sure that if he ever gave me a high five or a hug, if he ever congratulated me after I won or reassured me after a bad game, it would make me complacent.

Despite *The Hockey Handbook*, my father didn't have a master plan. Everything he did to me and had me do, on and off the ice, had just one intended purpose: to toughen me up. But in his mind, it didn't work—like he said to the writer from ESPN, he wished I had become as tough as him. I believe that what he did probably worked too well.

When I see those parent-child scenes play out as I drive by the sports complex every day—when I feel those same wrenching feelings, that familiar pain—I get an important reminder that my recovery from my father's abuse will never be complete. It will never be over. It's going to be something I have to work on the rest of my life. There's no denying or erasing the damage. It's about managing the effects. I show affection with my wife and with my sons, but it didn't come naturally at first. I had never experienced it. I had no model for it at home. Not with my father, of course, but not with my mother either—she didn't console me even though she must have known that my father had slapped me around and abused me. Maybe she believed that if she did, she would have been acknowledging that she knew what was going on. I don't know. For whatever reason, she acted as if she was completely in the dark and without any reason to feel the tug of conscience.

* * *

When I get home one day, the boys are in the backyard kicking a ball around. My younger son is making about as much contact as you'd expect for a kid who not long ago had two candles on his birthday cake, but my older son is a little more practiced. He's turning four soon.

"Should we have soccer shoes on the list of presents?" Sophie asks.

"If that's what you think he'd like," I say.

This is going to be my first brush with being a sports parent, something I had thought about. I'm not exactly dreading it, but I'm not looking forward to it either.

I don't think I'd be excited about my kids following me into hockey. I have a love-hate relationship with the game and I always have. Everything good in my life came from hockey. Without it, I would never have met Sophie. I met most of my closest friends through the game as well. Still, I feel like hockey robbed me of the chance to have a happy childhood. I feel like it wrecked my family life growing up. When Sophie and our sons came along, I realized that I didn't want the game to define me. I wanted more for myself and, more importantly, more for them. I'd like to see our sons take up other games or have a passionate interest outside of sports. But no matter what they choose, the same question remains: How do I encourage my sons without pushing them? It's not like I could ever push them the way my father pushed me. If I manage to stay halfway sensible, that shouldn't be an issue. If anything, I'll likely just let them play.

I'm not worried only about how I'll act as a sports parent. I'm worried about what I'll see. My father was extreme, but I know that other parents also crush their kids' spirits and desire to play sports. I wasn't the first young athlete to take out a restraining order against a parent. Mary Pierce, the Grand Slam tennis champion, did the same with her father twenty years ago. I'm not the only one who has become estranged from his family. Just the other day I read about Patrick Reed, a PGA golfer who had security guards remove his parents from the course at a tournament. Even my former Los Angeles teammate Jack Johnson broke off relations with his parents after he signed over power of attorney to them and they drove him into bankruptcy.

Once upon a time, Mary Pierce's father bought her first racquet, Patrick Reed's parents cheered for him on the eighteenth green of a youth tournament and the Johnsons signed up Jack for youth-league teams. It always begins with good intentions, I guess.

"Soccer would be something to start with," Sophie says. "Everybody's kid starts out playing it, boys or girls. And every kid is out there on the field. There's nobody stuck on the bench. We could make a couple of calls about signing him up."

"Yeah, I guess," I say.

I know where the conversation is heading. I think that maybe if I shut down, Sophie will change the subject. She doesn't. She asks what she can't know is a loaded question.

"Yeah, I played it one summer," I reply. "I was probably seven, I guess."

"Did you like it?" she says.

"I guess I did," I say. "It wasn't like I had to be forced to go to practice or games or anything."

"Why did you stop?" she asks.

I knew all along that it had to come to this. I'm not going to avoid the story though. I'm not going to lie. Sophie asked an honest question and I could only give her an honest answer.

"I remember one game I didn't play so well. My father was giving it to me on the drive home from the field. He talked about me wasting his time and money. I told him that I wanted to play and that I'd play better next time. But then he said, 'If you're not going to take it seriously, you're not going to fuckin' play, period.' And then he threw my soccer shoes out the window on the highway and we just kept going. That was the last soccer game I ever played."

My personal history is once again a conversation killer.

"You never told me about that," Sophie says. Even though she knows more about me than anybody, she's still surprised and hurt when she hears about an incident like this for the first time. She can't imagine any parent treating a kid this way.

"It never came up, I guess," I say. "It's been years since I thought about that day, really."

That's the truth. What my father did that day is something that I could never think about doing to one of my sons—not just tossing their soccer boots out the window, but also being that mean-spirited and domineering. I'll never cut them out of any positive activity that they have a passion for. Likewise, I'll never become the "involved" father, the one who makes officials and other parents roll their eyes and makes his child feel embarrassed or ashamed. I'll never deny them their childhood or impose my ambitions on them.

I just wonder how I'll react when I see someone like that on the sidelines of one of my kids' games. I want to believe that I'll step in and say something the way that Dwight Foster and Moe Mantha did—

something stronger if there's real cause. It doesn't have to be criminal, like the assault that put my father behind bars. If I see parents go off on their kids, it will trigger something in me, no doubt. It won't be a response that I should completely suppress—I will feel obliged to act, as anyone witnessing abusive behavior should. If I see parents physically abusing kids, I'm really not sure how I'll handle it. I hope I'll remain in control enough to step in and protect the kid and be able to give a coherent account to authorities when they get to the scene—again, as anyone should.

I know there's no avoiding it. I know that I'm going to see sports parents mistreating their children. I have no illusions. My father wasn't the only one. I saw enough growing up to know that he wasn't alone. And I saw enough to know that only a few people ever tried to get in his way—more people did little while my father put me through hell.

I'll be a good father to my sons, but not only that. I'll look at other families and ask the hard question: Would I treat my kids that way? And if I don't like what I see, I'll say something and do something about it. If I see a kid in trouble, it won't be left to that kid to call 911 in the middle of the night.